AF560652

DESIGN PLANNING AND MANAGEMENT IN FINANCE AND INVESTMENT

DESIGN PLANNING AND MANAGEMENT IN FINANCE AND INVESTMENT

D.K. Sharma

RANDOM PUBLICATIONS

NEW DELHI - 110 002 (INDIA)

Design Planning and Management in Finance and Investment

ISBN 978-93-51117-21-6

Published in 2015 in India by

RANDOM PUBLICATIONS

4376-A/4B, Gali Murari Lal, Ansari Road
New Delhi-110 002
Phone: +9111-43580356, 23289044
E-mail: randomexports@gmail.com; sales@randompublications.com;
info@randompublications.com

Reprinted 2018

Type Setting by: Friends Media, Delhi-110089
Digitally Pritnted at : Replika Press Pvt. Ltd.

Preface

Financial planning is the task of determining how a business will afford to achieve its strategic goals and objectives. Usually, a company creates a Financial Plan immediately after the vision and objectives have been set. The Financial Plan describes each of the activities, resources, equipment and materials that are needed to achieve these objectives, as well as the timeframes involved. Performing Financial Planning is critical to the success of any organization. It provides the Business Plan with rigor, by confirming that the objectives set are achievable from a financial point of view. It also helps the CEO to set financial targets for the organization, and reward staff for meeting objectives within the budget set. When drafting a financial plan, the company should establish the planning horizon, which is the time period of the plan, whether it be on a short-term (usually 12 months) or long-term (2–5 years) basis. Also, the individual projects and investment proposals of each operational unit within the company should be totalled and treated as one large project. This process is called aggregation.

Investment management is the professional asset management of various securities (shares, bonds and other securities) and other assets (e.g., real estate) in order to meet specified investment goals for the benefit of the investors. Investors may be institutions (insurance companies, pension funds, corporations, charities, educational establishments etc.) or private investors (both directly via investment contracts and more commonly via collective investment schemes e.g. mutual funds or exchange-traded funds). The term asset management is often used to refer to the investment management of collective investments, while the more generic fund management may refer to all forms of institutional investment as well as investment management for private investors. Investment managers who specialize in advisory or discretionary management on behalf of (normally wealthy) private investors may often refer to their services as money management or portfolio management often within the context of so-called "private banking". The provision of investment management services includes elements of financial statement analysis, asset selection, stock selection, plan implementation and ongoing monitoring of investments. Coming under the remit of financial services many of the world's largest companies are at least in part investment managers and employ millions of staff. The business of investment has several facets, the employment of professional fund managers, research (of individual assets and asset classes), dealing, settlement, marketing, internal auditing, and the preparation of reports for clients. The largest financial fund managers are firms that exhibit all the complexity their size demands. Apart from the people who bring in the money (marketers) and the people who direct investment (the fund managers), there are compliance staff (to ensure accord with legislative and regulatory constraints), internal auditors of various kinds (to examine internal systems and controls), financial controllers (to account for the institutions' own money and costs), computer experts, and "back office" employees.

This book covers the fundamentals of finance - including an overview of business finance, the basics of accountancy, financial risk and investment vehicles. Designed for savvy investors and professional advisors, this book offers the vital information needed for developing and implementing an overall strategic financial plan.

I thank all members of my team who have helped in the preparation of the book. My special thanks go to "Random Publications" who have published the book.

— D.K. Sharma

Contents

Chapter 1

Introduction of Financial Plan

In general usage, a financial plan is a comprehensive evaluation of someone's current and future financial state by using currently known variables to predict future cash flows, asset values and withdrawal plans. This often includes a budget which organises an individual's finances and sometimes includes a series of steps or specific goals for spending and saving in the future . This plan allocates future income to various types of expenses, such as rent or utilities, and also reserves some income for short-term and long-term savings. A financial plan is sometimes referred to as an investment plan, but in personal finance a financial plan can focus on other specific areas such as risk management, estates, college, or retirement.

Context of Business

In business, a financial plan can refer to the three primary financial statements (balance sheet, income statement, and cash flow statement) created within a business plan. Financial forecast or financial plan can also refer to an annual projection of income and expenses for a company, division or department. A financial plan can also be an estimation of cash needs and a decision on how to raise the cash, such as through borrowing or issuing additional shares in a company.

While the common usage of the term "financial plan" often refers to a formal and defined series of steps or goals, there is some technical confusion about what the term "financial plan" actually means in the industry. For example, one of the industry's leading professional organisations, the Certified Financial Planner Board of Standards, lacks any definition for the term "financial plan" in its *Standards of Professional Conduct* publication. This publication outlines the professional financial planner's job, and explains the process of financial planning, but the term "financial plan" never appears in the publication's text.

Issues of Definition

Textbooks used in colleges offering financial planning-related courses also generally do not define the term 'financial plan'. For example, Sid Mittra, Anandi P. Sahu, and Robert A Crane, authors of *Practicing Financial Planning for Professionals* do not define what a financial plan is, but merely defer to the Certified Financial Planner Board of Standards' definition of 'financial planning'.

Because of the lack of a formal definition in industry literature, and in major textbooks on the subject, the term 'financial plan' is merely inferred from the defined process of 'financial planning'.

Finance Functions

The following explanation will help in understanding each finance function in detail

Investment Decision

One of the most important finance functions is to intelligently allocate capital to long term assets. This activity is also known as capital budgeting. It is important to allocate capital in those long term assets so as to get maximum yield in future. Following are the two aspects of investment decision

a. Evaluation of new investment in terms of profitability
b. Comparison of cut off rate against new investment and prevailing investment.

Since the future is uncertain therefore there are difficulties in calculation of expected return. Along with uncertainty comes the risk factor which has to be taken into consideration. This risk factor plays a very significant role in calculating the expected return of the prospective investment. Therefore while considering investment proposal it is important to take into consideration both expected return and the risk involved.

Investment decision not only involves allocating capital to long term assets but also involves decisions of using funds which are obtained by selling those assets which become less profitable and less productive. It wise decisions to decompose depreciated assets which are not adding value and utilise those funds in securing other beneficial assets. An opportunity cost of capital needs to be calculating while dissolving such assets. The correct cut off rate is calculated by using this opportunity cost of the required rate of return (RRR).

Financial Decision

Financial decision is yet another important function which a financial manger must perform. It is important to make wise decisions about when, where and how should a business acquire funds. Funds can be acquired through many ways and channels. Broadly speaking a correct ratio of an equity and debt has to be maintained. This mix of equity capital and debt is known as a firm's capital structure. A firm tends to benefit most when the market value of a company's share maximizes this not only is a sign of growth for the firm but also maximizes shareholders wealth. On the other hand the use of debt affects the risk and return of a shareholder. It is more risky though it may increase the return on equity funds. A sound financial structure is said to be one which aims at maximizing shareholders return with minimum risk. In such a scenario the market value of the firm will maximize and hence an optimum capital structure would be achieved. Other than equity and debt there are several other tools which are used in deciding a firm capital structure.

Dividend Decision

Earning profit or a positive return is a common aim of all the businesses. But the key function a financial manger performs in case of profitability is to decide whether to distribute all the profits to the shareholder or retain all the profits or distribute part of the profits to the shareholder and retain the other half in the business. It's the financial manager's responsibility to decide a optimum dividend policy which maximizes the market value of the firm. Hence an optimum dividend payout ratio is calculated. It is a common practice to pay regular dividends in case of profitability Another way is to issue bonus shares to existing shareholders.

Liquidity Decision

It is very important to maintain a liquidity position of a firm to avoid insolvency. Firm's profitability, liquidity and risk all are associated with the investment in current assets. In order to maintain a tradeoff between profitability and liquidity it is important to invest sufficient funds in current assets. But since current assets do not earn anything for business therefore a proper calculation must be done before investing in current assets. Current assets should properly be valued and disposed of from time to time once they become non profitable.

Currents assets must be used in times of liquidity problems and times of insolvency.

The Finance Function and the Project Office

Contemporary organisations need to practice cost control if they are to survive the recessionary times. Given the fact that many top tier companies are currently mired in low growth and less activity situations, it is imperative that they control their costs as much as possible. This can happen only when the finance function in these companies is diligent and has a hawk eye towards the costs being incurred. Apart from this, companies also have to introduce efficiencies in the way their processes operate and this is another role for the finance function in modern day organisations. Further, there must be synergies between the various processes and this is where the finance function can play a critical role. Lest one thinks that the finance function, which is essentially a support function, has to do this all by themselves, it is useful to note that, many contemporary organisations have dedicated project office teams for each division, which perform this function. In other words, whereas the finance function oversees the organisational processes at a macro level, the project office teams indulge in the same at the micro level. This is the reason why finance and project budgeting and cost control have assumed significance because after all, companies exist to make profits and finance is the lifeblood that determines whether organisations are profitable or failures.

The Pension Fund Management and Tax Activities of the Finance Function

The next role of the finance function is in payroll, claims processing, and acting as the repository of pension schemes and gratuity. If the US follow the 401(k) rule and the finance function manages the defined benefit and defined contribution schemes, in India it is the EPF or the Employee Provident Funds that are managed by the finance function. Of course, only large organisations have dedicated EPF trusts to take care of these aspects and the norm in most other organisations is to act as facilitators for the EPF scheme with the local or regional PF (Provident Fund) commissioner. The third aspect of the role of the finance function is to manage the taxes and their collection at source from the employees. Whereas in the US, TDS or Tax Deduction at Source works differently from other countries, in India and much of the Western world, it is mandatory for organisations to deduct tax at source from the employees commensurate with their pay and benefits. The finance function also has to coordinate with the tax authorities and hand out the annual tax statements that form the basis of the employee's tax returns. Often, this is a sensitive and critical process since the tax rules mandate very strict principles for generating the tax statements.

Payroll, Claims Processing, and Automation

We have discussed the pension fund management and the tax deduction. The other role of the finance function is to process payroll and associated benefits in time and in tune with the regulatory requirements. Further, claims made by the employees with respect to medical, and transport allowances have to be processed by the finance function. Often, many organisations automate this routine activity wherein the use of ERP (Enterprise Resource Planning) software and financial workflow automation software make the job and the task of claims processing easier. Having said that, it must be remembered that the finance function has to do its due diligence on the claims being submitted to ensure that bogus claims and suspicious activities are found out and stopped. This is the reason why many organisations have experienced chartered accountants and financial professionals in charge of the finance function so that these aspects can be managed professionally and in a trustworthy manner. The key aspect here is that the finance function must be headed by persons of high integrity and trust that the management reposes in them must not be misused. In conclusion, the finance function though a non-core process in many organisations has come to occupy a place of prominence because of these aspects.

Role of a Financial Manager

Financial activities of a firm is one of the most important and complex activities of a firm. Therefore in order to take care of these activities a financial manager performs all the requisite financial activities.

A financial manger is a person who takes care of all the important financial functions of an organisation. The person in charge should maintain a far sightedness in order to ensure that the funds are utilised in the most efficient manner. His actions directly affect the Profitability, growth and goodwill of the firm.

Following are the Main Functions of a Financial Manager

Raising of Funds: In order to meet the obligation of the business it is important to have enough cash and liquidity. A firm can raise funds by the way of equity and debt. It is the responsibility of a financial manager to decide the ratio between debt and equity. It is important to maintain a good balance between equity and debt.

Allocation of Funds

Once the funds are raised through different channels the next important function is to allocate the funds. The funds should be allocated in such a manner that they are optimally used. In order to allocate funds in the best possible manner the following point must be considered

- The size of the firm and its growth capability
- Status of assets whether they are long term or short tem
- Mode by which the funds are raised.

These financial decisions directly and indirectly influence other managerial activities. Hence formation of a good asset mix and proper allocation of funds is one of the most important activity

Profit Planning

Profit earning is one of the prime functions of any business organisation. Profit earning is important for survival and sustenance of any organisation. Profit planning refers to proper usage of the profit generated by the firm. Profit arises due to many factors such as pricing, industry competition, state of the economy, mechanism of demand and supply, cost and output. A healthy mix of variable and fixed factors of production can lead to an increase in the profitability of the firm. Fixed costs are incurred by the use of fixed factors of production such as land and machinery. In order to maintain a tandem it is important to continuously value the depreciation cost of fixed cost of production. An opportunity cost must be calculated in order to replace those factors of production which has gone thrown wear and tear. If this is not noted then these fixed cost can cause huge fluctuations in profit.

Understanding Capital Markets

Shares of a company are traded on stock exchange and there is a continuous sale and purchase of securities. Hence a clear understanding of capital market is an important function of a financial manager. When securities are traded on stock market there involves a huge amount of risk involved. Therefore a financial manger understands and calculates the risk involved in this trading of shares and debentures. Its on the discretion of a financial manager as to how distribute the profits. Many investors do not like the firm to distribute the profits amongst share holders as dividend instead invest in the business itself to enhance growth. The practices of a financial manager directly impact the operation in capital market.

Financial Planning (Business)

Financial planning is the task of determining how a business will afford to achieve its strategic goals and objectives. Usually, a company creates a Financial Plan immediately after the vision and objectives have been set. The Financial Plan describes each of the activities, resources, equipment and materials that are needed to achieve these objectives, as well as the timeframes involved.

The Financial Planning activity involves the following tasks;-

- Assess the business environment
- Confirm the business vision and objectives
- Identify the types of resources needed to achieve these objectives
- Quantify the amount of resource (labour, equipment, materials)
- Calculate the total cost of each type of resource
- Summarize the costs to create a budget
- Identify any risks and issues with the budget set

Performing Financial Planning is critical to the success of any organisation. It provides the Business Plan with rigor, by confirming that the objectives set are achievable from a financial point of view. It also helps the CEO to set financial targets for the organisation, and reward staff for meeting objectives within the budget set.

The Role of Financial Planning includes Three Categories

1. Strategic role of financial management
2. Objectives of financial management
3. The planning cycle

When drafting a financial plan, the company should establish the planning horizon, which is the time period of the plan, whether it be on a short-term (usually 12 months) or long-term (2–5 years) basis. Also, the individual projects and investment proposals of each operational unit within the company should be totaled and treated as one large project. This process is called aggregation.

Financial Statement

A financial statement (or financial report) is a formal record of the financial activities of a business, person, or other entity.

Relevant financial information is presented in a structured manner and in a form easy to understand. They typically include basic financial statements, accompanied by a management discussion and analysis:

1. A balance sheet, also referred to as a statement of financial position, reports on a company's assets, liabilities, and ownership equity at a given point in time.
2. An income statement, also known as a statement of comprehensive income, statement of revenue & expense, P&L or profit and loss report, reports on a company's income, expenses, and profits over a period of time. A profit and loss statement provides information on the operation of the enterprise. These include sales and the various expenses incurred during the stated period.
3. A statement of cash flows reports on a company's cash flow activities, particularly its operating, investing and financing activities.

For large corporations, these statements may be complex and may include an extensive set of footnotes to the financial statements and management discussion and analysis. The notes typically describe each item on the balance sheet, income statement and cash flow statement in further detail. Notes to financial statements are considered an integral part of the financial statements.

Purpose of Financial Statements by Business Entities

"The objective of financial statements is to provide information about the financial position, performance and changes in financial position of an enterprise that is useful to a wide range of users in making economic decisions." Financial statements should be understandable, relevant, reliable and comparable. Reported assets, liabilities, equity, income and expenses are directly related to an organisation's financial position.

Financial statements are intended to be understandable by readers who have "a reasonable knowledge of business and economic activities and accounting and who are willing to study the information diligently." Financial statements may be used by users for different purposes:

- Owners and managers require financial statements to make important business decisions that affect its continued operations. Financial analysis is then performed on these statements to provide management with a more detailed understanding of the figures. These statements are also used as part of management's annual report to the stockholders.

- Employees also need these reports in making collective bargaining agreements (CBA) with the management, in the case of labour unions or for individuals in discussing their compensation, promotion and rankings.
- Prospective investors make use of financial statements to assess the viability of investing in a business. Financial analyses are often used by investors and are prepared by professionals (financial analysts), thus providing them with the basis for making investment decisions.
- Financial institutions (banks and other lending companies) use them to decide whether to grant a company with fresh working capital or extend debt securities (such as a long-term bank loan or debentures) to finance expansion and other significant expenditures.

Consolidated Financial Statements

Consolidated financial statements are defined as "Financial statements of a group in which the assets, liabilities, equity, income, expenses and cash flows of the parent (company) and its subsidiaries are presented as those of a single economic entity", according to International Accounting Standard 27 "Consolidated and separate financial statements", and International Financial Reporting Standard 10 "Consolidated financial statements".

Government Financial Statements

The rules for the recording, measurement and presentation of government financial statements may be different from those required for business and even for non-profit organisations. They may use either of two accounting methods: accrual accounting, or cost accounting, or a combination of the two (OCBOA). A complete set of chart of accounts is also used that is substantially different from the chart of a profit-oriented business.

Personal Financial Statements

Personal financial statements may be required from persons applying for a personal loan or financial aid. Typically, a personal financial statement consists of a single form for reporting personally held assets and liabilities (debts), or personal sources of income and expenses, or both. The form to be filled out is determined by the organisation supplying the loan or aid.

Audit and Legal Implications

Although laws differ from country to country, an audit of the financial statements of a public company is usually required for investment, financing, and tax purposes. These are usually performed by independent accountants or auditing firms. Results of the audit are summarized in an audit report that either provide an unqualified opinion on the financial statements or qualifications as to its fairness and accuracy. The audit opinion on the financial statements is usually included in the annual report.

There has been much legal debate over who an auditor is liable to. Since audit reports tend to be addressed to the current shareholders, it is commonly thought that they owe a legal duty of care to them. But this may not be the case as determined by common law precedent. In Canada, auditors are liable only to investors using a prospectus to buy shares in the primary market. In the United Kingdom, they have been held liable to potential investors when the auditor was aware of the potential investor and how they would use the information in the financial statements. Nowadays auditors tend to include in their report liability restricting language, discouraging anyone other than the addressees of their report from relying on it. Liability is an important issue: in the UK, for example, auditors have unlimited liability.

In the United States, especially in the post-Enron era there has been substantial concern about the accuracy of financial statements. Corporate officers (the chief executive officer (CEO) and chief financial officer (CFO)) are personally responsible for fair financial reporting allowing those reading the report to have a good sense of the organisation.

Standards and Regulations

Different countries have developed their own accounting principles over time, making international comparisons of companies difficult. To ensure uniformity and comparability between financial statements prepared by different companies, a set of guidelines and rules are used. Commonly referred to as Generally Accepted Accounting Principles (GAAP), these set of guidelines provide the basis in the preparation of financial statements, although many companies voluntarily disclose information beyond the scope of such requirements.

Recently there has been a push towards standardizing accounting rules made by the International Accounting Standards Board ("IASB"). IASB develops International Financial Reporting Standards that have been adopted by Australia, Canada and the European Union (for publicly quoted companies only), are under consideration in South Africa and other countries. The United States Financial Accounting Standards Board has made a commitment to converge the U.S. GAAP and IFRS over time.

Inclusion in Annual Reports

To entice new investors, public companies assemble their financial statements on fine paper with pleasing graphics and photos in an annual report to shareholders, attempting to capture the excitement and culture of the organisation in a "marketing brochure" of sorts. Usually the company's chief executive will write a letter to shareholders, describing management's performance and the company's financial highlights.

In the United States, prior to the advent of the internet, the annual report was considered the most effective way for corporations to communicate with individual shareholders. Blue chip companies went to great expense to produce and mail out attractive annual reports to every shareholder. The annual report was often prepared in the style of a coffee table book.

Notes to Financial Statements

Notes to financial statements (notes) are additional information added to the end of financial statements that help explain specific items in the statements as well as provide a more comprehensive assessment of a company's financial condition. Notes to financial statements can include information on debt, going concern criteria, accounts, contingent liabilities or contextual information explaining the financial numbers (e.g. to indicate a lawsuit).

The notes clarify individual statement line-items. For example, if a company lists a loss on a fixed asset impairment line in their income statement, notes could corroborate the reason for the impairment by describing how the asset became impaired. Notes are also used to explain the accounting methods used to prepare the statements and they support valuations for how particular accounts have been computed. In consolidated financial statements, all subsidiaries are listed as well as the amount of ownership (controlling interest) that the parent company has in the subsidiaries. Any items within the financial statements that are valuated by estimation are part of the notes if a substantial difference exists between the amount of the estimate previously reported and the actual result. Full disclosure of the effects of the differences between the estimate and actual results should be included.

Management Discussion and Analysis

Management discussion and analysis or MD&A is an integrated part of a company's annual financial statements. The purpose of the MD&A is to provide a narrative explanation, through the eyes of management, of how an entity has performed in the past, its financial condition, and its future prospects. In so doing, the MD&A attempt to provide investors with complete, fair, and balanced information to help them decide whether to invest or continue to invest in an entity.

The section contains a description of the year gone by and some of the key factors that influenced the business of the company in that year, as well as a fair and unbiased overview of the company's past, present, and future.

MD&A typically describes the corporation's liquidity position, capital resources, results of its operations, underlying causes of material changes in financial statement items (such as asset impairment and restructuring charges), events of unusual or infrequent nature (such as mergers and acquisitions or share buybacks), positive and negative trends, effects of inflation, domestic and international market risks, and significant uncertainties.

Moving to Electronic Financial Statements

Financial statements have been created on paper for hundreds of years. The growth of the Web has seen more and more financial statements created in an electronic form which is exchangeable over the Web. Common forms of electronic financial statements are PDF and HTML. These types of electronic financial statements have their drawbacks in that it still takes a human to read the information in order to reuse the information contained in a financial statement.

More recently a market driven global standard, XBRL (Extensible Business Reporting Language), which can be used for creating financial statements in a structured and computer readable format, has become more popular as a format for creating financial statements. Many regulators around the world such as the U.S. Securities and Exchange Commission have mandated XBRL for the submission of financial information.

The UN/CEFACT created, with respect to Generally Accepted Accounting Principles, (GAAP), internal or external financial reporting XML messages to be used between enterprises and their partners, such as private interested parties (e.g. bank) and public collecting bodies (e.g. taxation authorities). Many regulators use such messages to collect financial and economic information.

Balance Sheet

In financial accounting, a balance sheet or statement of financial position is a summary of the financial balances of a sole proprietorship, a business partnership, a corporation or other business organisation, such as an LLC or an LLP. Assets, liabilities and ownership equity are listed as of a specific date, such as the end of its financial year. A balance sheet is often described as a "snapshot of a company's financial condition". Of the three basic financial statements, the balance sheet is the only statement which applies to a single point in time of a business' calendar year.

A standard company balance sheet has three parts: assets, liabilities and ownership equity. The main categories of assets are usually listed first, and typically in order of liquidity. Assets are followed by the liabilities. The difference between the assets and the liabilities is known as equity or the net assets or the net worth or capital of the company and according to the accounting equation, net worth must equal assets minus liabilities. Another way to look at the balance sheet equation is that total assets equals liabilities plus owner's equity. Looking at the equation in this way shows how assets were financed: either by borrowing money (liability) or by using the owner's money (owner's or shareholders' equity). Balance sheets are usually presented with assets in one section and liabilities and net worth in the other section with the two sections "balancing".

A business operating entirely in cash can measure its profits by withdrawing the entire bank balance at the end of the period, plus any cash in hand. However, many businesses are not paid immediately; they build up inventories of goods and they acquire buildings and equipment. In other words: businesses have assets and so they cannot, even if they want to, immediately turn these into cash at the end of each period. Often, these businesses owe money to suppliers and to tax authorities, and the proprietors do not withdraw all their original capital and profits at the end of each period. In other words businesses also have liabilities.

Types

A balance sheet summarizes an organisation or individual's assets, equity and liabilities at a specific point in time. Two forms of balance sheet exist. They are the report form and the account form. Individuals and small businesses tend to have simple balance sheets. Larger businesses tend to have more complex balance sheets, and these are presented in the organisation's annual report. Large businesses also may prepare balance sheets for segments of their businesses. A balance sheet is often presented alongside one for a different point in time (typically the previous year) for comparison.

Personal Balance Sheet

A personal balance sheet lists current assets such as cash in checking accounts and savings accounts, long-term assets such as common stock and real estate, current liabilities such as loan debt and mortgage debt due, or overdue, long-term liabilities such as mortgage and other loan debt. Securities and real estate values are listed at market value rather than at historical cost or cost basis. Personal net worth is the difference between an individual's total assets and total liabilities.

US Small Business Balance Sheet

Sample Small Business Balance Sheet				
Assets (current)		***Liabilities and Owners' Equity***		
Cash	$6,600	Liabilities		
Accounts Receivable	$6,200	Notes Payable	$5,000	
Assets (non-current)		Accounts Payable $25,000		
Tools and equipment	$25,000	*Total liabilities*		$30,000
		Owners' equity		
		Capital Stock	$7,000	
		Retained Earnings	$800	
		Total owners' equity		$7,800
Total	$37,800	*Total*		$37,800

A small business balance sheet lists current assets such as cash, accounts receivable, and inventory, fixed assets such as land, buildings, and equipment, intangible assets such as patents, and liabilities such as accounts payable, accrued expenses, and long-term debt. Contingent liabilities such as warranties are noted in the footnotes to the balance sheet. The small business's equity is the difference between total assets and total liabilities.

Public Business Entities Balance Sheet Structure

Guidelines for balance sheets of public business entities are given by the International Accounting Standards Board and numerous country-specific organisations/companys. The standard used by companies in the USA adhere to U.S. Generally Accepted Accounting Principles (GAAP). The Federal Accounting Standards Advisory Board (FASAB) is a United States federal advisory committee whose mission is to develop generally accepted accounting principles (GAAP) for federal financial reporting entities.

Balance sheet account names and usage depend on the organisation's country and the type of organisation. Government organisations do not generally follow standards established for individuals or businesses. If applicable to the business, summary values for the following items should be included in the balance sheet: Assets are all the things the business owns. This will include property, tools, cars, desks, chairs, machinery, and so on.

Assets

Current Assets:

1. Cash and cash equivalents
2. Accounts receivable
3. Prepaid expenses for future services that will be used within a year

Non-Current Assets (Fixed Assets):

1. Property, plant and equipment
2. Investment property, such as real estate held for investment purposes
3. Intangible assets
4. Financial assets (excluding investments accounted for using the equity method, accounts receivables, and cash and cash equivalents)
5. Investments accounted for using the equity method
6. Biological assets, which are living plants or animals. Bearer biological assets are plants or animals which bear agricultural produce for harvest, such as apple trees grown to produce apples and sheep raised to produce wool.

Liabilities:

1. Accounts payable
2. Provisions for warranties or court decisions
3. Financial liabilities (excluding provisions and accounts payable), such as promissory notes and corporate bonds
4. Liabilities and assets for current tax
5. Deferred tax liabilities and deferred tax assets
6. Unearned revenue for services paid for by customers but not yet provided

Equity

The net assets shown by the balance sheet equals the third part of the balance sheet, which is known as the shareholders' equity. It comprises:

1. Issued capital and reserves attributable to equity holders of the parent company (controlling interest)
2. Non-controlling interest in equity

Formally, shareholders' equity is part of the company's liabilities: they are funds "owing" to shareholders (after payment of all other liabilities); usually, however, "liabilities" is used in the more restrictive sense of liabilities excluding shareholders' equity. The balance of assets and liabilities (including shareholders' equity) is not a coincidence. Records of the values of each account in the balance sheet are maintained using a system of accounting known as double-entry bookkeeping. In this sense, shareholders' equity by construction must equal assets minus liabilities, and thus the shareholders' equity is considered to be a residual.

Regarding the Items in Equity Section, the Following Disclosures are Required

1. Numbers of shares authorized, issued and fully paid, and issued but not fully paid
2. Par value of shares
3. Reconciliation of shares outstanding at the beginning and the end of the period
4. Description of rights, preferences, and restrictions of shares
5. Treasury shares, including shares held by subsidiaries and associates
6. Shares reserved for issuance under options and contracts
7. A description of the nature and purpose of each reserve within owners' equity

Balance Sheet Substantiation

Balance Sheet Substantiation is the accounting process conducted by businesses on a regular basis to confirm that the balances held in the primary accounting system of record (e.g. SAP, Oracle, other ERP system's General Ledger) are reconciled (in balance with) with the balance and transaction records held in the same or supporting sub-systems.

Balance Sheet Substantiation includes multiple processes including reconciliation (at a transactional or at a balance level) of the account, a process of review of the reconciliation and any pertinent supporting documentation and a formal certification (sign-off) of the account in a predetermined form driven by corporate policy.

Balance Sheet Substantiation is an important process that is typically carried out on a monthly, quarterly and year-end basis. The results help to drive the regulatory balance sheet reporting obligations of the organisation.

Historically, Balance Sheet Substantiation has been a wholly manual process, driven by spreadsheets, email and manual monitoring and reporting. In recent years software solutions have been developed to bring a level of process automation, standardization and enhanced control to the Balance Sheet Substantiation or account certification process. These solutions are suitable for organisations with a high volume of accounts and/or personnel involved in the Balance Sheet Substantiation process and can be used to drive efficiencies, improve transparency and help to reduce risk. Balance Sheet Substantiation is a key control process in the SOX 404 top-down risk assessment.

Income Statement

An income statement (US English) or profit and loss account (UK English) (also referred to as a *profit and loss statement* (P&L), *revenue statement, statement of financial performance, earnings statement, operating statement*, or *statement of operations*) is one of the financial statements of a company and shows the company's revenues and expenses during a particular period. It indicates how the revenues (money received from the sale of products and services before expenses are taken out, also known as the "top line") are transformed into the net income (the result after all revenues and expenses have been accounted for, also known as "net profit" or the "bottom line"). It displays the revenues recognised for a specific period, and the cost and expenses charged against these revenues, including write-offs (e.g., depreciation and amortization of various assets) and taxes. The purpose of the income statement is to show managers and investors whether the company made or lost money during the period being reported.

One important thing to remember about an income statement is that it represents a period of time like the cash flow statement. This contrasts with the balance sheet, which represents a single moment in time. Charitable organisations that are required to publish financial statements do not produce an income statement. Instead, they produce a similar statement that reflects funding sources compared against program expenses, administrative costs, and other operating commitments. This statement is commonly referred to as the statement of activities. Revenues and expenses are further categorized in the statement of activities by the donor restrictions on the funds received and expended.

The income statement can be prepared in one of two methods. The Single Step income statement takes a simpler approach, totaling revenues and subtracting expenses to find the bottom line. The more complex Multi-Step income statement (as the name implies) takes several steps to find the bottom line, starting with the gross profit. It then calculates operating expenses and, when deducted from the gross profit, yields income from operations. Adding to income from operations is the difference of other revenues and other expenses. When combined with income from operations, this yields income before taxes. The final step is to deduct taxes, which finally produces the net income for the period measured.

Usefulness and Limitations of Income Statement

Income statements should help investors and creditors determine the past financial performance of the enterprise, predict future performance, and assess the capability of generating future cash flows through report of the income and expenses.

However, Information of an Income Statement has Several Limitations

- Items that might be relevant but cannot be reliably measured are not reported (*e.g.* brand recognition and loyalty).
- Some numbers depend on accounting methods used (*e.g.* using FIFO or LIFO accounting to measure inventory level).
- Some numbers depend on judgments and estimates (*e.g.* depreciation expense depends on estimated useful life and salvage value).

- INCOME STATEMENT GREENHARBOR LLC -
For the year ended DECEMBER 31 2010

	€ Debit	€ Credit
Revenues		
GROSS REVENUES (including INTEREST income)		296,397

Expenses:		
ADVERTISING	6,300	
BANK & CREDIT CARD FEES	144	
BOOKKEEPING	2,350	
SUBCONTRACTORS	88,000	
ENTERTAINMENT	5,550	
INSURANCE	750	
LEGAL & PROFESSIONAL SERVICES	1,575	
LICENSES	632	
PRINTING, POSTAGE & STATIONERY	320	
RENT	13,000	
MATERIALS	74,400	
TELEPHONE	1,000	
UTILITIES	1,491	

TOTAL EXPENSES		(195,513)

NET INCOME		100,885

Guidelines for statements of comprehensive income and income statements of business entities are formulated by the International Accounting Standards Board and numerous country-specific organisations, for example the FASB in the U.S. Names and usage of different accounts in the income statement depend on the type of organisation, industry practices and the requirements of different jurisdictions.

If applicable to the business, summary values for the following items should be included in the income statement:

Operating Section

- Revenue - Cash inflows or other enhancements of assets of an entity during a period from delivering or producing goods, rendering services, or other activities that constitute the entity's ongoing major operations. It is usually presented as sales minus sales discounts, returns, and allowances. Every time a business sells a product or performs a service, it obtains revenue. This often is referred to as gross revenue or sales revenue.
- Expenses - Cash outflows or other using-up of assets or incurrence of liabilities during a period from delivering or producing goods, rendering services, or carrying out other activities that constitute the entity's ongoing major operations.
  - Cost of Goods Sold (COGS) / Cost of Sales - represents the direct costs attributable to goods produced and sold by a business (manufacturing or merchandizing). It includes *material costs*, *direct labour*, and *overhead costs* (as in absorption costing), and excludes operating costs (period costs) such as selling, administrative, advertising or R&D, etc.
  - Selling, General and Administrative expenses (SG&A or SGA) - consist of the combined payroll costs. SGA is usually understood as a major portion of non-production related costs, in contrast to production costs such as direct labour.
    - Selling expenses - represent expenses needed to sell products (e.g. *salaries of sales people, commissions and travel expenses, advertising, freight, shipping, depreciation of sales store buildings and equipment*, etc.).
    - General and Administrative (G&A) expenses - represent expenses to manage the business (*salaries of officers / executives, legal and professional fees, utilities, insurance, depreciation of office building and equipment, office rents, office supplies*, etc.).

- o Depreciation / Amortization - the charge with respect to fixed assets / intangible assets that have been capitalised on the balance sheet for a specific (accounting) period. It is a systematic and rational allocation of cost rather than the recognition of market value decrement.
- o Research & Development (R&D) expenses - represent expenses included in research and development.

Expenses recognised in the income statement should be analysed either by nature (raw materials, transport costs, staffing costs, depreciation, employee benefit etc.) or by function (cost of sales, selling, administrative, etc.). (IAS 1.99) If an entity categorises by function, then additional information on the nature of expenses, at least, – depreciation, amortisation and employee benefits expense – must be disclosed. (IAS 1.104) The major exclusive of costs of goods sold, are classified as operating expenses. These represent the resources expended, except for inventory purchases, in generating the revenue for the period. Expenses often are divided into two broad sub classifications selling expenses and administrative expenses.

Non-Operating Section

- Other revenues or gains - revenues and gains from other than primary business activities (e.g. *rent, income from patents,* goodwill). It also includes unusual gains that are either unusual or infrequent, but not both (e.g. *gain from sale of securities* or *gain from disposal of fixed assets*)
- Other expenses or losses - expenses or losses not related to primary business operations, (e.g. *foreign exchange loss*).
- Finance costs - costs of borrowing from various creditors (e.g. *interest expenses, bank charges*).
- Income tax expense - sum of the amount of tax payable to tax authorities in the current reporting period (current tax liabilities/ tax payable) and the amount of deferred tax liabilities (or assets).

Irregular Items

They are reported separately because this way users can better predict future cash flows - irregular items most likely will not recur. These are reported *net of taxes.*

- Discontinued operations is the most common type of irregular items. Shifting business location(s), stopping production temporarily, or changes due to technological improvement do not qualify as discontinued operations. Discontinued operations *must* be shown separately.

Cumulative effect of changes in accounting policies (principles) is the difference between the book value of the affected assets (or liabilities) under the old policy (principle) and what the book value would have been if the new principle had been applied in the prior periods. For example, valuation of inventories using LIFO instead of weighted average method. The changes should be applied retrospectively and shown as adjustments to the *beginning* balance of affected components in Equity. All comparative financial statements should be restated. (IAS 8)

However, *changes in estimates* (e.g. estimated useful life of a fixed asset) only requires prospective changes. (IAS 8)

No items may be presented in the income statement as extraordinary items under IFRS regulations, but are permissible under US GAAP. (IAS 1.87) *Extraordinary items* are both unusual (abnormal) and infrequent, for example, unexpected natural disaster, expropriation, prohibitions under new regulations. [Note: natural disaster might not qualify depending on location (e.g. frost damage would not qualify in Canada but would in the tropics).]

Additional items may be needed to fairly present the entity's results of operations. (IAS 1.85)

Disclosures

Certain items must be disclosed separately in the notes (or the statement of comprehensive income), if material, including: (IAS 1.98)

- Write-downs of inventories to net realisable value or of property, plant and equipment to recoverable amount, as well as *reversals* of such write-downs
- Restructurings of the activities of an entity and *reversals* of any provisions for the costs of restructuring
- Disposals of items of property, plant and equipment
- Disposals of investments
- Discontinued operations
- Litigation settlements
- Other reversals of provisions

Earnings Per Share

Because of its importance, earnings per share (EPS) are required to be disclosed on the face of the income statement. A company which reports any of the irregular items must also report EPS for these items either in the statement or in the notes.

$$\text{Earnings per share} = \frac{\text{Net income} - \text{Preferred stock dividends}}{\text{Weighted average of common stock shares outstanding}}$$

There are two forms of EPS reported:

- Basic: in this case "weighted average of shares outstanding" includes only actual stocks outstanding.
- Diluted: in this case "weighted average of shares outstanding" is calculated as if all stock options, warrants, convertible bonds, and other securities that could be transformed into shares *are* transformed. This increases the number of shares and so EPS decreases. Diluted EPS is considered to be a more reliable way to measure EPS.

Requirements of IFRS

On 6 September 2007, the International Accounting Standards Board issued a revised *IAS 1: Presentation of Financial Statements*, which is effective for annual periods beginning on or after 1 January 2009.

A business entity adopting IFRS must include:

- a statement of comprehensive income or
- *two* separate statements comprising:

1. an income statement displaying components of profit or loss *and*
2. a *statement of comprehensive income* that *begins* with profit or loss (bottom line of the income statement) and displays the items of other comprehensive income for the reporting period. (IAS1.81)

All non-owner changes in equity (i.e. *comprehensive income*) shall be presented in either in the statement of comprehensive income (or in a separate income statement and a statement of comprehensive income). Components of comprehensive income may not be presented in the statement of changes in equity.

Comprehensive income for a period includes profit or loss (net income) for that period and other comprehensive income recognised in that period.

All items of income and expense recognised in a period must be included in profit or loss unless a Standard or an Interpretation requires otherwise. (IAS 1.88) Some IFRSs require or permit that some components to be excluded from profit or loss and instead to be included in other comprehensive income. (IAS 1.89)

Items and Disclosures

The statement of comprehensive income should include: (IAS 1.82)

1. Revenue
2. Finance costs (including interest expenses)
3. Share of the profit or loss of associates and joint ventures accounted for using the equity method
4. Tax expense
5. A *single* amount comprising the total of (1) the *post-tax* profit or loss of *discontinued operations* and (2) the *post-tax* gain or loss recognised on the disposal of the assets or disposal group(s) constituting the *discontinued operation*
6. Profit or loss
7. Each component of other comprehensive income classified by nature
8. Share of the other comprehensive income of associates and joint ventures accounted for using the equity method
9. Total comprehensive income

The following items must also be disclosed in the statement of comprehensive income as allocations for the period: (IAS 1.83)

- Profit or loss for the period attributable to non-controlling interests and owners of the parent
- Total comprehensive income attributable to non-controlling interests and owners of the parent

No items may be presented in the statement of comprehensive income (or in the income statement, if separately presented) or in the notes as *extraordinary items*.

Cash Flow Statement

In financial accounting, a cash flow statement, also known as *statement of cash flows*, is a financial statement that shows how changes in balance sheet accounts and income affect cash and cash equivalents, and breaks the analysis down to operating, investing and financing activities. Essentially, the cash flow statement is concerned with the flow of cash in and out of the business. The statement captures both the current operating results and the accompanying changes in the balance sheet. As an analytical tool, the statement of cash flows is useful in determining the short-term viability of a company, particularly its ability to pay bills. International Accounting Standard 7 (IAS 7), is the International Accounting Standard that deals with cash flow statements.

People and groups interested in cash flow statements include:

- Accounting personnel, who need to know whether the organisation will be able to cover payroll and other immediate expenses
- Potential lenders or creditors, who want a clear picture of a company's ability to repay
- Potential investors, who need to judge whether the company is financially sound
- Potential employees or contractors, who need to know whether the company will be able to afford compensation
- Shareholders of the business.

Purpose

Statement of Cash Flow - Simple Example for the period 1 Jan 2006 to 31 Dec 2006	
Cash flow from operations	$4,000
Cash flow from investing	($1,000)
Cash flow from financing	($2,000)
Net cash flow	$1,000
Parentheses indicate negative values	

The cash flow statement was previously known as the flow of Cash statement. The cash flow statement reflects a firm's liquidity.

The balance sheet is a snapshot of a firm's financial resources and obligations at a single point in time, and the income statement summarizes a firm's financial transactions over an interval of time. These two financial statements reflect the accrual basis accounting used by firms to match revenues with the expenses associated with generating those revenues. The cash flow statement includes only inflows and outflows of cash and cash equivalents; it excludes transactions that do not directly affect cash receipts and payments. These non-cash transactions include depreciation or write-offs on bad debts or credit losses to name a few. The cash flow statement is a cash basis report on three types of financial activities: operating activities, investing activities, and financing activities. Non-cash activities are usually reported in footnotes.

The cash flow statement is intended to

1. provide information on a firm's liquidity and solvency and its ability to change cash flows in future circumstances

2. provide additional information for evaluating changes in assets, liabilities and equity
3. improve the comparability of different firms' operating performance by eliminating the effects of different accounting methods
4. indicate the amount, timing and probability of future cash flows

The cash flow statement has been adopted as a standard financial statement because it eliminates allocations, which might be derived from different accounting methods, such as various timeframes for depreciating fixed assets.

History and Variations

Cash basis financial statements were very common before accrual basis financial statements. The "flow of funds" statements of the past were cash flow statements.

In 1863, the Dowlais Iron Company had recovered from a business slump, but had no cash to invest for a new blast furnace, despite having made a profit. To explain why there were no funds to invest, the manager made a new financial statement that was called a *comparison balance sheet*, which showed that the company was holding too much inventory. This new financial statement was the genesis of cash flow statement that is used today.

In the United States in 1973, the Financial Accounting Standards Board (FASB) defined rules that made it mandatory under Generally Accepted Accounting Principles (US GAAP) to report sources and uses of funds, but the definition of "funds" was not clear. Net working capital might be cash or might be the difference between current assets and current liabilities. From the late 1970 to the mid-1980s, the FASB discussed the usefulness of predicting future cash flows. In 1987, FASB Statement No. 95 (FAS 95) mandated that firms provide cash flow statements. In 1992, the International Accounting Standards Board issued International Accounting Standard 7 (IAS 7), *Cash Flow Statement*, which became effective in 1994, mandating that firms provide cash flow statements.

US GAAP and IAS 7 rules for cash flow statements are similar, but some of the differences are:

- IAS 7 requires that the cash flow statement include changes in both cash and cash equivalents. US GAAP permits using cash alone or cash and cash equivalents.
- IAS 7 permits bank borrowings (overdraft) in certain countries to be included in cash equivalents rather than being considered a part of financing activities.

- IAS 7 allows interest paid to be included in operating activities or financing activities. US GAAP requires that interest paid be included in operating activities.
- US GAAP (FAS 95) requires that when the direct method is used to present the operating activities of the cash flow statement, a supplemental schedule must also present a cash flow statement using the indirect method. The IASC strongly recommends the direct method but allows either method. The IASC considers the indirect method less clear to users of financial statements. Cash flow statements are most commonly prepared using the indirect method, which is not especially useful in projecting future cash flows.

Cash Flow Activities

The cash flow statement is partitioned into three segments, namely:

1. cash flow resulting from operating activities;
2. cash flow resulting from investing activities;
3. cash flow resulting from financing activities.

The money coming into the business is called cash inflow, and money going out from the business is called cash outflow.

Operating Activities

Operating activities include the production, sales and delivery of the company's product as well as collecting payment from its customers. This could include purchasing raw materials, building inventory, advertising, and shipping the product.

Under IAS 7, Operating Cash Flows Include:

- Receipts from the sale of goods or services
- Receipts for the sale of loans, debt or equity instruments in a trading portfolio
- Interest received on loans
- Payments to suppliers for goods and services
- Payments to employees or on behalf of employees
- Interest payments (alternatively, this can be reported under financing activities in IAS 7, and US GAAP)
- buying Merchandise

Items which are added back to [or subtracted from, as appropriate] the net income figure (which is found on the Income Statement) to arrive at cash flows from operations generally include:

- Depreciation (loss of tangible asset value over time)
- Deferred tax
- Amortization (loss of intangible asset value over time)
- Any gains or losses associated with the sale of a non-current asset, because associated cash flows do not belong in the operating section (unrealised gains/losses are also added back from the income statement).
- Dividends received
- Revenue received from certain investing activities

Investing Activities

Examples of Investing Activities are:

- Purchase or Sale of an asset (assets can be land, building, equipment, marketable securities, etc.)
- Loans made to suppliers or received from customers
- Payments related to mergers and acquisition.

Financing Activities

Financing activities include the inflow of cash from investors such as banks and shareholders, as well as the outflow of cash to shareholders as dividends as the company generates income. Other activities which impact the long-term liabilities and equity of the company are also listed in the financing activities section of the cash flow statement.

Under IAS 7,

- Payments of dividends
- Payments for repurchase of company shares
- For non-profit organisations, receipts of donor-restricted cash that is limited to long-term purposes

Items Under the Financing Activities Section include:

- Dividends paid
- Sale or repurchase of the company's stock
- Net borrowings
- Payment of dividend tax
- Repayment of debt principal, including capital leases

Disclosure of Non-Cash Activities

Under IAS 7, non-cash investing and financing activities are disclosed in footnotes to the financial statements. Under US General Accepted Accounting Principles (GAAP), non-cash activities may be disclosed in a footnote or within the cash flow statement itself. Non-cash financing activities may include

- Leasing to purchase an asset
- Converting debt to equity
- Exchanging non-cash assets or liabilities for other non-cash assets or liabilities
- Issuing shares in exchange for assets

Preparation Methods

The direct method of preparing a cash flow statement results in a more easily understood report. The indirect method is almost universally used, because FAS 95 requires a supplementary report similar to the indirect method if a company chooses to use the direct method.

Direct Method

The direct method for creating a cash flow statement reports major classes of gross cash receipts and payments. Under IAS 7, dividends received may be reported under operating activities or under investing activities. If taxes paid are directly linked to operating activities, they are reported under operating activities; if the taxes are directly linked to investing activities or financing activities, they are reported under investing or financing activities. Generally Accepted Accounting Principles (GAAP) vary from International Financial Reporting Standards in that under GAAP rules, dividends received from a company's investing activities is reported as an "operating activity," not an "investing activity."

Sample Cash Flow Statement Using the Direct Method

Cash flows from (used in) operating activities		
Cash receipts from customers	9,500	
Cash paid to suppliers and employees	(2,000)	
Cash generated from operations (sum)	7,500	
Interest paid	(2,000)	
Income taxes paid	(3,000)	
Net cash flows from operating activities		2,500
Cash flows from (used in) investing activities		
Proceeds from the sale of equipment	7,500	
Dividends received	3,000	
Net cash flows from investing activities		10,500
Cash flows from (used in) financing activities		
Dividends paid	(2,500)	
Net cash flows used in financing activities		(2,500)
.		
Net increase in cash and cash equivalents		10,500
Cash and cash equivalents, beginning of year		1,000
Cash and cash equivalents, end of year		$11,500

Indirect Method

The indirect method uses net-income as a starting point, makes adjustments for all transactions for non-cash items, then adjusts from all cash-based transactions. An increase in an asset account is subtracted from net income, and an increase in a liability account is added back to net income. This method converts accrual-basis net income (or loss) into cash flow by using a series of additions and deductions.

Rules (Operating Activities)

To Find Cash Flows from Operating Activities using the Balance Sheet and Net Income	
For Increases in	Net Inc Adj
Current Assets (Non-Cash)	Decrease
Current Liabilities	Increase
For All Non-Cash...	
**Expenses* (Decreases in Fixed Assets)	Increase
**Non-cash expenses must be added back to NI. Such expenses may be represented on the balance sheet as decreases in long term asset accounts. Thus decreases in fixed assets increase NI.*	

The following rules can be followed to calculate Cash Flows from Operating Activities when given only a two-year comparative balance sheet and the Net Income figure. Cash Flows from Operating Activities can be found by adjusting Net Income relative to the change in beginning and ending balances of Current Assets, Current Liabilities, and sometimes Long Term Assets. When comparing the change in long term assets over a year, the accountant must be certain that these changes were caused entirely by their devaluation rather than purchases or sales (i.e. they must be operating items not providing or using cash) or if they are nonoperating items.

- Decrease in non-cash current assets are added to net income
- Increase in non-cash current asset are subtracted from net income
- Increase in current liabilities are added to net income
- Decrease in current liabilities are subtracted from net income
- Expenses with no cash outflows are added back to net income (depreciation and/or amortization expense are the only operating items that have no effect on cash flows in the period)
- Revenues with no cash inflows are subtracted from net income
- Non operating losses are added back to net income
- Non operating gains are subtracted from net income

The intricacies of this procedure might be seen as,

Net Cash Flows from Operating Activities = Net Income + Rule Items

For example, consider a company that has a net income of $100 this year, and its A/R increased by $25 since the beginning of the year. If the balances of all other current assets, long term assets and current liabilities did not change over the year, the cash flows could be determined by the rules above as $100 – $25 = Cash Flows from Operating Activities = $75.

The logic is that, if the company made $100 that year (net income), and they are using the accrual accounting system (not cash based) then any income they generated that year which has not yet been paid for in cash should be subtracted from the net income figure in order to find cash flows from operating activities. And the increase in A/R meant that $25 of sales occurred on credit and have not yet been paid for in cash.

In the case of finding Cash Flows when there is a change in a fixed asset account, say the Buildings and Equipment account decreases, the change is added back to Net Income. The reasoning behind this is that because Net Income is calculated by, Net Income = Rev - Cogs - Depreciation Exp - Other Exp then the Net Income figure will be decreased by the building's depreciation that year. This depreciation is not associated with an exchange of cash, therefore the depreciation is added back into net income to remove the non-cash activity.

Rules (Financing Activities)

Finding the Cash Flows from Financing Activities is much more intuitive and needs little explanation. Generally, the things to account for are financing activities:

- Include as outflows, reductions of long term notes payable (as would represent the cash repayment of debt on the balance sheet)
- Or as inflows, the issuance of new notes payable
- Include as outflows, all dividends paid by the entity to outside parties
- Or as inflows, dividend payments received from outside parties
- Include as outflows, the purchase of notes stocks or bonds
- Or as inflows, the receipt of payments on such financing vehicles.

In the case of more advanced accounting situations, such as when dealing with subsidiaries, the accountant must

- Exclude intra-company dividend payments.
- Exclude intra-company bond interest.

A traditional equation for this might look something like,

Net Cash Flows from Financing Activities =

[Divs received from 3rd parties] − [Divs paid to 3rd parties]

−{Divs paid to NCI but not intracompany div payments}

Example: cash flow of XYZ:

XYZ co. Ltd. Cash Flow Statement (all numbers in millions of Rs.)			
Period ending	*31 Mar 2010*	*31 Mar 2009*	*31 Mar 2008*
Net income	21,538	24,589	17,046
Operating activities, cash flows provided by or used in:			
Depreciation and amortization	2,790	2,592	2,747
Adjustments to net income	4,617	621	2,910
Decrease (increase) in accounts receivable	12,503	17,236	--
Increase (decrease) in liabilities (A/P, taxes payable)	131,622	19,822	37,856
Decrease (increase) in inventories	--	--	--
Increase (decrease) in other operating activities	(173,057)	(33,061)	(62,963)
Net cash flow from operating activities	13	31,799	(2,404)
Investing activities, cash flows provided by or used in:			
Capital expenditures	(4,035)	(3,724)	(3,011)
Investments	(201,777)	(71,710)	(75,649)
Other cash flows from investing activities	1,606	17,009	(571)
Net cash flows from investing activities	(204,206)	(58,425)	(79,231)
Financing activities, cash flows provided by or used in:			
Dividends paid	(9,826)	(9,188)	(8,375)
Sale (repurchase) of stock	(5,327)	(12,090)	133
Increase (decrease) in debt	101,122	26,651	21,204
Other cash flows from financing activities	120,461	27,910	70,349
Net cash flows from financing activities	206,430	33,283	83,311
Effect of exchange rate changes	645	(1,840)	731
Net increase (decrease) in cash and cash equivalents	2,882	4,817	2,407

Discounted Cash Flow

In finance, discounted cash flow (DCF) analysis is a method of valuing a project, company, or asset using the concepts of the time value of money. All future cash flows are estimated and discounted to give their present values (PVs)—the sum of all future cash flows, both incoming and outgoing, is the net present value (NPV), which is taken as the value or price of the cash flows in question.

Using DCF analysis to compute the NPV takes as input cash flows and a discount rate and gives as output a present value; the opposite process—takes cash flows and a price (present value) as inputs, and provides as output the discount rate—this is used in bond markets to obtain the yield. Discounted cash flow analysis is widely used in investment finance, real estate development, corporate financial management and patent valuation.

Discount Rate

The most widely used method of discounting is exponential discounting, which values future cash flows as "how much money would have to be invested currently, at a given rate of return, to yield the cash flow in future." Other methods of discounting, such as hyperbolic discounting, are studied in academia and said to reflect intuitive decision-making, but are not generally used in industry.

The discount rate used is generally the appropriate weighted average cost of capital (WACC), that reflects the risk of the cashflows. The discount rate reflects two things:

1. Time value of money (risk-free rate) – according to the theory of time preference, investors would rather have cash immediately than having to wait and must therefore be compensated by paying for the delay
2. Risk premium – reflects the extra return investors demand because they want to be compensated for the risk that the cash flow might not materialize after all

History

Discounted cash flow calculations have been used in some form since money was first lent at interest in ancient times. As a method of asset valuation it has often been opposed to accounting book value, which is based on the amount paid for the asset. Following the stock market crash of 1929, discounted cash flow analysis gained popularity as a valuation method for stocks. Irving Fisher in his 1930 book *The Theory of Interest* and John Burr Williams's 1938 text *The Theory of Investment Value* first formally expressed the DCF method in modern economic terms.

Mathematics

Discounted Cash Flows

The discounted cash flow formula is derived from the future value formula for calculating the time value of money and compounding returns.

$$DCF = \frac{CF_1}{(1+r)^1} + \frac{CF_2}{(1+r)^2} + \cdots + \frac{CF_n}{(1+r)^n}$$

$$FV = DCF \cdot (1+r)^n$$

Thus the discounted present value (for one cash flow in one future period) is expressed as:

$$DPV = \frac{FV}{(1+r)^n}$$

where

- *DPV* is the discounted present value of the future cash flow (*FV*), or *FV* adjusted for the delay in receipt;
- *FV* is the nominal value of a cash flow amount in a future period;
- *r* is the interest rate or discount rate, which reflects the cost of tying up capital and may also allow for the risk that the payment may not be received in full;
- *n* is the time in years before the future cash flow occurs.

Where multiple cash flows in multiple time periods are discounted, it is necessary to sum them as follows:

$$DPV = \sum_{t=0}^{N} \frac{FV_t}{(1+r)^t}$$

for each future cash flow (*FV*) at any time period (*t*) in years from the present time, summed over all time periods. The sum can then be used as a net present value figure. If the amount to be paid at time 0 (now) for all the future cash flows is known, then that amount can be substituted for *DPV* and the equation can be solved for *r*, that is the internal rate of return.

All the above assumes that the interest rate remains constant throughout the whole period.

Continuous Cash Flows

For continuous cash flows, the summation in the above formula is replaced by an integration:

$$DPV = \int_0^T FV(t)e^{-\lambda t}dt,$$

where $FV(t)$ is now the *rate* of cash flow, and $\lambda = log(1+r)$.

Example DCF

To show how discounted cash flow analysis is performed, consider the following simplified example.

- John Doe buys a house for \$100,000. Three years later, he expects to be able to sell this house for \$150,000.

Simple subtraction suggests that the value of his profit on such a transaction would be \$150,000 " \$100,000 = \$50,000, or 50%. If that \$50,000 is amortized over the three years, his implied annual return (known as the internal rate of return) would be about 14.5%. Looking at those figures, he might be justified in thinking that the purchase looked like a good idea.

$$1.145^3 \times 100000 = 150000 \text{ approximately.}$$

However, since three years have passed between the purchase and the sale, any cash flow from the sale must be discounted accordingly. At the time John Doe buys the house, the 3-year US Treasury Note rate is 5% per annum. Treasury Notes are generally considered to be inherently less risky than real estate, since the value of the Note is guaranteed by the US Government and there is a liquid market for the purchase and sale of T-Notes. If he hadn't put his money into buying the house, he could have invested it in the relatively safe T-Notes instead. This 5% per annum can therefore be regarded as the risk-free interest rate for the relevant period (3 years).

Using the DPV formula above (FV=$150,000, i=0.05, n=3), that means that the value of $150,000 received in three years actually has a present value of $129,576 (rounded off). In other words we would need to invest $129,576 in a T-Bond now to get $150,000 in 3 years almost risk free. This is a quantitative way of showing that money in the future is not as valuable as money in the present ($150,000 in 3 years isn't worth the same as $150,000 now; it is worth $129,576 now).

Subtracting the purchase price of the house ($100,000) from the present value results in the net present value of the whole transaction, which would be $29,576 or a little more than 29% of the purchase price.

Another way of looking at the deal as the excess return achieved (over the risk-free rate) is (114.5 - 105)/(100 + 5) or approximately 9.0% (still very respectable).

But What about Risk?

We assume that the $150,000 is John's best estimate of the sale price that he will be able to achieve in 3 years time (after deducting all expenses, of course). There is of course a lot of uncertainty about house prices, and the outcome may end up higher or lower than this estimate.

(The house John is buying is in a "good neighbourhood," but market values have been rising quite a lot lately and the real estate market analysts in the media are talking about a slow-down and higher interest rates. There is a probability that John might not be able to get the full $150,000 he is expecting in three years due to a slowing of price appreciation, or that loss of liquidity in the real estate market might make it very hard for him to sell at all.)

Under normal circumstances, people entering into such transactions are risk-averse, that is to say that they are prepared to accept a lower expected return for the sake of avoiding risk. For the sake of the example (and this is a gross simplification), let's assume that he values this particular risk at 5% per annum (we could perform a more precise probabilistic analysis of the risk, but that is beyond the scope of this article). Therefore, allowing for this risk, his expected return is now 9.0% per annum (the arithmetic is the same as above).

And the excess return over the risk-free rate is now (109 - 105)/(100 + 5) which comes to approximately 3.8% per annum.

That return rate may seem low, but it is still positive after all of our discounting, suggesting that the investment decision is probably a good one: it produces enough profit to compensate for tying up capital and incurring risk with a little extra left over. When investors and managers perform DCF analysis, the important thing is that the net present value of the decision after discounting all future cash flows at least be positive (more than zero). If it is negative, that means that the investment decision would actually *lose* money even if it appears to generate a nominal profit. For instance, if the expected sale price of John Doe's house in the example above was not $150,000 in three years, but *$130,000* in three years or $150,000 in *five* years, then on the above assumptions buying the house would actually cause John to *lose* money in present-value terms (about $3,000 in the first case, and about $8,000 in the second). Similarly, if the house was located in an undesirable neighbourhood and the Federal Reserve Bank was about to raise interest rates by five percentage points, then the risk factor would be a lot higher than 5%: it might not be possible for him to predict a profit in discounted terms even if he thinks he could sell the house for *$200,000* in three years.

In this example, only one future cash flow was considered. For a decision which generates multiple cash flows in multiple time periods, all the cash flows must be discounted and then summed into a single net present value.

Methods of Appraisal of a Company or Project

This is necessarily a simple treatment of a complex subject: more detail is beyond the scope of this article.

For these valuation purposes, a number of different DCF methods are distinguished today, some of which are outlined below. The details are likely to vary depending on the capital structure of the company. However the assumptions used in the appraisal (especially the equity discount rate and the projection of the cash flows to be achieved) are likely to be at least as important as the precise model used.

Both the income stream selected and the associated cost of capital model determine the valuation result obtained with each method. This is one reason these valuation methods are formally referred to as the Discounted Future Economic Income methods.

- Equity-Approach
  - *Flows to equity approach (FTE):*Discount the cash flows available to the holders of equity capital, after allowing for cost of servicing debt capital

Advantages: Makes explicit allowance for the cost of debt capital

Disadvantages: Requires judgement on choice of discount rate

- Entity-Approach:
  - *Adjusted present value approach (APV):* Discount the cash flows before allowing for the debt capital (but allowing for the tax relief obtained on the debt capital)

Advantages: Simpler to apply if a specific project is being valued which does not have earmarked debt capital finance

Disadvantages: Requires judgement on choice of discount rate; no explicit allowance for cost of debt capital, which may be much higher than a "risk-free" rate

  - *Weighted average cost of capital approach (WACC):* Derive a weighted cost of the capital obtained from the various sources and use that discount rate to discount the cash flows from the project

Advantages: Overcomes the requirement for debt capital finance to be earmarked to particular projects

Disadvantages: Care must be exercised in the selection of the appropriate income stream. The net cash flow to total invested capital is the generally accepted choice.

  - *Total cash flow approach (TCF):* This distinction illustrates that the Discounted Cash Flow method can be used to determine the value of various business ownership interests. These can include equity or debt holders.

Alternatively, the method can be used to value the company based on the value of total invested capital. In each case, the differences lie in the choice of the income stream and discount rate. For example, the net cash flow to total invested capital and WACC are appropriate when valuing a company based on the market value of all invested capital.

Shortcomings

Commercial banks have widely used discounted cash flow as a method of valuing commercial real estate construction projects. This practice has two substantial shortcomings. 1) The discount rate assumption relies on the market for competing investments at the time of the analysis, which would likely change, perhaps dramatically, over time, and 2) straight line assumptions about income increasing over ten years are generally based upon historic increases in market rent but never factors in the cyclical nature of many real estate markets. Most loans are made during boom real estate markets and these markets usually last fewer than ten years. Using DCF to analyze commercial real estate during any but the early years of a boom market will lead to overvaluation of the asset.

Discounted cash flow models are powerful, but they do have shortcomings. DCF is merely a mechanical valuation tool, which makes it subject to the principle "garbage in, garbage out". Small changes in inputs can result in large changes in the value of a company. Instead of trying to project the cash flows to infinity, terminal value techniques are often used. A simple annuity is used to estimate the terminal value past 10 years, for example. This is done because it is harder to come to a realistic estimate of the cash flows as time goes on involves calculating the period of time likely to recoup the initial outlay.

Marginal Cost

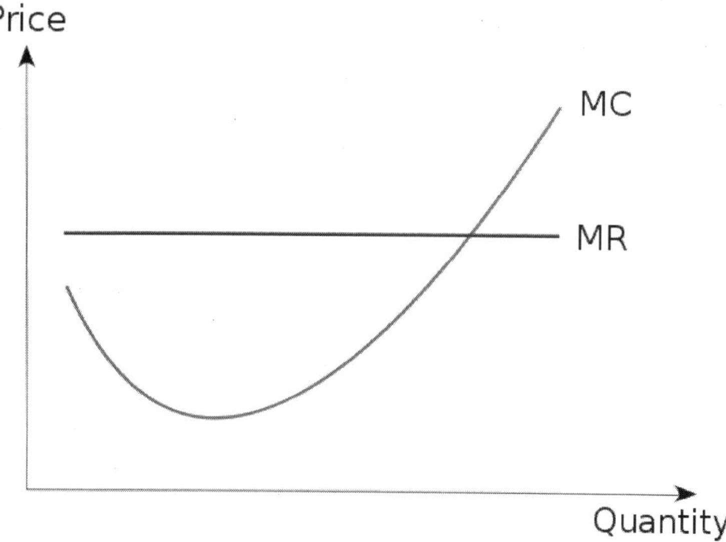

Figure: *A typical marginal cost curve with marginal revenue overlaid*

In economics and finance, marginal cost is the change in the total cost that arises when the quantity produced has an increment by unit. That is, it is the cost of producing one more unit of a good. In general terms, marginal cost at each level of production includes any additional costs required to produce the next unit. For example, if producing additional vehicles requires building a new factory, the marginal cost of the *extra* vehicles includes the cost of the new factory. In practice, this analysis is segregated into short and long-run cases, so that over the longest run, all costs become marginal. At each level of production and time period being considered, marginal costs include all costs that vary with the level of production, whereas other costs that do not vary with production are considered fixed.

If the good being produced is infinitely divisible, so the size of a marginal cost will change with volume, as a non-linear and non-proportional cost function includes the following:

- variable terms dependent to volume,
- constant terms independent to volume and occurring with the respective lot size,
- jump fix cost increase or decrease dependent to steps of volume increase.

In practice the above definition of marginal cost as the change in total cost as a result of an increase in output of one unit is inconsistent with the differential definition of marginal cost for virtually all non-linear functions. This is as the definition finds the tangent to the total cost curve at the point q which assumes that costs increase at the same rate as they were at q. A new definition may be useful for marginal unit cost (MUC) using the current definition of the change in total cost as a result of an increase of one unit of output defined as: TC(q+1)-TC(q) and redefining marginal cost to be the change in total as a result of an infinitesimally small increase in q which is consistent with its use in economic literature and can be calculated differentially.

If the cost function is differentiable joining, the marginal cost is the cost of the next unit produced referring to the basic volume.

$$\text{Marginal Cost } (MC) = \frac{dC}{dQ}$$

If the cost function is not differentiable, the marginal cost can be expressed as follows.

$$MC = \frac{\Delta C}{\Delta Q}$$

A number of other factors can affect marginal cost and its applicability to real world problems. Some of these may be considered market failures. These may include information asymmetries, the presence of negative or positive externalities, transaction costs, price discrimination and others.

Cost Functions and Relationship to Average Cost

In the simplest case, the total cost function and its derivative are expressed as follows, where Q represents the production quantity, VC represents variable costs, FC represents fixed costs and TC represents total costs.

$$\frac{\mathrm{d}C}{\mathrm{d}Q} = \frac{\mathrm{d}(C_0 + \Delta C)}{\mathrm{d}Q} = \frac{\mathrm{d}\Delta C}{\mathrm{d}Q}$$

Since (by definition) fixed costs do not vary with production quantity, it drops out of the equation when it is differentiated. The important conclusion is that marginal cost *is not related to* fixed costs. This can be compared with average total cost or ATC, which is the total cost divided by the number of units produced and *does* include fixed costs.

$$ATC = \frac{C_0 + \Delta C}{Q}$$

For discrete calculation without calculus, marginal cost equals the change in total (or variable) cost that comes with each additional unit produced. In contrast, incremental cost is the composition of total cost from the surrogate of contributions, where any increment is determined by the contribution of the cost factors, not necessarily by single units.

For instance, suppose the total cost of making 1 shoe is $30 and the total cost of making 2 shoes is $40. The marginal cost of producing the second shoe is $40 – $30 = $10.

Marginal cost is not the cost of producing the “next” or “last” unit. As Silberberg and Suen note, the cost of the last unit is the same as the cost of the first unit and every other unit. In the short run, increasing production requires using more of the variable input — conventionally assumed to be labour. Adding more labour to a fixed capital stock reduces the marginal product of labour because of the diminishing marginal returns. This reduction in productivity is not limited to the additional labour needed to produce the marginal unit - the productivity of every unit of labour is reduced. Thus the costs of producing the marginal unit of output has two components: the cost associated with producing the marginal unit and the increase in average costs for all units produced due to the "damage" to the entire productive process $\left(\partial AC / \partial q\right)$ q. The first component is the per unit or average cost. The second unit is the small increase in costs due to the law of diminishing marginal returns which increases the costs of all units of sold. Therefore, the precise formula is: MC = AC + (∂ AC/∂ q)q.

Marginal costs can also be expressed as the cost per unit of labour divided by the marginal product of labour.

$$MC = \frac{\Delta VC}{\Delta Q}$$

$$\Delta VC = w\Delta L$$

$$MC = \frac{w\Delta L}{\Delta Q}$$

Because $\frac{\Delta L}{\Delta Q}$ is the change in quantity of labour that affects a one unit change in output, this implies that this equals $\frac{1}{MPL}$. Therefore $MC = \frac{w}{MPL}$ Since the wage rate is assumed constant, marginal cost and marginal product of labour have an inverse relationship—if marginal cost is increasing (decreasing) the marginal product of labour is decreasing (increasing).

Economies of Scale

Economies of scale is a concept that applies to the long run, a span of time in which all inputs can be varied by the firm so that there are no fixed inputs or fixed costs. Production may be subject to economies of scale (or diseconomies of scale).

Economies of scale are said to exist if an additional unit of output can be produced for less than the average of all previous units— that is, if long-run marginal cost is below long-run average cost, so the latter is falling. Conversely, there may be levels of production where marginal cost is higher than average cost, and average cost is an increasing function of output. For this generic case, minimum average cost occurs at the point where average cost and marginal cost are equal (when plotted, the marginal cost curve intersects the average cost curve from below); this point will *not* be at the minimum for marginal cost if fixed costs are greater than 0.

Perfectly Competitive Supply Curve

The portion of the marginal cost curve above its intersection with the average variable cost curve is the supply curve for a firm operating in a perfectly competitive market. (the portion of the MC curve below its intersection with the AVC curve is not part of the supply curve because a firm would not operate at price below the shut down point) This is not true for firms operating in other market structures. For example, while a monopoly "has" an MC curve it does not have a supply curve. In a perfectly competitive market, a supply curve shows the quantity a seller's willing and able to supply at each price - for each price there is a unique quantity that would be supplied. The one-to-one relationship simply is absent in the case of a monopoly. With a monopoly there could be an infinite number of prices associated with a given quantity. It all depends on the shape and position of the demand curve and its accompanying marginal revenue curve.

Decisions Taken Based on Marginal Costs

In perfectly competitive markets, firms decide the quantity to be produced based on marginal costs and sale price. If the sale price is higher than the marginal cost, then they supply the unit and sell it. If the marginal cost is higher than the price, it would not be profitable to produce it. So the production will be carried out until the marginal cost is equal to the sale price. In other words, firms refuse to sell if the marginal cost is higher than the market price.

Relationship to Fixed Costs

Marginal costs are not affected by changes in fixed cost. Marginal costs can be expressed as $\Delta C(q)$—ΔQ. Since fixed costs do not vary with (depend on) changes in quantity, MC is ΔVC—ΔQ. Thus if fixed cost were to double MC would not be affected and consequently the profit maximizing quantity and price would not change. This can be illustrated by graphing the short run total cost curve and the short run variable cost curve. The shape of the curves are identical. Each curve initially decreases at a decreasing rate, reaches an inflection point, then increases at an increasing rate. The only difference between the curves is that the SRVC curve begins from the origin while the SRTC curve originates on the y-axis. The distance of the origin of the SRTC above the origin represents the fixed cost - the vertical distance between the curves. This distance remains constant as the quantity produced, Q, increases. MC is the slope of the SRVC curve. A change in fixed cost would be reflected by a change in the vertical distance between the SRTC and SRVC curve. Any such change would have no effect on the shape of the SRVC curve and therefore its slope at any point - MC.

Externalities

Externalities are costs (or benefits) that are not borne by the parties to the economic transaction. A producer may, for example, pollute the environment, and others may bear those costs. A consumer may consume a good which produces benefits for society, such as education; because the individual does not receive all of the benefits, he may consume less than efficiency would suggest. Alternatively, an individual may be a smoker or alcoholic and impose costs on others. In these cases, production or consumption of the good in question may differ from the optimum level.

Negative Externalities of Production

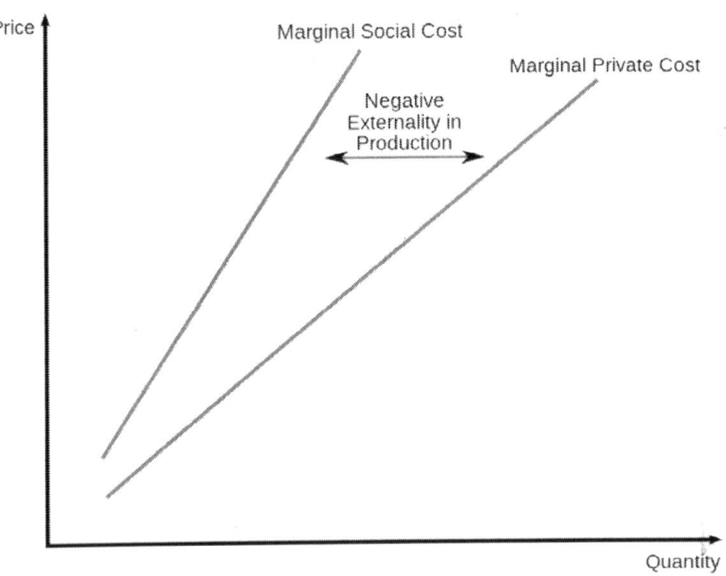

Figure: *Negative Externalities of Production*

Much of the time, private and social costs do not diverge from one another, but at times social costs may be either greater or less than private costs. When marginal social costs of production are greater than that of the private cost function, we see the occurrence of a negative externality of production. Productive processes that result in pollution are a textbook example of production that creates negative externalities.

Such externalities are a result of firms externalising their costs onto a third party in order to reduce their own total cost. As a result of externalising such costs we see that members of society will be negatively affected by such behaviour of the firm. In this case, we see that an increased cost of production on society creates a social cost curve that depicts a greater cost than the private cost curve.

In an equilibrium state we see that markets creating negative externalities of production will overproduce that good. As a result, the socially optimal production level would be lower than that observed.

Positive Externalities of Production

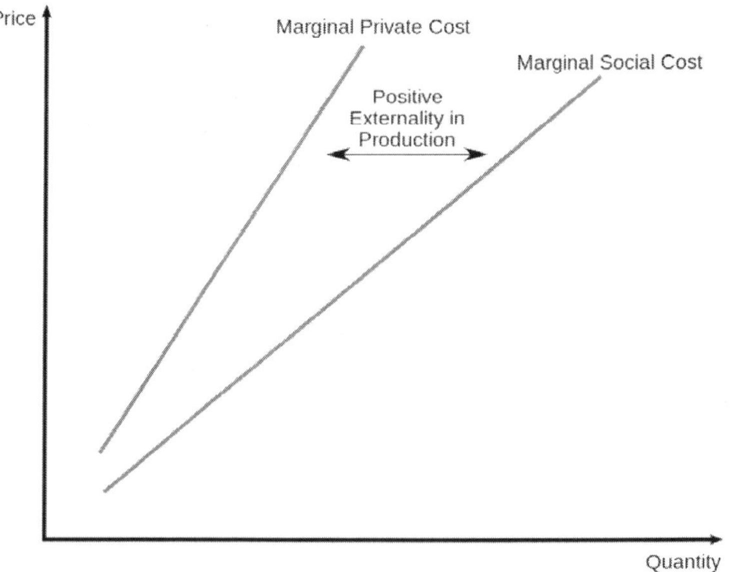

Figure: *Positive Externalities of Production*

When marginal social costs of production are less than that of the private cost function, we see the occurrence of a positive externality of production. Production of public goods are a textbook example of production that create positive externalities. An example of such a public good, which creates a divergence in social and private costs, includes the production of education. It is often seen that education is a positive for any whole society, as well as a positive for those directly involved in the market.

Examining the relevant diagram we see that such production creates a social cost curve that is less than that of the private curve. In an equilibrium state we see that markets creating positive externalities of production will under produce that good. As a result, the socially optimal production level would be greater than that observed.

Social Costs

Of great importance in the theory of marginal cost is the distinction between the marginal *private* and *social* costs. The marginal private cost shows the cost associated to the firm in question. It is the marginal private cost that is used by business decision makers in their profit maximization goals.

Marginal social cost is similar to private cost in that it includes the cost of private enterprise but *also* any other cost (or offsetting benefit) to society to parties having no direct association with purchase or sale of the product. It incorporates all negative and positive externalities, of both production and consumption. Examples might include a social cost from air pollution affecting third parties or a social benefit from flu shots protecting others from infection.

Chapter 2

Analyzing the Financial Resources of the Business

Financial Issues

One of the most critical aspects of management pertains to the finances of running a firm. Although there are numerous issues facing modern managers with respect to financial management, the following sections will address three of the most ubiquitous—acquisition of outside capital for start-up and growth, management of working capital and cash flow, and the construction and implementation of a capital budgeting process. Accessing the capital markets is fundamental for procuring funds that allow the firm to grow. Working capital involves managing the current assets and liabilities of the firm. Capital budgeting is the process of making long-term fixed asset investments.

Accessing the Financial Markets

In the initial start-up of any firm, management must procure the funds needed to get the business off the ground. These funds may come from a variety of sources, but managers should be aware that all assets are initially financed with either of two sources of capital—equity and debt. The capital markets represent the method by which external funds are made available to firms requiring outside capital infusions.

Equity Markets

The equity markets are the means by which managers may raise capital by selling portions of the firm's ownership. The most common method is selling common stock in the firm. Outside investors provide the firm with new investment capital in exchange for ownership rights in the firm. As owners, stockholders receive voting rights and may participate in the financial success of the firm. In corporations, stockholders are protected by limited liability, meaning they are liable only for losses limited to the amount invested in the firm's stock; personal assets are protected against liability. Other sources of equity capital include contributions by the individual owner or owners from their own resources, and those made by family and friends of originators of the business.

Another method of raising equity capital involves the sale of preferred stock in the firm. Preferred stock promises to pay investors a stated dividend amount, and may also offer the opportunity for eventual conversion into common shares, commonly called convertible preferred stock. Preferred stock is particularly important for larger corporations as a source of funds because current tax law subsidizes the investment by one corporation in another corporation's preferred stock by exempting a portion of dividend income from taxation.

Other methods of equity capital attainment include the selling of warrants and rights. Warrants are securities that grant the holder the right to purchase a fixed number of common shares in the firm at a specified price for a specified period of time. Because warrants are stand-alone securities that may be traded among investors, the firm may raise new capital immediately through the sale of warrants while delaying the dilution of existing stockholders's interests until the warrants are exercised.

Rights are similar to warrants in that firms issue rights as a method of raising new equity capital. In a rights offering, the firm issues additional common stock to raise new capital. Rights are then issued to all outstanding shareholders, giving them the right to purchase shares in the new offering to avoid dilution of their pro-rata ownership in the firm. Through the use of rights, the firm is able to directly access the group of investors who are already interested in the firm's financial success, namely existing shareholders. Because rights have value in that they allow the purchase of new shares at a set subscription price, they are desired by shareholders and may be sold to others if the shareholder decides not to use the rights.

Debt Markets

The other major market for outside capital is the debt market. The debt market is often vital to the financial success of a firm and managers must be familiar with, and have access to, outside sources of debt capital to ensure the survival of the firm. A common method of debt financing is borrowing from financial institutions. Banks, finance companies, and other lenders offer loans of varying terms that are critical for financial management, particularly short-term debt to alleviate temporary cash flow problems. A firm that experiences seasonal sales or uneven production schedules will sometimes utilise an established line of credit to borrow during times of capital needs and repay during times of cash surplus. By arranging credit lines prior to the capital need, managers assure that the firm will not experience sales or production interruptions due to cash shortages. For longer-term needs, negotiated notes from lenders serve as an intermediate source of debt financing.

For longer-term capital, the bond markets represent the primary source of debt financing. Bonds are debt securities in which investors become creditors of the firm in exchange for the right to receive payments of interest at regular intervals. For firms desiring to grow beyond local or regional status, access to the bond markets is critical for long-term capital needs, especially when firms do not desire to dilute existing ownership by offering additional equity financing.

Short-term Financial Issues

Short-term financial issues for managers revolve around two primary areas; the management of current assets and current liabilities. Together, they constitute the overall management of cash flow for the firm. Cash flow management is absolutely critical to the financial survival of a firm, since a shortage of cash may result in a firm that shows a profit on its income statement actually going bankrupt by being unable to meet its financial obligations.

Current Assets

Management of a firm's current assets starts with the management of cash. Cash provides the liquidity needed to meet everyday obligations owed to creditors and suppliers and the flexibility to take advantage of new opportunities that may arise. Managing cash is a tricky issue for many firms; cash is a necessary component of daily operations, yet cash is a non-earning asset. Dollars tied up in cash (checking accounts) could be earning higher rates of return if invested in other areas. Larger corporations spend considerable time and resources in cash management, whereby dollars are transferred back and forth between cash accounts and marketable securities that earn a higher rate of return. As previously mentioned, negotiated credit lines serve to supplement depleted cash during periods of shortage.

Another critical issue is the management of accounts receivable. Receivables are money owed to the firm that has not yet been collected.

They represent an important investment for the firm, since dollars not yet received cannot earn a positive return. The management of accounts receivable involves the determination and implementation of the firm's credit policy such as how long customers are allowed to pay for merchandise or services received and cash discounts for immediate rather than deferred payment. These are important financial issues for any manager: to whom does the company extend credit, for how much, and for how long? A tight credit policy may result in missed sales opportunities, since fewer potential customers will qualify for credit sales. Conversely, liberal credit terms may result in longer average collection periods and greater uncollected accounts. There are real costs associated with these issues, and managers must work to find appropriate trade-offs that result not only in higher sales, but also in the greatest profitability.

A third aspect of current asset management involves the management of inventories. Like receivables, inventory represents an investment of resources by the firm that has yet to pay off. On one hand, adequate inventory levels are necessary to ensure uninterrupted production schedules and to meet unexpected sales demand. However, too much inventory means dollars tied up in non-earning assets that could be devoted to more profitable investments. Managers must decide whether to attempt to coordinate production with sales patterns, or maintain level production regardless of current demand. These decisions spill over into other areas such as employee morale, since uneven or random production scheduling may result in temporary layoffs or overtime requirements. Again, managers utilise negotiated credit lines to access capital to maintain needed inventory materials when production and sales patterns differ.

Current Liabilities

Management of current liabilities involves accounts payable, short-term bank loans, lines of credit, and, for larger corporations, commercial paper. While the importance of short-term credit lines has already been discussed, accounts payable management is a critical issue, particularly for smaller firms. The longer a firm takes to pay its creditors, the longer it maintains access to and has the use of the funds. Thus, managers have every incentive to pay outstanding bills as slowly as possible. However, taking too long to pay may result in suppliers declining to offer future credit. Trade credit offered by suppliers is one of the most important sources of short-term financing for small firms that have limited access to other capital market sources. It is incumbent on managers to seek and negotiate the most favourable trade credit terms possible, since longer payment periods reduce potential cash flow problems and provide greater financial flexibility.

Larger corporations are able to issue commercial paper to provide short-term financial liquidity. Commercial paper is a short-term, unsecured note backed only by the firm's ability to repay. As such, only large, established firms find a market for their commercial paper. Firms such as General Motors use commercial paper as a regular source of short-term debt financing to cover cash flow shortages and provide the firm with ready liquidity.

Cash Budget

Pulling together the management of current assets and liabilities results in the development of a cash budget. A cash budget is a schedule of expected cash inflows and outflows by a period that allows managers the ability to plan for and cover cash shortfalls and surpluses. A successful cash budget prevents the types of surprises or shortages that can result in financial crises such as the inability to pay creditors or purchase additional inventory to meet production needs.

Likewise, managers should work to monitor and manage the firm's cash conversion cycle. The cash conversion cycle consists, primarily, of three elements: the inventory conversion period, the receivable collections period, and the payables deferral period. The goal of effective cash management is to minimize the inventory conversion and receivables collection periods, and to maximize the payables deferral period. Through the successful management of current assets and liabilities, managers can maintain a cash conversion cycle that provides the firm with liquidity and profitability while avoiding the cash flow problems that so often result in financial distress.

Capital Budgeting Analysis

The third major financial issue for managers involves long-term investments. This area, collectively known as capital budgeting, involves investment in fixed assets such as plant and equipment, new product and business analysis, and expansion and merger analysis. Capital budgeting is extremely important, because the decisions made involve the direction and opportunities for the future growth of the firm. The goal of corporate management is to maximize shareholder wealth; profitable capital projects result in increased firm value.

Discounted Cash Flow

This process is also known as discounted cash flow analysis. The first step in evaluating a long-term investment opportunity is to estimate the net cash flows that would accrue to the firm. Managers should take care to use economically-sound techniques in cash flow analysis. All cash flows should be incremental (i.e., those that would otherwise not accrue to the firm unless this project or investment is undertaken). They should be on an after-tax basis; the only relevant cash flows are those that the firm will actually receive after all expenses and taxes are paid.

Finally, sunk costs should not be included in the net cash flows associated with the project or investment. Only those cash flows associated with the future profitability of the investment should be included in the decision analysis. The proper economic decision is whether or not to invest today, and that decision is based on how the future cash flows will affect the present value of the firm. Past expenditures are not part of the analysis.

Once the project's net cash flows are determined, the timing of the cash flows should be considered. This is the discounted portion of discounted cash flow analysis. The decision of whether or not to invest is made in the present, so all dollars associated with the investment should be converted into present-value dollars. Managers must determine the proper interest rate at which to discount future cash flows. The discount rate should represent the opportunity cost of capital—the rate of return that could be earned on alternative investment projects of similar risk. Many firms set an internal "hurdle rate" for capital budgeting analysis, in effect saying no long-term investments will be undertaken that offer an expected rate of return lower than the hurdle rate. Normally, this rate is the weighted average cost of capital, which incorporates the firm's capital structure in determining the required rate of return on investment.

Net Present Value Analysis

Once the net cash flows are determined and the discount rate has been established, managers should utilise a discounted cash flow method to evaluate and rank investment alternatives. The most economically-sound technique is net present value analysis (NPV), which involves discounting all future project cash flows back to the present using the firm's discount rate, then subtracting the net cost of the investment project. If the present value of the future cash-flow stream exceeds the present cost, then undertaking the project would add value to the firm today. The NPV method is congruent with the idea of management's goal to maximize the present value, which represents shareholder wealth, of the firm.

Internal Rate of Return

Another popular technique is the internal rate of return (IRR) method. The IRR is actually a special case of the NPV method. The internal rate of return is the unique discount rate that equates the present value of the future cash flow stream to the net cost of the project. If the IRR of the project is greater than the firm's hurdle rate, then the project offers a chance to earn a profitable return on investment and should be undertaken.

Payback Method

Finally, a third technique often used is the payback method. The payback method attempts to determine how long it will take for the project to recoup the total investment costs. Unlike the NPV and the IRR methods, the payback method is not a measure of profitability. Instead, it is a measure of time. Firms and managers often set a (subjective) hurdle period, such as no projects will be undertaken which do not recoup their initial costs in less than five years. The analysis then involves comparing the pay-back of the proposed investment to the firm's hurdle period. The payback method is popular because it provides an answer to a frequently-asked question—namely "how long before this investment pays for itself?" However, it is a flawed method because it does not consider all of the project's cash flows and does not consider the time value of money. Managers should employ the payback technique only in tandem with at least one of either the NPV or IRR discounted cash-flow methods.

Financial management is an integral aspect of managing a company. Accessing the capital markets to provide investment dollars, managing the working capital of the firm to ensure liquidity and flexibility, and making long-term investment decisions are all important issues that managers should address to allow the firm to grow and prosper.

Internal Control

Internal control, as defined in accounting and auditing, is a process for assuring achievement of an organisation's objectives in operational effectiveness and efficiency, reliable financial reporting, and compliance with laws, regulations and policies. A broad concept, internal control involves everything that controls risks to an organisation.

It is a means by which an organisation's resources are directed, monitored, and measured. It plays an important role in detecting and preventing fraud and protecting the organisation's resources, both physical (e.g., machinery and property) and intangible (e.g., reputation or intellectual property such as trademarks).

At the organisational level, internal control objectives relate to the reliability of financial reporting, timely feedback on the achievement of operational or strategic goals, and compliance with laws and regulations. At the specific transaction level, internal control refers to the actions taken to achieve a specific objective (e.g., how to ensure the organisation's payments to third parties are for valid services rendered.) Internal control procedures reduce process variation, leading to more predictable outcomes. Internal control is a key element of the Foreign Corrupt Practices Act (FCPA) of 1977 and the Sarbanes–Oxley Act of 2002, which required improvements in internal control in United States public corporations. Internal controls within business entities are also referred to as operational controls.

Early History of Internal Control

Internal controls have existed from ancient times. In Hellenistic Egypt there was a dual administration, with one set of bureaucrats charged with collecting taxes and another with supervising them. In the Republic of China, the Control *Yuan* (γvß[b–; pinyin: Jiânchá Yùan), one of the five branches of government, is an investigatory agency that monitors the other branches of government.

Definitions

There are many definitions of internal control, as it affects the various constituencies (stakeholders) of an organisation in various ways and at different levels of aggregation.

Under the COSO Internal Control-Integrated Framework, a widely used framework in not only the United States but around the world, internal control is broadly defined as a process, effected by an entity's board of directors, management, and other personnel, designed to provide reasonable assurance regarding the achievement of objectives relating to operations, reporting, and compliance..

COSO Defines Internal Control as Having Five Components

1. Control Environment-sets the tone for the organisation, influencing the control consciousness of its people. It is the foundation for all other components of internal control.
2. Risk Assessment-the identification and analysis of relevant risks to the achievement of objectives, forming a basis for how the risks should be managed

3. Information and Communication-systems or processes that support the identification, capture, and exchange of information in a form and time frame that enable people to carry out their responsibilities
4. Control Activities-the policies and procedures that help ensure management directives are carried out.
5. Monitoring-processes used to assess the quality of internal control performance over time.

The COSO definition relates to the aggregate control system of the organisation, which is composed of many individual control procedures.

Discrete control procedures, or *controls* are defined by the SEC as: "...a specific set of policies, procedures, and activities designed to meet an objective. A control may exist within a designated function or activity in a process. A control's impact...may be entity-wide or specific to an account balance, class of transactions or application. Controls have unique characteristics – for example, they can be: automated or manual; reconciliations; segregation of duties; review and approval authorizations; safeguarding and accountability of assets; preventing or detecting error or fraud. Controls within a process may consist of financial reporting controls and operational controls (that is, those designed to achieve operational objectives)."

Context

More generally, setting objectives, budgets, plans and other expectations establish criteria for control. Control itself exists to keep performance or a state of affairs within what is expected, allowed or accepted. Control built within a process is internal in nature. It takes place with a combination of interrelated components – such as social environment effecting behaviour of employees, information necessary in control, and policies and procedures. Internal control structure is a plan determining how internal control consists of these elements.

The concepts of corporate governance also heavily rely on the necessity of internal controls. Internal controls help ensure that processes operate as designed and that risk responses (risk treatments) in risk management are carried out (COSO II). In addition, there needs to be in place circumstances ensuring that the aforementioned procedures will be performed as intended: right attitudes, integrity and competence, and monitoring by managers.

Roles and Responsibilities in Internal Control

According to the COSO Framework, everyone in an organisation has responsibility for internal control to some extent. Virtually all employees produce information used in the internal control system or take other actions needed to affect control. Also, all personnel should be responsible for communicating upward problems in operations, noncompliance with the code of conduct, or other policy violations or illegal actions. Each major entity in corporate governance has a particular role to play:

Management

The Chief Executive Officer (the top manager) of the organisation has overall responsibility for designing and implementing effective internal control. More than any other individual, the chief executive sets the "tone at the top" that affects integrity and ethics and other factors of a positive control environment. In a large company, the chief executive fulfills this duty by providing leadership and direction to senior managers and reviewing the way they're controlling the business. Senior managers, in turn, assign responsibility for establishment of more specific internal control policies and procedures to personnel responsible for the unit's functions. In a smaller entity, the influence of the chief executive, often an owner-manager, is usually more direct. In any event, in a cascading responsibility, a manager is effectively a chief executive of his or her sphere of responsibility. Of particular significance are financial officers and their staffs, whose control activities cut across, as well as up and down, the operating and other units of an enterprise.

Board of Directors

Management is accountable to the board of directors, which provides governance, guidance and oversight. Effective board members are objective, capable and inquisitive. They also have a knowledge of the entity's activities and environment, and commit the time necessary to fulfil their board responsibilities. Management may be in a position to override controls and ignore or stifle communications from subordinates, enabling a dishonest management which intentionally misrepresents results to cover its tracks. A strong, active board, particularly when coupled with effective upward communications channels and capable financial, legal and internal audit functions, is often best able to identify and correct such a problem.

Auditors

The internal auditors and external auditors of the organisation also measure the effectiveness of internal control through their efforts. They assess whether the controls are properly designed, implemented and working effectively, and make recommendations on how to improve internal control. They may also review Information technology controls, which relate to the IT systems of the organisation. There are laws and regulations on internal control related to financial reporting in a number of jurisdictions. In the U.S. these regulations are specifically established by Sections 404 and 302 of the Sarbanes-Oxley Act. Guidance on auditing these controls is specified in PCAOB *Auditing Standard No. 5* and SEC guidance, further discussed in SOX 404 top-down risk assessment. To provide reasonable assurance that internal controls involved in the financial reporting process are effective, they are tested by the external auditor (the organisation's public accountants), who are required to opine on the internal controls of the company and the reliability of its financial reporting.

Audit Committee

The role and the responsibilities of the audit committee, in general terms, are to: (a) Discuss with management, internal and external auditors and major stakeholders the quality and adequacy of the organisation's internal controls system and risk management process, and their effectiveness and outcomes, and meet regularly and privately with the Director of Internal Audit; (b) Review and discuss with management and the external auditors and approve the audited financial statements of the organisation and make a recommendation regarding inclusion of those financial statements in any public filing. Also review with management and the independent auditor the effect of regulatory and accounting initiatives as well as off-balance sheet issues in the organisation's financial statements; (c) Review and discuss with management the types of information to be disclosed and the types of presentations to be made with respect to the Company's earning press release and financial information and earnings guidance provided to analysts and rating agencies; (d) Confirm the scope of audits to be performed by the external and internal auditors, monitor progress and review results and review fees and expenses. Review significant findings or unsatisfactory internal audit reports, or audit problems or difficulties encountered by the external independent auditor. Monitor management's response to all audit findings; (e) Manage complaints concerning accounting, internal accounting controls or auditing matters; (f) Receive regular reports from the Chief Executive Officer, Chief Financial Officer and the Company's other Control Committees regarding deficiencies in the design or operation of internal controls and any fraud that involves management or other employees with a significant role in internal controls; and (g) Support management in resolving conflicts of interest. Monitor the adequacy of the organisation's internal controls and ensure that all fraud cases are acted upon.

Personnel Benefits Committee

The role and the responsibilities of the personnel benefits, in general terms, are to: (a) Approve and oversee administration of the Company's Executive Compensation Program; (b) Review and approve specific compensation matters for the Chief Executive Officer, Chief Operating Officer (if applicable), Chief Financial Officer, General Counsel, Senior Human Resources Officer, Treasurer, Director, Corporate Relations and Management, and Company Directors; (c) Review, as appropriate, any changes to compensation matters for the officers listed above with the Board; and (d)Review and monitor all human-resource related performance and compliance activities and reports, including the performance management system. They also ensure that benefit-related performance measures are properly used by the management of the organisation.

Operating Staff

All staff members should be responsible for reporting problems of operations, monitoring and improving their performance, and monitoring non-compliance with the corporate policies and various professional codes, or violations of policies, standards, practices and procedures. Their particular responsibilities should be documented in their individual personnel files. In performance management activities they take part in all compliance and performance data collection and processing activities as they are part of various organisational units and may also be responsible for various compliance and operational-related activities of the organisation.

Staff and junior managers may be involved in evaluating the controls within their own organisational unit using a control self-assessment.

Limitations

Internal control can provide reasonable, not absolute, assurance that the objectives of an organisation will be met. The concept of reasonable assurance implies a high degree of assurance, constrained by the costs and benefits of establishing incremental control procedures.

Effective internal control implies the organisation generates reliable financial reporting and substantially complies with the laws and regulations that apply to it. However, whether an organisation achieves operational and strategic objectives may depend on factors outside the enterprise, such as competition or technological innovation. These factors are outside the scope of internal control; therefore, effective internal control provides only timely information or feedback on progress towards the achievement of operational and strategic objectives, but cannot guarantee their achievement.

Describing Internal Controls

Internal controls may be described in terms of: a) the pertinent objective or financial statement assertion; and b) the nature of the control activity itself.

Objective or Assertions Categorization

Controls may be defined against the particular financial statement assertion to which they relate. There are five such assertions:

1. Existence/Occurrence/Validity: Only valid or authorized transactions are processed.
2. Completeness: All transactions are processed that should be.
3. Rights and obligations: Assets are the rights of the organisation and the liabilities are its obligations as of a given date.
4. Valuation: Transactions are valued accurately using the proper methodology, such as a specified means of computation or formula.
5. Presentation and disclosure: Accounts and disclosures are properly described in the financial statements of the organisation.

For example, a validity control objective might be: "Payments are made only for authorized products and services received." A typical control procedure would be: "The payable system compares the purchase order, receiving record, and vendor invoice prior to authorizing payment." Management is responsible for implementing appropriate controls that apply to all transactions in their areas of responsibility.

Activity Categorization

Control activities may also be explained by the type or nature of activity. These include (but are not limited to):

- Segregation of duties – separating authorization, custody, and record keeping roles to prevent fraud or error by one person.
- Authorization of transactions – review of particular transactions by an appropriate person.
- Retention of records – maintaining documentation to substantiate transactions.
- Supervision or monitoring of operations – observation or review of ongoing operational activity.

- Physical safeguards – usage of cameras, locks, physical barriers, etc. to protect property, such as merchandise inventory.
- Top-level reviews-analysis of actual results versus organisational goals or plans, periodic and regular operational reviews, metrics, and other key performance indicators (KPIs).
- IT general controls – Controls related to: a) Security, to ensure access to systems and data is restricted to authorized personnel, such as usage of passwords and review of access logs; and b) Change management, to ensure program code is properly controlled, such as separation of production and test environments, system and user testing of changes prior to acceptance, and controls over migration of code into production.
- IT application controls – Controls over information processing enforced by IT applications, such as edit checks to validate data entry, accounting for transactions in numerical sequences, and comparing file totals with control accounts.

Control Precision

Control precision describes the alignment or correlation between a particular control procedure and a given control objective or risk. A control with direct impact on the achievement of an objective (or mitigation of a risk) is said to be more precise than one with indirect impact on the objective or risk. Precision is distinct from sufficiency; that is, multiple controls with varying degrees of precision may be involved in achieving a control objective or mitigating a risk.

Precision is an important factor in performing a SOX 404 top-down risk assessment. After identifying specific financial reporting material misstatement risks, management and the external auditors are required to identify and test controls that mitigate the risks. This involves making judgments regarding both precision and sufficiency of controls required to mitigate the risks.

Risks and controls may be entity-level or assertion-level under the PCAOB guidance. Entity-level controls are identified to address entity-level risks. However, a combination of entity-level and assertion-level controls are typically identified to address assertion-level risks. The PCAOB set forth a three-level hierarchy for considering the precision of entity-level controls. Later guidance by the PCAOB regarding small public firms provided several factors to consider in assessing precision.

Fraud and Internal Control

Internal control plays an important role in the prevention and detection of fraud. Under the Sarbanes-Oxley Act, companies are required to perform a fraud risk assessment and assess related controls. This typically involves identifying scenarios in which theft or loss could occur and determining if existing control procedures effectively manage the risk to an acceptable level. The risk that senior management might override important financial controls to manipulate financial reporting is also a key area of focus in fraud risk assessment.

The AICPA, IIA, and ACFE also sponsored a guide published during 2008 that includes a framework for helping organisations manage their fraud risk.

Internal Controls and Process Improvement

Controls can be evaluated and improved to make a business operation run more effectively and efficiently. For example, automating controls that are manual in nature can save costs and improve transaction processing. If the internal control system is thought of by executives as only a means of preventing fraud and complying with laws and regulations, an important opportunity may be missed. Internal controls can also be used to systematically improve businesses, particularly in regard to effectiveness and efficiency.

Continuous Controls Monitoring

Advances in technology and data analysis have led to the development of numerous tools which can automatically evaluate the effectiveness of internal controls. Used in conjunction with continuous auditing, continuous controls monitoring provides assurance on financial information flowing through the business processes.

Intangible Asset

Intangible asset is an asset that lacks physical substance and usually is very hard to evaluate. It includes patents, copyrights, franchises, goodwill, trademarks, trade names.

Definition

Intangible assets have been argued to be one possible contributor to the disparity between company value as per their accounting records, and company value as per their market capitalization. Considering this argument, it is important to understand what an intangible asset truly is in the eyes of an accountant. A number of attempts have been made to define intangible assets:

- Prior to 2005 the Australian Accounting Standards Board issued the Statement of Accounting Concepts number 4 (SAC 4). This statement did not provide a formal definition of an intangible asset but did provide that tangibility was not an essential characteristic of asset.

- International Accounting Standards Board standard 38 (IAS 38) defines an intangible asset as: "an identifiable non-monetary asset without physical substance." This definition is in addition to the standard definition of an asset which requires a *past event* that has given rise to a resource that the entity *controls* and from which *future economic benefits* are expected to flow. Thus, the extra requirement for an intangible asset under IAS 38 is *identifiability*. This criterion requires that an intangible asset is separable from the entity or that it arises from a contractual or legal right.
- The Financial Accounting Standards Board Accounting Standard Codification 350 (ASC 350) defines an intangible asset as an asset, other than a financial asset, that lacks physical substance.

The lack of physical substance would therefore seem to be a defining characteristic of an intangible asset. Both the IASB and FASB definitions specifically preclude monetary assets in their definition of an intangible asset. This is necessary in order to avoid the classification of items such as accounts receivable, derivatives and cash in the bank as an intangible asset. IAS 38 contains examples of intangible assets, including: computer software, copyright and patents.

Research and Development

IAS 38 requires any project that results in the generation of a resource to the entity be classified into two phases: a research phase, and a development phase.

Research is defined as "the original and planned investigation undertaken with the prospect of gaining new scientific or technical knowledge and understanding. For example, a company can carry a research on one of its products which it will use in the entity of which results in future economic income.

Development is defined as "the application of research findings to a plan or design for the production of new or substantially improved materials, devices, products, processes, systems, or services, before the start of commercial production or use."

The accounting treatment of such expenses depends on whether it is classified as research or development. Where the distinction cannot be made, IAS 38 requires that the entire project be treated as research and expensed through the Statement of Comprehensive Income.

As research expenditure is highly speculative, there is no certainty that future economic benefits will flow to the entity. As such, prudence dictates that research expenditure be expensed through the Statement of Comprehensive Income. Development expenditure, however, is less speculative and it becomes possible to predict the future economic benefits that will flow to the entity. The matching concept dictates that development expenditure be capitalised as the expenditure will generate future economic benefit to the entity.

The classification of research and development expenditure can be highly subjective, and it is important to note that organisations may have an ulterior motive in its classification of research and development expenditure. Less scrupulous directors may manipulate financial statements through their classification of research and development expenditure.

Financial Accounting

General Standards: The International Accounting Standards Board (IASB) offers some guidance (IAS 38) as to how intangible assets should be accounted for in financial statements. In general, legal intangibles that are developed internally are not recognised and legal intangibles that are purchased from third parties are recognised. Wordings are similar to IAS 9.

Under US GAAP, intangible assets are classified into: Purchased vs. internally created intangibles, and Limited-life vs. indefinite-life intangibles.

Expense Allocation

Intangible assets are typically expensed according to their respective life expectancy. Intangible assets have either an identifiable or indefinite useful life. Intangible assets with identifiable useful lives are amortized on a straight-line basis over their economic or legal life, whichever is shorter. Examples of intangible assets with identifiable useful lives include copyrights and patents. Intangible assets with indefinite useful lives are reassessed each year for impairment. If an impairment has occurred, then a loss must be recognised. An impairment loss is determined by subtracting the asset's fair value from the asset's book/carrying value. Trademarks and goodwill are examples of intangible assets with indefinite useful lives. Goodwill has to be tested for impairment rather than amortized. If impaired, goodwill is reduced and loss is recognised in the Income statement.

Taxation

For personal income tax purposes, some costs with respect to intangible assets must be capitalized rather than treated as deductible expenses. Treasury regulations generally require capitalization of costs associated with acquiring, creating, or enhancing intangible assets. For example, an amount paid to obtain a trademark must be capitalized. Certain amounts paid to facilitate these transactions are also capitalized. Some types of intangible assets are categorized based on whether the asset is acquired from another party or created by the taxpayer. The regulations contain many provisions intended to make it easier to determine when capitalization is required.

Definition of "intangibles" differs from standard accounting, in some US state governments. These governments may refer to stocks and bonds as "intangibles. "

Forecasting Demand

Forecasting

Forecasting involves the generation of a number, set of numbers, or scenario that corresponds to a future occurrence. It is absolutely essential to short-range and long-range planning. By definition, a forecast is based on past data, as opposed to a prediction, which is more subjective and based on instinct, gut feel, or guess. For example, the evening news gives the weather "forecast" not the weather "prediction." Regardless, the terms forecast and prediction are often used inter-changeably. For example, definitions of regression—a technique sometimes used in forecasting—generally state that its purpose is to explain or "predict."

Forecasting is Based on a Number of Assumptions:

1. The past will repeat itself. In other words, what has happened in the past will happen again in the future.
2. As the forecast horizon shortens, forecast accuracy increases. For instance, a forecast for tomorrow will be more accurate than a forecast for next month; a forecast for next month will be more accurate than a forecast for next year; and a forecast for next year will be more accurate than a forecast for ten years in the future.
3. Forecasting in the aggregate is more accurate than forecasting individual items. This means that a company will be able to forecast total demand over its entire spectrum of products more accurately than it will be able to forecast individual stock-keeping units (SKUs). For example, General Motors can more accurately forecast the total number of cars needed for next year than the total number of white Chevrolet Impalas with a certain option package.

4. Forecasts are seldom accurate. Furthermore, forecasts are almost never totally accurate. While some are very close, few are "right on the money." Therefore, it is wise to offer a forecast "range." If one were to forecast a demand of 100,000 units for the next month, it is extremely unlikely that demand would equal 100,000 exactly. However, a forecast of 90,000 to 110,000 would provide a much larger target for planning.

William J. Stevenson Lists a Number of Characteristics that are Common to a Good Forecast

- Accurate—some degree of accuracy should be determined and stated so that comparison can be made to alternative forecasts.
- Reliable—the forecast method should consistently provide a good forecast if the user is to establish some degree of confidence.
- Timely—a certain amount of time is needed to respond to the forecast so the forecasting horizon must allow for the time necessary to make changes.
- Easy to use and understand—users of the forecast must be confident and comfortable working with it.
- Cost-effective—the cost of making the forecast should not outweigh the benefits obtained from the forecast.

Forecasting techniques range from the simple to the extremely complex. These techniques are usually classified as being qualitative or quantitative.

Qualitative Techniques

Qualitative forecasting techniques are generally more subjective than their quantitative counterparts. Qualitative techniques are more useful in the earlier stages of the product life cycle, when less past data exists for use in quantitative methods. Qualitative methods include the Delphi technique, Nominal Group Technique (NGT), sales force opinions, executive opinions, and market research.

The Delphi Technique

The Delphi technique uses a panel of experts to produce a forecast. Each expert is asked to provide a forecast specific to the need at hand. After the initial forecasts are made, each expert reads what every other expert wrote and is, of course, influenced by their views. A subsequent forecast is then made by each expert. Each expert then reads again what every other expert wrote and is again influenced by the perceptions of the others. This process repeats itself until each expert nears agreement on the needed scenario or numbers.

Nominal Group Technique

Nominal Group Technique is similar to the Delphi technique in that it utilises a group of participants, usually experts. After the participants respond to forecast-related questions, they rank their responses in order of perceived relative importance. Then the rankings are collected and aggregated. Eventually, the group should reach a consensus regarding the priorities of the ranked issues.

Sales Force Opinions

The sales staff is often a good source of information regarding future demand. The sales manager may ask for input from each salesperson and aggregate their responses into a sales force composite forecast. Caution should be exercised when using this technique as the members of the sales force may not be able to distinguish between what customers say and what they actually do. Also, if the forecasts will be used to establish sales quotas, the sales force may be tempted to provide lower estimates.

Executive Opinions

Sometimes upper-levels managers meet and develop forecasts based on their knowledge of their areas of responsibility. This is sometimes referred to as a jury of executive opinion.

Market Research

In market research, consumer surveys are used to establish potential demand. Such marketing research usually involves constructing a questionnaire that solicits personal, demographic, economic, and marketing information. On occasion, market researchers collect such information in person at retail outlets and malls, where the consumer can experience—taste, feel, smell, and see—a particular product. The researcher must be careful that the sample of people surveyed is representative of the desired consumer target.

Quantitative Techniques

Quantitative forecasting techniques are generally more objective than their qualitative counterparts. Quantitative forecasts can be time-series forecasts (i.e., a projection of the past into the future) or forecasts based on associative models (i.e., based on one or more explanatory variables). Time-series data may have underlying behaviours that need to be identified by the forecaster. In addition, the forecast may need to identify the causes of the behaviour. Some of these behaviours may be patterns or simply random variations. Among the patterns are:

- Trends, which are long-term movements (up or down) in the data.
- Seasonality, which produces short-term variations that are usually related to the time of year, month, or even a particular day, as witnessed by retail sales at Christmas or the spikes in banking activity on the first of the month and on Fridays.
- Cycles, which are wavelike variations lasting more than a year that are usually tied to economic or political conditions.
- Irregular variations that do not reflect typical behaviour, such as a period of extreme weather or a union strike.
- Random variations, which encompass all non-typical behaviours not accounted for by the other classifications.

Among the time-series models, the simplest is the naïve forecast. A naïve forecast simply uses the actual demand for the past period as the forecasted demand for the next period. This, of course, makes the assumption that the past will repeat. It also assumes that any trends, seasonality, or cycles are either reflected in the previous period's demand or do not exist.

***Table:** Naïve Forecasting*

Period	***Actual Demand (000's)***	***Forecast (000's)***
January	45	
February	60	45
March	72	60
April	58	72
May	40	58
June		40

Another simple technique is the use of averaging. To make a forecast using averaging, one simply takes the average of some number of periods of past data by summing each period and dividing the result by the number of periods. This technique has been found to be very effective for short-range forecasting.

Variations of averaging include the moving average, the weighted average, and the weighted moving average. A moving average takes a predetermined number of periods, sums their actual demand, and divides by the number of periods to reach a forecast. For each subsequent period, the oldest period of data drops off and the latest period is added. Assuming a three-month moving average and using the data from Table, one would simply add 45 (January), 60 (February), and 72 (March) and divide by three to arrive at a forecast for April:

$$45 + 60 + 72 = 177 \div 3 = 59$$

To arrive at a forecast for May, one would drop January's demand from the equation and add the demand from April.

Table: *Three Month Moving Average Forecast*

Period	***Actual Demand (000's)***	***Forecast (000's)***
January	45	
February	60	
March	72	
April	58	59
May	40	63
June		57

A weighted average applies a predetermined weight to each month of past data, sums the past data from each period, and divides by the total of the weights. If the forecaster adjusts the weights so that their sum is equal to 1, then the weights are multiplied by the actual demand of each applicable period. The results are then summed to achieve a weighted forecast. Generally, the more recent the data the higher the weight, and the older the data the smaller the weight. Using the demand example, a weighted average using weights of .4, .3, .2, and .1 would yield the forecast for June as:

$$60(.1) + 72(.2) + 58(.3) + 40(.4) = 53.8$$

Forecasters may also use a combination of the weighted average and moving average forecasts. A weighted moving average forecast assigns weights to a predetermined number of periods of actual data and computes the forecast the same way as described above. As with all moving forecasts, as each new period is added, the data from the oldest period is discarded.

Table: *Three–Month Weighted Moving Average Forecast*

Period	***Actual Demand (000's)***	***Forecast (000's)***
January	45	
February	60	
March	72	
April	58	55
May	40	63
June		61

A more complex form of weighted moving average is exponential smoothing, so named because the weight falls off exponentially as the data ages. Exponential smoothing takes the previous period's forecast and adjusts it by a predetermined smoothing constant, α (called alpha;

the value for alpha is less than one) multiplied by the difference in the previous forecast and the demand that actually occurred during the previously forecasted period (called forecast error). Exponential smoothing is expressed formulaically as such:

New forecast = previous forecast + alpha (actual demand " previous forecast)

$$F = F + \alpha(A - F)$$

Exponential smoothing requires the forecaster to begin the forecast in a past period and work forward to the period for which a current forecast is needed. A substantial amount of past data and a beginning or initial forecast are also necessary. The initial forecast can be an actual forecast from a previous period, the actual demand from a previous period, or it can be estimated by averaging all or part of the past data. Some heuristics exist for computing an initial forecast. For example, the heuristic $N = (2 \div \alpha) - 1$ and an alpha of .5 would yield an N of 3, indicating the user would average the first three periods of data to get an initial forecast. However, the accuracy of the initial forecast is not critical if one is using large amounts of data, since exponential smoothing is "self-correcting." Given enough periods of past data, exponential smoothing will eventually make enough corrections to compensate for a reasonably inaccurate initial forecast. Using the data used in other examples, an initial forecast of 50, and an alpha of .7, a forecast for February is computed as such:

New forecast (February) = 50 + .7(45 – 50) = 41.5

Next, the forecast for March:

New forecast (March) = 41.5 + .7(60 – 41.5) = 54.45

This process continues until the forecaster reaches the desired period. In Table this would be for the month of June, since the actual demand for June is not known.

Table:

Period	*Actual Demand (000's)*	*Forecast (000's)*
January	45	50
February	60	41.5
March	72	54.45
April	58	66.74
May	40	60.62
June		46.19

An extension of exponential smoothing can be used when time-series data exhibits a linear trend. This method is known by several names: double smoothing; trend-adjusted exponential smoothing; forecast including trend (FIT); and Holt's Model. Without adjustment, simple exponential smoothing results will lag the trend, that is, the forecast will always be low if the trend is increasing, or high if the trend is decreasing. With this model there are two smoothing constants, α and β with β representing the trend component.

An extension of Holt's Model, called Holt-Winter's Method, takes into account both trend and seasonality. There are two versions, multiplicative and additive, with the multiplicative being the most widely used. In the additive model, seasonality is expressed as a quantity to be added to or subtracted from the series average. The multiplicative model expresses seasonality as a percentage—known as seasonal relatives or seasonal indexes—of the average (or trend). These are then multiplied times values in order to incorporate seasonality. A relative of 0.8 would indicate demand that is 80 percent of the average, while 1.10 would indicate demand that is 10 percent above the average. Detailed information regarding this method can be found in most operations management textbooks or one of a number of books on forecasting.

Associative or causal techniques involve the identification of variables that can be used to predict another variable of interest. For example, interest rates may be used to forecast the demand for home refinancing. Typically, this involves the use of linear regression, where the objective is to develop an equation that summarizes the effects of the predictor (independent) variables upon the forecasted (dependent) variable. If the predictor variable were plotted, the object would be to obtain an equation of a straight line that minimizes the sum of the squared deviations from the line (with deviation being the distance from each point to the line). The equation would appear as: $y = a + bx$, where y is the predicted (dependent) variable, x is the predictor (independent) variable, b is the slope of the line, and a is equal to the height of the line at the y-intercept. Once the equation is determined, the user can insert current values for the predictor (independent) variable to arrive at a forecast (dependent variable).

If there is more than one predictor variable or if the relationship between predictor and forecast is not linear, simple linear regression will be inadequate. For situations with multiple predictors, multiple regression should be employed, while non-linear relationships call for the use of curvilinear regression.

Econometric Forecasting

Econometric methods, such as autoregressive integrated moving-average model (ARIMA), use complex mathematical equations to show past relationships between demand and variables that influence the demand. An equation is derived and then tested and fine-tuned to ensure that it is as reliable a representation of the past relationship as possible. Once this is done, projected values of the influencing variables (income, prices, etc.) are inserted into the equation to make a forecast.

Evaluating Forecasts

Forecast accuracy can be determined by computing the bias, mean absolute deviation (MAD), mean square error (MSE), or mean absolute percent error (MAPE) for the forecast using different values for alpha. Bias is the sum of the forecast errors [Σ(FE)]. For the exponential smoothing example above, the computed bias would be:

$$(60 - 41.5) + (72 - 54.45) + (58 - 66.74) + (40 - 60.62) = 6.69$$

If one assumes that a low bias indicates an overall low forecast error, one could compute the bias for a number of potential values of alpha and assume that the one with the lowest bias would be the most accurate. However, caution must be observed in that wildly inaccurate forecasts may yield a low bias if they tend to be both over forecast and under forecast (negative and positive). For example, over three periods a firm may use a particular value of alpha to over forecast by 75,000 units (–75,000), under forecast by 100,000 units (+100,000), and then over forecast by 25,000 units (–25,000), yielding a bias of zero (–75,000 + 100,000 – 25,000 = 0). By comparison, another alpha yielding over forecasts of 2,000 units, 1,000 units, and 3,000 units would result in a bias of 5,000 units. If normal demand was 100,000 units per period, the first alpha would yield forecasts that were off by as much as 100 percent while the second alpha would be off by a maximum of only 3 percent, even though the bias in the first forecast was zero.

A safer measure of forecast accuracy is the mean absolute deviation (MAD). To compute the MAD, the forecaster sums the absolute value of the forecast errors and then divides by the number of forecasts ($\Sigma |FE| \div N$). By taking the absolute value of the forecast errors, the offsetting of positive and negative values are avoided. This means that both an over forecast of 50 and an under forecast of 50 are off by 50. Using the data from the exponential smoothing example, MAD can be computed as follows:

$$(|60 - 41.5| + |72 - 54.45| + |58 - 66.74| + |40 - 60.62|) \div 4 = 16.35$$

Therefore, the forecaster is off an average of 16.35 units per forecast. When compared to the result of other alphas, the forecaster will know that the alpha with the lowest MAD is yielding the most accurate forecast.

Mean square error (MSE) can also be utilised in the same fashion. MSE is the sum of the forecast errors squared divided by N-1 [(Σ(FE)) ÷ (N-1)]. Squaring the forecast errors eliminates the possibility of offsetting negative numbers, since none of the results can be negative. Utilising the same data as above, the MSE would be:

$$[(18.5) + (17.55) + (-8.74) + (-20.62)] \div 3 = 383.94$$

As with MAD, the forecaster may compare the MSE of forecasts derived using various values of alpha and assume the alpha with the lowest MSE is yielding the most accurate forecast.

The mean absolute percent error (MAPE) is the average absolute percent error. To arrive at the MAPE one must take the sum of the ratios between forecast error and actual demand times 100 (to get the percentage) and divide by N [(Σ | Actual demand – forecast | ÷ Actual demand) × 100 ÷ N]. Using the data from the exponential smoothing example, MAPE can be computed as follows:

$$[(18.5/60 + 17.55/72 + 8.74/58 + 20.62/48) \times 100] \div 4 = 28.33\%$$

As with MAD and MSE, the lower the relative error the more accurate the forecast.

It should be noted that in some cases the ability of the forecast to change quickly to respond to changes in data patterns is considered to be more important than accuracy. Therefore, one's choice of forecasting method should reflect the relative balance of importance between accuracy and responsiveness, as determined by the forecaster.

Making a Forecast

William J. Stevenson lists the following as the basic steps in the forecasting process:

- Determine the forecast's purpose. Factors such as how and when the forecast will be used, the degree of accuracy needed, and the level of detail desired determine the cost (time, money, employees) that can be dedicated to the forecast and the type of forecasting method to be utilised.
- Establish a time horizon. This occurs after one has determined the purpose of the forecast. Longer-term forecasts require longer time horizons and vice versa. Accuracy is again a consideration.
- Select a forecasting technique. The technique selected depends upon the purpose of the forecast, the time horizon desired, and the allowed cost.
- Gather and analyze data. The amount and type of data needed is governed by the forecast's purpose, the forecasting technique selected, and any cost considerations.

- Make the forecast.
- Monitor the forecast. Evaluate the performance of the forecast and modify, if necessary.

Pricing Policy and Strategy

Managers should start setting prices during the development stage as part of strategic pricing to avoid launching products or services that cannot sustain profitable prices in the market. This approach to pricing enables companies to either fit costs to prices or scrap products or services that cannot be generated cost-effectively. Through systematic pricing policies and strategies, companies can reap greater profits and increase or defend their market shares. Setting prices is one of the principal tasks of marketing and finance managers in that the price of a product or service often plays a significant role in that product's or service's success, not to mention in a company's profitability. Generally, pricing policy refers how a company sets the prices of its products and services based on costs, value, demand, and competition. Pricing strategy, on the other hand, refers to how a company uses pricing to achieve its strategic goals, such as offering lower prices to increase sales volume or higher prices to decrease backlog. Despite some degree of difference, pricing policy and strategy tend to overlap, and the different policies and strategies are not necessarily mutually exclusive.

After establishing the bases for their prices, managers can begin developing pricing strategies by determining company pricing goals, such as increasing short-term and long-term profits, stabilizing prices, increasing cash flow, and warding off competition. Managers also must take into account current market conditions when developing pricing strategies to ensure that the prices they choose fit market conditions. In addition, effective pricing strategy involves considering customers, costs, competition, and different market segments.

Pricing strategy entails more than reacting to market conditions, such as reducing pricing because competitors have reduced their prices. Instead, it encompasses more thorough planning and consideration of customers, competitors, and company goals. Furthermore, pricing strategies tend to vary depending on whether a company is a new entrant into a market or an established firm. New entrants sometimes offer products at low cost to attract market share, while incumbents' reactions vary. Incumbents that fear the new entrant will challenge the incumbents' customer base may match prices or go even lower than the new entrant to protect its market share. If incumbents do not view the new entrant as a serious threat, incumbents may simply resort to increased advertising aimed at enhancing customer loyalty, but have no change in price in efforts to keep the new entrant from stealing away customers.

The following sections explain various ways companies develop pricing policy and strategy. First, cost-based pricing is considered. This is followed by the second topic of value-based pricing. Third, demand-based pricing is addressed followed by competition-based pricing. After this, several strategies for new and established pricing strategies are explained.

Cost-based Pricing

The traditional pricing policy can be summarized by the formula:

Cost + Fixed profit percentage = Selling price.

Cost-based pricing involves the determination of all fixed and variable costs associated with a product or service. After the total costs attributable to the product or service have been determined, managers add a desired profit margin to each unit such as a 5 or 10 percent markup. The goal of the cost-oriented approach is to cover all costs incurred in producing or delivering products or services and to achieve a targeted level of profit.

By itself, this method is simple and straightforward, requiring only that managers study financial and accounting records to determine prices. This pricing approach does not involve examining the market or considering the competition and other factors that might have an impact on pricing. Cost-oriented pricing also is popular because it is an age-old practice that uses internal information that managers can obtain easily. In addition, a company can defend its prices based on costs, and demonstrate that its prices cover costs plus a markup for profit.

However, critics contend that the cost-oriented strategy fails to provide a company with an effective pricing policy. One problem with the cost-plus strategy is that determining a unit's cost before its price is difficult in many industries because unit costs may vary depending on volume. As a result, many business analysts have criticized this method, arguing that it is no longer appropriate for modern market conditions. Cost-based pricing generally leads to high prices in weak markets and low prices in strong markets, thereby impeding profitability because these prices are the exact opposites of what strategic prices would be if market conditions were taken into consideration.

While managers must consider costs when developing a pricing policy and strategy, costs alone should not determine prices. Many managers of industrial goods and service companies sell their products and services at incremental cost, and make their substantial profits from their best customers and from short-notice deliveries. When considering costs, managers should ask what costs they can afford to pay, taking into account the prices the market allows, and still allow for a profit on the sale. In addition, managers must consider production costs in order to determine what goods to produce and in what amounts. Nevertheless, pricing generally involves determining what prices customers can afford before determining what amount of products to produce. By bearing in mind the prices they can charge and the costs they can afford to pay, managers can determine whether their costs enable them to compete in the low-cost market, where customers are concerned primarily with price, or whether they must compete in the premium-price market, in which customers are primarily concerned with quality and features.

Value-Based Pricing

Value pricers adhere to the thinking that the optimal selling price is a reflection of a product or service's perceived value by customers, not just the company's costs to produce or provide a product or service. The value of a product or service is derived from customer needs, preferences, expectations, and financial resources as well as from competitors' offerings. Consequently, this approach calls for managers to query customers and research the market to determine how much they value a product or service. In addition, managers must compare their products or services with those of their competitors to identify their value advantages and disadvantages.

Yet, value-based pricing is not just creating customer satisfaction or making sales because customer satisfaction may be achieved through discounting alone, a pricing strategy that could also lead to greater sales. However, discounting may not necessarily lead to profitability. Value pricing involves setting prices to increase profitability by tapping into more of a product or service's value attributes. This approach to pricing also depends heavily on strong advertising, especially for new products or services, in order to communicate the value of products or services to customers and to motivate customers to pay more if necessary for the value provided by these products or services.

Demand-based Pricing

Managers adopting demand-based pricing policies are, like value pricers, not fully concerned with costs. Instead, they concentrate on the behaviour and characteristics of customers and the quality and characteristics of their products or services. Demand-oriented pricing focuses on the level of demand for a product or service, not on the cost of materials, labour, and so forth.

According to this pricing policy, managers try to determine the amount of products or services they can sell at different prices. Managers need demand schedules in order to determine prices based on demand. Using demand schedules, managers can figure out which production and sales levels would be the most profitable. To determine the most profitable production and sales levels, managers examine production and marketing costs estimates at different sales levels. The prices are determined by considering the cost estimates at different sales levels and expected revenues from sales volumes associated with projected prices.

The success of this strategy depends on the reliability of demand estimates. Hence, the crucial obstacle managers face with this approach is accurately gauging demand, which requires extensive knowledge of the manifold market factors that may have an impact on the number of products sold. Two common options managers have for obtaining accurate estimates are enlisting the help from either sales representatives or market experts. Managers frequently ask sales representatives to estimate increases or decreases in demand stemming from specific increases or decreases in a product or service's price, since sales representatives generally are attuned to market trends and customer demands. Alternatively, managers can seek the assistance of experts such as market researchers or consultants to provide estimates of sales levels at various unit prices.

Competition-Based Pricing

With a competition-based pricing policy, a company sets its prices by determining what other companies competing in the market charge. A company begins developing competition-based prices by identifying its present competitors. Next, a company assesses its own product or service. After this step, a company sets it prices higher than, lower than, or on par with the competitors based on the advantages and disadvantages of a company's product or service as well as on the expected response by competitors to the set price. This last consideration-the response of competitors-is an important part of competition-based pricing, especially in markets with only a few competitors. In such a market, if one competitor lowers its price, the others will most likely lower theirs as well.

This pricing policy allows companies to set prices quickly with relatively little effort, since it does not require as accurate market data as the demand pricing. Competitive pricing also makes distributors more receptive to a company's products because they are priced within the range the distributor already handles. Furthermore, this pricing policy enables companies to select from a variety of different pricing strategies to achieve their strategic goals. In other words, companies can choose to mark their prices above, below, or on par with their competitors' prices and thereby influence customer perceptions of their products. For example, if a Company A sets its prices above those of its competitors, the higher price could suggest that Company A's products or services are superior in quality. Harley Davidson used this with great success. Although Harley-Davidson uses many of the same parts suppliers as Honda, Kawasaki, Yamaha, and Honda, they price well above the competitive price of these competitors. Harley's high prices combined with its customer loyalty and mystique help overcome buyer resistance to higher prices. Production efficiencies over the last two decades, however, have made quality among motorcycle producers about equal, but pricing above the market signals quality to buyers, whether or not they get the quality premium they pay for.

Strategies for New

Product pricing strategies frequently depend on the stage a product or service is in its life cycle; that is, new products often require different pricing strategies than established products or mature products.

New Product Pricing Strategy

Entrants often rely on pricing strategies that allow them to capture market share quickly. When there are several competitors in a market, entrants usually use lower pricing to change consumer spending habits and acquire market share. To appeal to customers effectively, entrants generally implement a simple or transparent pricing structure, which enables customers to compare prices easily and understand that the entrants have lower prices than established incumbent companies.

Complex pricing arrangements, however, prevent lower pricing from being a successful strategy in that customers cannot readily compare prices with hidden and contingent costs. The long-distance telephone market illustrates this point; large corporations have lengthy telephone bills that include numerous contingent costs, which depend on location, use, and service features. Consequently, competitors in the corporate long-distance telephone service market do not use lower pricing as the primary pricing strategy, as they do in the consumer and small-business markets, where telephone billing is much simpler.

Another example is the computer industry. Dell, Fujitsu, HP, and many others personal computer makers offer bundles of products that make it more difficult for consumers to sort out the true differences among these competitors. For example, consumers purchasing an HP computer from the retailer, Best Buy, will have not only the computer itself, but also six months of "free" Internet access bundled into the price. Comparing the absolute value of each personal computer become more difficult as an increasing number of other products such as Quicken, Adobe's Photoshop Elements, and other software are sold together with the purchase. For Macintosh users or for those who might consider switching from a personal computer to a Macintosh, Apple announced in 2005 that it would begin selling the Mac Mini, a Macintosh that, as with PC makers, bundles its iLife software into the mix. By extending its brand to non-premium price tiers, Apple will compete head-to-head with established firms. And although the Mac Mini is at a low price point, starting at $499, it will be difficult for consumers to directly compare the bundled products of PCs directly with the bundled products of Apple's Mac Mini. The complexity of these comparisons is what can make such new product pricing successful.

Established Product Pricing Strategy

Sometimes established companies need not adjust their prices at all in response to entrants and their lower prices, because customers frequently are willing to pay more for the products or services of an established company to avoid perceived risks associated with switching products or services.

However, when established companies do not have this advantage, they must implement other pricing strategies to preserve their market share and profits. When entrants are involved, established companies sometimes attempt to hide their actual prices by embedding them in complex prices. This tactic makes it difficult for customers to compare prices, which is advantageous to established companies competing with entrants that have lower prices. In addition, established companies also may use a more complex pricing plan, such as a two-part pricing tactic. This tactic especially benefits companies with significant market power. Local telephone companies, for example, use this strategy, charging both fixed and per-minute charges.

Market Segmentation

Because all customers do not have the same needs, expectations, and financial resources, managers can improve their pricing strategies by segmenting markets. Successful segmentation comes about when managers determine what motivates particular markets and what differences exist in the market when taken as a whole. For example, some customers may be motivated largely by price, while others are motivated by functionality and utility. The idea behind segmentation is to divide a large group into a set of smaller groups that share significant characteristics such as age, income, geographic location, lifestyle, and so on. By dividing a market into two or more segments, a company can devise a pricing scheme that will appeal to the motivations of each of the different market segments or it can decide to target only particular segments of the market that best correspond to its products or services and their prices.

Managers can use market segmentation strategically to price products or services in order to attain company objectives. Companies can set prices differently for different segments based on factors such as location, time of sale, quantity of sale, product design, and a number of others, depending on the way companies divide up the market. By doing so, companies can increase their profits, market share, cash flow, and so forth.

Product Life Cycle and Industry Life Cycle

Recognising that all living things go through a cycle of birth, growth, maturity, and death, the inspiration for the concepts of product life cycle and industry life cycle comes from biology. The life-cycle concept is an appropriate description of what happens to products and industries over time. When applied to organisations, the product life cycle and industry life cycle contain the four stages of introduction, growth, maturity, and decline.

This concept is much more than an interesting analogy of business and biology. In biology, a living organism's position in its life cycle leads to different courses of action concerning the organism's future. An industry's position and a product's position in their life cycles also lead to very different decisions concerning their futures. Consequently, the life-cycle concept was adopted from biology for use as a strategic planning tool for products and industries.

The following sections define the terms, explain why products have a life cycle, describe the stages of the product life cycle, and examine the strategic implications of the product life cycle.

Definitions

The life cycle can be used to observe the behaviour of many concepts in business. In its classic form, which is described in a later section, it is best applied to products and industries. Used in this form, a product is not individual but a group of similar products. For example, the Chevrolet Malibu, Ford Taurus, and Honda Accord are a product group of mid-sized sedans.

Industry is a much broader classification than product; an industry consists of many similar groups of products. The product groups of mid-size sedan, pickup truck, and sport-utility vehicle all belong to the automobile industry.

Generally, industries have longer life cycles than products. The automobile industry has lasted more than 100 years and shows no signs of declining. However, the large family-sedan appears to be well into the decline stage. After decades of dominance in the automobile industry, only a few large cars, such as Ford's Crown Victoria, are being manufactured.

The life-cycle concept also describes individual brand products, such as the Ford Taurus. However, individual products in a group of products usually have much shorter life cycles, and they do not always follow the classic shape of the product life cycle. They may be introduced and die, and then be reintroduced again at a latter point. For example, the Chevrolet Nova has had more than one life cycle. Consequently, products are defined as groups of similar products, and industries defined as a collection of comparable product groups.

The discussion that follows is applicable to both industries and products. The terms product life cycle and industry life cycle both refer to the four stages of introduction, growth, maturity, and decline. To simplify the discussion, both the product life cycle and industry life cycle will be combined and simply called the product life cycle.

Rationale for the Product Life Cycle

Since products are not living beings, why do they have life cycles? The reason is that society accepts products at different rates, but all go through similar stages of societal acceptance. This acceptance of innovations by societies is called the diffusion of innovations. As society begins to adopt and accept an innovation, the new product grows, eventually reaching maturity. When there is a better alternative to the product or when public preference changes, the products will enter a decline, possibly ending with the death of the product.

The diffusion-of-innovations concept categorizes society by the speed with which the individual members adopt a new product. It classifies people into the five categories of innovators, early adopters, early majority, late majority, and laggards.

Innovators

The first people in a society to adopt a new product are the innovators. These people are risk takers and may be looking for new products to try. They represent only 2.5 percent of the population. Though these people are the first to try a product, they are not usually opinion leaders. Consequently, they do not pass information about the product to the rest of the population.

Early Adopters

The early adopters have many opinion leaders in their ranks. They are the first people in the neighbourhood to try a new product, and many of them willingly pass the information about the product onto other people. Their experiences can determine whether a product will have a long or short life cycle. They represent about 13.5 percent of the population.

Early Majority

Once the early adopters have tried and given their approval to a product, the early majority will begin to follow. Thirty-four percent of the population is in this category. Since they represent such a large percent of the population, the adoption by the early majority causes the new product to enter a period of rapid growth.

Late Majority

After a significant portion of the population has adopted a product, the late majority will consider its use. These people are not risk takers; they typically wait until they see the product approved by others. They also represent about 34 percent of the population. Once they have adopted the product, the innovators, early adopters, early majority, and late majority represent a total of about 84 percent of the population. By this point, the new product will have reached its maturity.

Laggards

The last category of society to adopt a new product is generally fearful about trying new things. Often, they wait until being forced to adopt because the alternate product is no longer being produced. The laggards represent about 16 percent of the population.

New-product Development

Although product development is not usually recognised as a formal stage in the product life cycle, many ideas for long-term product planning are derived from the concepts that are generated through this preliminary process. Product development is defined as a strategy for company growth by offering modified or new products to current market segments. Additionally, product development focuses on turning product concepts into a physical product, while ensuring that the idea can be turned into a workable product through each stage.

In the product development stage, costs begin to accumulate due to the investment in proposed concepts and ideas. Before introduction, a successful product in the marketplace will go through the following eight distinct stages of new product development: idea generation, idea screening, concept development, marketing strategy, business analysis, product development, test marketing, and commercialization.

Idea generation usually stems from the organisation's internal sources (R&D, engineering, marketing). Company employees will brainstorm new ideas to generate viable product concepts. Additionally, a company may also analyze their competition's new product offerings with the intention of differentiating and improving on existing designs.

Ideas are ultimately screened, reducing the number of unrealistic concepts and focusing on realistic, attainable concepts. A single idea is developed into a product concept. Concepts are then tested to measure how appealing the product might be to consumers from the anticipated target market. Testing may range from focus groups to random surveys.

After concept testing, a marketing strategy is needed to define how the product will be positioned in the marketplace. Identifying the product's anticipated target market, financial expectations, distribution channels, and pricing strategy are also determined at this time.

Business analysis, including sales forecasting, determines if the product will be profitable to manufacturer. Many factors are considered when judging the products anticipated profitability. Managers will look at the length of time it takes for the product to be profitable, cost of capital, and other financial considerations when deciding weather to proceed with development. If the concept is approved, a prototype is created from the product concept.

The prototype undergoes rigorous testing to ensure safety and effectiveness of the product. These tests are a good measure for determining whether or not a product is safe and if it should if the designers should move forward with the creation of the product.

Once a successful prototype is developed, companies perform test marketing on the product. Typically, a company will conduct formal research on a product concept to see if the proposed idea has validity with the targeted audience. Again, customer surveys and focus groups are conducted with the intention of testing the product on a sample of the targeted demographic. The testing is then analyzed to measure consumer reaction to the product. Once all the information is available and the company decides to introduce the product, high commercialization costs are incurred.

Stages of the Product Life Cycle

As stated above, the product life cycle consists of four stages: introduction, growth, maturity, and decline. Determination of a product's stage in its life cycle is not based on age, but on the relationship of sales, costs, profits, and number of competitors. Each of these stages is described below.

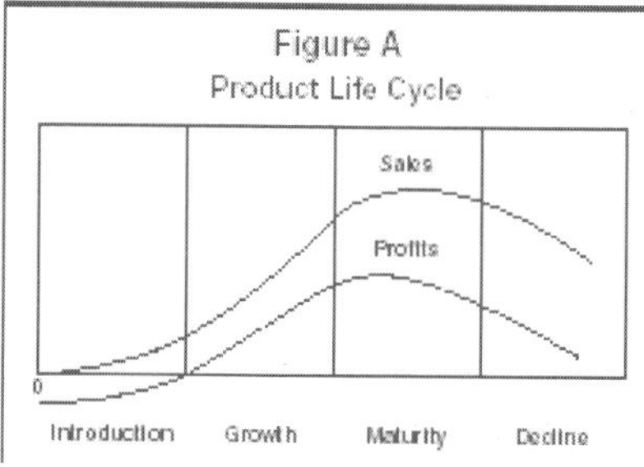

***Figure:** A Product Life Cycle*

Introduction

When a new product is introduced to a market, the innovators may be the only people aware of the new product. If the product is a new product class, the innovators may not know what the product uses are. Recalling that the innovators represent only a small percent of the population, the sales of the new product will be low. However, there is an advantage in this situation in that the new product does not yet have any competition. During the introduction stage of a new product, the developer enjoys a monopoly.

Unfortunately, the product monopoly does not usually translate to immediate profits. The product may have been in development for a long time and considerable development costs are still in the recovery phase. Also, an expensive marketing effort may be needed to introduce the product to the public. With low sales and high expenses, the introduction stage of the life cycle is usually a money loser for the company. However, the hope is for the future of the product, and the company usually is more than willing to incur the losses.

Growth

As the early adopters begin to try the product, a sale begins to grow and profits usually start to follow. This is a great time for a company introducing a new product because the company still enjoys a monopoly early in the growth stage. The company is reaping all the sales and profits of the new product. When Chrysler introduced the idea of the minivan, they were in this enviable position of having the only minivan on the market.

As the early adopters begin influencing the early majority, sales and profits sore. The competition has also been watching from the new product's inception. Unfortunately for the original firm, the competition has also noticed the new product's success. Although they cannot be the first, the competition races to offer their own products and gain a share of a growing market. Chrysler's minivan did not maintain its monopoly for long; soon, the other major automobile manufacturers offered models to compete with Chrysler. Although total sales and profits continue to grow throughout the growth stage, they are divided among many manufacturers.

Maturity

By the end of the growth stage of the life cycle, the market is beginning to become very competitive, and this trend continues into the early period of the maturity stage. Besides many more manufacturers offering their products, the producers continue the product-differentiation process begun in the growth stage. The result is a market saturated with many manufacturers offering many models of the product. These manufacturers produce a multitude of models, from desktop computers to notebooks.

With so many companies now in the market, the competition for customers becomes fierce. Although total sales continue to grow during the first part of the maturity stage, the increased competition causes profits to peak at the end of the growth stage and beginning of the maturity stage. Profits then decline during the remainder of the maturity stage. The declining profits mean that the market is not as attractive to companies as it was in the growth stage.

In the growth stage, even inefficient companies made money. However, only the best companies and their products survive in the maturity stage. Manufacturers begin to drop out as they see profits turn to losses. Though there is still competition in the computer industry, for example, companies such as Dell and Apple have emerged as the leaders in the market. During the later part of the maturity stage, even sales begin to dip, putting more pressure on the remaining manufacturers.

Decline

The number of companies abandoning the market continues and accelerates in the decline stage. Not only does the efficiency of the company play a factor in the decline, but also the product category itself now becomes a factor. By this time, the market may perceive the product as "old," and it may no longer be in demand. For example, the public replaced their preference for station wagons with their desire for minivans. Advancing technology may also bypass and replace a product, as when tapes and CDs replaced the vinyl record.

The product will continue to exist as long as a few manufacturers can maintain profitability. The laggards will resist switching to the alternative, and manufacturers who can profitably serve this niche will continue to do so. Eventually, even the laggards will switch, and the last companies producing the product will be forced to withdraw, thereby killing the product group.

Product Strategies During the Product Life Cycle

Depending on the stage of the product life cycle, the marketing strategy should vary to meet the changing conditions. The marketing mix consists of the product, promotion, price, and distribution. Each element must change with the product life cycle if the company expects to maximize sales and profits. It is important to note that as products move through each stage of the life cycle, they should be monitored and re-evaluated in terms of reducing both production costs and the time it takes to make a product or service profitable with its new position.

Strategic options for products during the product life cycle are examined below.

Introduction Stage

In the introduction stage, the product's novelty and lack of competition dominate the marketing strategy. The public is not aware of the product and does not know what benefits it offers them.

Product strategy is focused on introducing one model. Since the public is unaware of the product, to offer more models could confuse them as they learn the purpose of the product. This model may offer various options, but there are usually no major variations on the basic idea of the product. The cost of development may also prohibit the company from developing more models for introduction. With no competition yet in the product category, one model is adequate for introduction.

Since the product is new, persuading the market to buy the product is of secondary importance to informing the public that the product exists. It is the innovators who will begin to buy the product, and they need to be informed. With only one company offering the product, those innovators that decide to purchase the product have only one company from which they can purchase the product. Consequently, the promotion efforts concentrate on informing the public of the product benefits and the company producing the product. Persuasion to buy a particular brand is not needed in the introduction stage.

The pricing policy offers the company an opportunity to regain some development costs. Since the company's product is not only new to the company, but also introduces a new product, the company can use a skimming pricing strategy; that is, a very high price for the new product. Though the high price of the new product may deter some potential customers, many innovators and early adopters will pay the high price to own the new product. The first electronic calculators, for example, were quite expensive. If the product is easily copied, however, the developer may want to use a low-price penetration policy to deter future competition.

Since there are few purchasers in the introduction stage, the distribution does not need to be widespread. The innovators are risk takers and desire to purchase something new. Consequently, they may seek out the distributors carrying the new product, and only a few distributors will suffice.

Growth Stage

In the growth stage, the early adopters, followed by the early majority, begin to consume the product in growing numbers. The increasing sales result in the emergence of profits rather than losses.

During the early part of the growth stage, the company can continue its product policy of offering one basic model. However, if the new product group is successful, eventually competitors will offer their own products to compete in the new category. At that point, the original company will need to offer more models. The models should be differentiated from one another so that the company can continue to attract the new customers coming into the market.

Even with competition beginning to offer their products in the new category, the original company still dominates the market. However, as the market leader rather than a monopoly, the company will need to change its promotion policy of informing the public about their new product and new product category.

With an informing policy, the market leader would still receive the majority of new sales. Unfortunately for the original company, the competition will not be using an informative policy. They will be trying to persuade the public why their product is better than the market leader's product. Consequently, the market leader should switch to a persuasive promotion policy.

As the competition enters the market, they will probably be offering products at prices lower than the price of the original product. This is a penetration pricing policy designed to take sales away from the market leader. If the original company used a skimming pricing policy, its continued use would surely lead to rapid lost sales to the competition unless it is altered. Prices should be lowered so that sales can continue to grow, and the competition kept at bay.

In a growing market, the company's exclusive distribution policy would limit the potential growth for the firm, and sales would go to the competition. Consequently, the company must increase its product distribution to maintain its leadership in the market.

Maturity Stage

Many competitors characterize the maturity stage. With the large number of firms producing products, the competition for customers becomes quite intense, and profits decline. The strategy for firms during the maturity stage becomes one of survival, as many competitors will eventually withdraw from the market.

With many companies offering several models of the product, the number of products on the market becomes tremendous. The original company must continue differentiating their models so that the market is aware of the differences in the company's products and the competitors' products. The customers are going to ask why they should buy a particular company's product; just because the product was the first on the market is not going to persuade the customers to continue buying the product. Quality, styling, and product features are a few of the means of differentiating the product from the competition.

During the maturity stage, the need to inform the public has long since passed. Now, the promotion strategy focus is on continuing the persuasion tactics started during the growth stage. The purpose of persuasion is to position the product to the market, which involves creating an image for a product. The image should not be an advertiser's creation, but based on the reality of the product.

The differentiation methods of quality, styling, and features are excellent means of positioning a product. For example, a Chevrolet

Corvette and Porsche Boxster are both sports cars, but consumers see the different positions of the cars. The company differentiates its products and uses promotion to create the different position image. Each company hopes that its position is preferred by the consumers.

With the intense competition, management keeps the price of the product to its lowest possible level. For example, the competition for entry-level personal computers has now shifted to offering the lowest price. All of the companies in a mature market must now watch costs carefully.

Every aspect from development through production through marketing is designed to offer the lowest cost possible. A cost and a price advantage over competitors in this stage are significant competitive advantages. Consumers are aware of prices and will reward the company with the lower price, all else being equal. The firm that does not have a significant cost advantage risks losing customers and going out of business.

The absence of a company's product in a particular location may result in lost sales during the maturity period. Widespread distribution is essential. If the company's product is not in a particular location, one or more of the competitors' products are likely to be there. The firm cannot risk losing sales simply because their products were not available.

Decline Stage

During the decline stage, sales and profits begin an even sharper drop, and the number of competitors is reduced even further. With public preference for this product waning, the decline stage continues until the last of the producers cannot make a profit, and the product category dies.

The product strategy now becomes one of reducing the number of models offered. With the public abandoning the product and competition declining, the need for many models is no longer there. The company now focuses its attention on the costs and profitability of the remaining models. Costs, such as research and development and production, are cut to the minimal amount necessary. After the cost cuts, management eliminates those products that are no longer profitable.

The promotion efforts also include an examination of costs. Only the minimal amount of promotion necessary to keep the product selling is done. The remaining people in the market want the product and do not need to be convinced that they should buy the product. They only need to know that the product is still available. Consequently, the promotion effort shifts to reminder promotion.

Products' prices are also kept as low as possible during the decline stage. Since the number of competitors has dropped, it may seem that a company could raise prices. If the remaining customers maintain strong brand loyalty, this policy might be possible. However, the product has fallen out of favour, and customers have other product alternatives. A price increase that could not be justified by cost increases runs the risk of alienating even the few customers left purchasing the product. Consequently, the strategy should be to keep the prices as low as possible.

Cost is also an overriding factor in the distribution of the product during the decline stage. The declining sales may not justify the widespread distribution reached during the maturity stage. Only those areas or markets that are still profitable should be covered, and the unprofitable distribution outlets eliminated. Hopefully for the last companies producing the product, the brand-loyal customers or laggards will seek out the limited locations of the products and continue purchasing it.

Decline Stage Trap

Just because a product's sales begin to decline does not mean that the product life cycle has reached the decline stage. However, if the company believes that the product is in a decline, the implementation of the decline stage strategies may lead to the death of the product long before its time.

Before the strategies for declining products are tried, the company should definitely establish that the product is in decline. The company should first follow strategies to boost sales and not resign themselves to the cost-cutting strategies of the decline stage. For example, Arm & Hammer could have easily decided that their baking soda was dying, and implemented decline stage strategies. However, they chose to fight for its life. They differentiated the product by finding new uses—such as a deodorizer and an ingredient in toothpaste. They so successfully repositioned the product that many people now think about baking soda as a deodorizer first and disregard its original use in baking.

Borrowed from biology, the life-cycle concept has been adapted and applied to products and industries. The product life cycle maintains that products and industries move through the stages of introduction, growth, maturity, and decline. By viewing a product from the perspective of its product-life-cycle position, management can use the product life cycle as a valuable decision-making tool. As the product moves through its life cycle, the appropriate strategies for its future development vary greatly. Knowledge of the appropriate strategies can help guide management actions.

New Product Development

In business and engineering, new product development (NPD) is the complete process of bringing a new product to market. New product development is described in the literature as the transformation of a market opportunity into a product available for sale and it can be tangible (that is, something physical you can touch) or intangible (like a service, experience, or belief). A good understanding of customer needs and wants, the competitive environment and the nature of the market represent the top required factors for the success of a new product. Cost, time and quality are the main variables that drive the customer needs. Aimed at these three variables, companies develop continuous practices and strategies to better satisfy the customer requirements and increase their market share by a regulate development of new products. There are many uncertainties and challenges throughout the process which companies must face. The use of best practices and the elimination of barriers to communication are the main concerns for the management of NPD process.

NPD Process Structure

The NPD process consists of a series of activities that firms employ in the complex process of delivering new products to the market. Every new product will pass through a series of stages from ideation through design, manufacturing and market introduction. The development process basically has three main phases:

1. Fuzzy front-end (FFE) is the set of activities employed before the formal and well defined NPD or stage-gate process
2. Product design starts with the development of the new product and it ends at pre-commercialization analysis stage.
3. Fuzzy back-end or commercialization phase represent the action steps where the production and market launch occur.

The front-end phase have been very well researched, with valuable models proposed. Peter Koen et. al. provides a five step front end activity called front end innovation: opportunity identification, opportunity analysis, idea genesis, idea selection, and idea and technology development. He also includes an engine in the middle of the five front end stages and the possible outside barriers that can influence the process outcome. The engine represents the management driving the activities described. The front end of the innovation is the greatest area of weakness in the NPD process. This is mainly because the FFE is often chaotic, unpredictable and unstructured. Engineering design is the process whereby a technical solution is developed to solve a given problem The design stage is very important because at this stage most of the product life cycle costs are engaged. Previous research shows that 70% - 80% of the final product quality and 70% of the product entire life-cycle cost are determined in the product design phase, therefore the design-manufacturing interface represent the greatest opportunity for cost reduction. Design projects last from a few weeks to three years with an average of one year. Design and Commercialization phases usually start a very early collaboration. When the concept design is finished it will be sent to manufacturing plant for prototyping, developing a Concurrent Engineering approach by implementing practices such as QFD, DFM/DFA and more. The output of the design (engineering) is a set of product and process specifications – mostly in the form of drawings, and the output of manufacturing is the product ready for sale. Basically, the design team will develop drawings with technical specifications representing the future product, and will send it to the manufacturing plant to be executed. Solving product/process fit problems is of high priority in information communication design because 90% of the development effort must be scrapped if any changes are made after the release to manufacturing.

NPD Models

Conceptual models have been designed in order to facilitate a smooth process. The concept adopted by IDEO, a successful design and consulting firm, is one of the most researched processes in regard to new product development and is a five step procedure. These steps are listed in chronological order: 1. understand and observe the market, the client, the technology, and the limitations of the problem; 2. synthesize the information collected at the first step; 3. Visualise new customers using the product; 4. prototype, evaluate and improve the concept; 5. implementation of design changes which are associated with more technologically advanced procedures and therefore this step will require more time.

One of the first developed models that today companies still use in the NPD process is the Booz, Allen and Hamilton (BAH) Model, published in 1982. This is the best known model because it underlies the NPD systems that have been put forward later. This model represent the foundation of all the other models that have been developed afterwards. Significant work has been conducted in order to propose better models, but in fact these models can be easily linked to BAH model. The seven steps of BAH model are: new product strategy, idea generation, screening and evaluation, business analysis, development, testing, and commercialization.

A pioneer of NPD research is Robert G. Cooper. Over the last two decades he conducted significant work in the area of NPD. The Stage-Gate model developed in the 1980's was proposed as a new tool for managing new products development processes. The 2010 APQC benchmarking study reveals that 88% of U.S. businesses employ a stage-gate system to manage new products, from idea to launch. In return, the companies that adopt this system are reported to receive benefits such as improved team work, shorter cycle time, improved success rates, earlier detection of failure, a better launch, and even shorter cycle times – reduced by about 30%. These findings highlight the importance of the stage-gate model, making it the single most important discovery in the area of new product development.

Marketing Considerations

There have been a number of approaches proposed for analyzing and responding to the marketing challenges of new product development. Two of these are *the eight stages* process of Koen and a process known as *the fuzzy front end.*

The Eight Stages

1. Idea Generation is often called the "NPD" of the NPD process.
   - Ideas for new products can be obtained from basic research using a SWOT analysis (Strengths, Weaknesses, Opportunities & Threats). Market and consumer trends, company's R&D department, competitors, focus groups, employees, salespeople, corporate spies, trade shows, or ethnographic discovery methods (searching for user patterns and habits) may also be used to get an insight into new product lines or product features.
   - Lots of ideas are generated about the new product. Out of these ideas many are implemented. The ideas are generated in many forms. Many reasons are responsible for generation of an idea.
   - Idea Generation or Brainstorming of new product, service, or store concepts - idea generation techniques can begin when you have done your OPPORTUNITY ANALYSIS to support your ideas in the Idea Screening Phase (shown in the next development step).

2. Idea Screening
   - o The object is to eliminate unsound concepts prior to devoting resources to them.
   - o The screeners should ask several questions:
     - Will the customer in the target market benefit from the product?
     - What is the size and growth forecasts of the market segment / target market?
     - What is the current or expected competitive pressure for the product idea?
     - What are the industry sales and market trends the product idea is based on?
     - Is it technically feasible to manufacture the product?
     - Will the product be profitable when manufactured and delivered to the customer at the target price?
3. Idea Development and Testing
   - o Develop the marketing and engineering details
     - Investigate intellectual property issues and search patent databases
     - Who is the target market and who is the decision maker in the purchasing process?
     - What product features must the product incorporate?
     - What benefits will the product provide?
     - How will consumers react to the product?
     - How will the product be produced most cost effectively?
     - Prove feasibility through virtual computer aided rendering and rapid prototyping
     - What will it cost to produce it?
   - o Testing the Idea may involve asking a number of prospective customers to evaluate the idea
4. Business Analysis
   - o Estimate likely selling price based upon competition and customer feedback
   - o Estimate sales volume based upon size of market and such tools as the Fourt-Woodlock equation
   - o Estimate profitability and break-even point

5. Beta Testing and Market Testing
   - o Produce a physical prototype or mock-up
   - o Test the product (and its packaging) in typical usage situations
   - o Conduct focus group customer interviews or introduce at trade show
   - o Make adjustments where necessary
   - o Produce an initial run of the product and sell it in a test market area to determine customer acceptance
6. Technical Implementation
   - o New program initiation
   - o Finalize Quality management system
   - o Resource estimation
   - o Requirement publication
   - o Publish technical communications such as data sheets
   - o Engineering operations planning
   - o Department scheduling
   - o Supplier collaboration
   - o Logistics plan
   - o Resource plan publication
   - o Program review and monitoring
   - o Contingencies - what-if planning
7. Commercialization (often considered post-NPD)
   - o Launch the product
   - o Produce and place advertisements and other promotions
   - o Fill the distribution pipeline with product
   - o Critical path analysis is most useful at this stage
8. New Product Pricing
   - o Impact of new product on the entire product portfolio
   - o Value Analysis (internal & external)
   - o Competition and alternative competitive technologies
   - o Differing value segments (price, value and need)
   - o Product Costs (fixed & variable)
   - o Forecast of unit volumes, revenue, and profit

These steps may be iterated as needed. Some steps may be eliminated. To reduce the time that the NPD process takes, many companies are completing several steps at the same time (referred to as concurrent engineering or time to market). Most industry leaders see new product development as a *proactive* process where resources are allocated to identify market changes and seize upon new product opportunities before they occur (in contrast to a *reactive strategy* in which nothing is done until problems occur or the competitor introduces an innovation). Many industry leaders see new product development as an ongoing process (referred to as *continuous development*) in which the entire organisation is always looking for opportunities.

For the more innovative products indicated on the diagram above, great amounts of uncertainty and change may exist which makes it difficult or impossible to plan the complete project before starting it. In this case, a more flexible approach may be advisable.

Because the NPD process typically requires both engineering and marketing expertise, cross-functional teams are a common way of organising projects. The team is responsible for all aspects of the project, from initial idea generation to final commercialization, and they usually report to senior management (often to a vice president or Program Manager). In those industries where products are technically complex, development research is typically expensive and product life cycles are relatively short, strategic alliances among several organisations helps to spread the costs, provide access to a wider skill set and speeds up the overall process.

Because both engineering and marketing expertise are usually critical to the process, choosing an appropriate blend of the two is important. Observe that this article is slanted more toward the marketing side. For more of an engineering slant.

A new product pricing process is important to reduce risk and increase confidence in the pricing and marketing decisions to be made. Processes have been proposed to break down the complex task of new product pricing into more manageable elements.

The Path to Developing Successful New Products points out three key processes that can play critical role in product development: Talk to the customer; Nurture a project culture; Keep it focused.

Fuzzy Front End

The Fuzzy Front End (FFE) is the messy "getting started" period of new product engineering development processes. It is in the front end where the organisation formulates a concept of the product to be developed and decides whether or not to invest resources in the further development of an idea. It is the phase between first consideration of an opportunity and when it is judged ready to enter the structured development process (Kim and Wilemon, 2007; Koen et al., 2001). It includes all activities from the search for new opportunities through the formation of a germ of an idea to the development of a precise concept. The Fuzzy Front End phase ends when an organisation approves and begins formal development of the concept.

Although the Fuzzy Front End may not be an expensive part of product development, it can consume 50% of development time, and it is where major commitments are typically made involving time, money, and the product's nature, thus setting the course for the entire project and final end product. Consequently, this phase should be considered as an essential part of development rather than something that happens "before development," and its cycle time should be included in the total development cycle time.

Koen et al. distinguish five different front-end elements (not necessarily in a particular order):

1. Opportunity Identification
2. Opportunity Analysis
3. Idea Genesis
4. Idea Selection
5. Idea and Technology Development

- The first element is the opportunity identification. In this element, large or incremental business and technological chances are identified in a more or less structured way. Using the guidelines established here, resources will eventually be allocated to new projects.... which then lead to a structured NPPD (New Product & Process Development) strategy.
- The second element is the opportunity analysis. It is done to translate the identified opportunities into implications for the business and technology specific context of the company. Here extensive efforts may be made to align ideas to target customer groups and do market studies and/or technical trials and research.
- The third element is the idea genesis, which is described as evolutionary and iterative process progressing from birth to maturation of the opportunity into a tangible idea. The process of the idea genesis can be made internally or come from outside inputs, e.g. a supplier offering a new material/technology or from a customer with an unusual request.

- The fourth element is the idea selection. Its purpose is to choose whether to pursue an idea by analyzing its potential business value.
- The fifth element is the idea and technology development. During this part of the front-end, the business case is developed based on estimates of the total available market, customer needs, investment requirements, competition analysis and project uncertainty. Some organisations consider this to be the first stage of the NPPD process (i.e., Stage 0).

The Fuzzy Front End is also described in literature as "Front End of Innovation", "Phase 0", "Stage 0" or "Pre-Project-Activities".

A universally acceptable definition for Fuzzy Front End or a dominant framework has not been developed so far. In a glossary of PDMA, it is mentioned that the Fuzzy Front End generally consists of three tasks: strategic planning, idea generation, and, especially, pre-technical evaluation. These activities are often chaotic, unpredictable, and unstructured. In comparison, the subsequent new product development process is typically structured, predictable, and formal. The term *Fuzzy Front End* was first popularized by Smith and Reinertsen (1991). R.G.Cooper (1988) describes the early stages of NPPD as a four step process in which ideas are generated (I), subjected to a preliminary technical and market assessment (II) and merged to coherent product concepts (III) which are finally judged for their fit with existing product strategies and portfolios (IV).

Other Approaches

Other authors have divided predevelopment product development activities differently:

1. Preliminary market assessment
2. Technical assessment
3. Source-of-supply assessment: suppliers and partners or alliances
4. Market research: market size and segmentation analysis, VoC (voice of the customer) research
5. Product idea testing
6. Customer value assessment
7. Product definition
8. Business and financial analysis

These activities yield essential information to make a Go/No-Go to Development decision.

One of the earliest studies using the case study method defined the front-end to include the interrelated activities of:

- product strategy formulation and communication
- opportunity identification and assessment
- idea generation
- product definition
- project planning
- executive reviews

Economical analysis, benchmarking of competitive products and modelling and prototyping are also important activities during the front-end activities. The outcomes of FFE are the:

- mission statement
- customer needs
- details of the selected idea
- product definition and specifications
- economic analysis of the product
- the development schedule
- project staffing and the budget
- a business plan aligned with corporate strategy

A conceptual model of Front-End Process was proposed which includes early phases of the innovation process. This model is structured in three phases and three gates:

- Phase 1: Environmental screening or opportunity identification stage in which external changes will be analysed and translated into potential business opportunities.
- Phase 2: Preliminary definition of an idea or concept.
- Phase 3: Detailed product, project or service definition, and Business planning.

The gates are:

- Opportunity screening
- Idea evaluation
- Go/No-Go for development

The final gate leads to a dedicated new product development project. Many professionals and academics consider that the general features of Fuzzy Front End (fuzziness, ambiguity, and uncertainty) make it difficult to see the FFE as a structured process, but rather as a set of interdependent activities (e.g. Kim and Wilemon, 2002). However, Husig et al., 2005 [10] argue that front-end not need to be fuzzy, but can be handled in a structured manner. In fact Carbone showed that when using the front end success factors in an integrated process, product success is increased. Peter Koen argues that in the FFE for incremental, platform and radical projects, three separate strategies and processes are typically involved. The traditional Stage Gate (TM) process was designed for incremental product development, namely for a single product. The FFE for developing a new platform must start out with a strategic vision of where the company wants to develop products and this will lead to a family of products. Projects for breakthrough products start out with a similar strategic vision, but are associated with technologies which require new discoveries.

Incremental, Platform and Breakthrough Products Include

- *Incremental products* are considered to be cost reductions, improvements to existing product lines, additions to existing platforms and repositioning of existing products introduced in markets.
- *Breakthrough products* are new to the company or new to the world and offer a 5-10 times or greater improvement in performance combined with a 30-50% or greater reduction in costs.
- *Platform products* establish a basic architecture for a next generation product or process and are substantially larger in scope and resources than incremental projects.

Chapter 3

Financial Management

Risk Management

Risk management is the identification, assessment, and prioritization of risks (defined in ISO 31000 as *the effect of uncertainty on objectives*) followed by coordinated and economical application of resources to minimize, monitor, and control the probability and/or impact of unfortunate events or to maximize the realisation of opportunities.

Risks can come from uncertainty in financial markets, threats from project failures (at any phase in design, development, production, or sustainment life-cycles), legal liabilities, credit risk, accidents, natural causes and disasters as well as deliberate attack from an adversary, or events of uncertain or unpredictable root-cause. Several risk management standards have been developed including the Project Management Institute, the National Institute of Standards and Technology, actuarial societies, and ISO standards. Methods, definitions and goals vary widely according to whether the risk management method is in the context of project management, security, engineering, industrial processes, financial portfolios, actuarial assessments, or public health and safety.

The strategies to manage threats (uncertainties with negative consequences) typically include transferring the threat to another party, avoiding the threat, reducing the negative effect or probability of the threat, or even accepting some or all of the potential or actual consequences of a particular threat, and the opposites for opportunities (uncertain future states with benefits).

Certain aspects of many of the risk management standards have come under criticism for having no measurable improvement on risk, whether the confidence in estimates and decisions seem to increase. For example, it has been shown that one in six IT projects experience cost overruns of 200% on average, and schedule overruns of 70%.

A widely used vocabulary for risk management is defined by ISO Guide 73, "Risk management. Vocabulary."

In ideal risk management, a prioritization process is followed whereby the risks with the greatest loss (or impact) and the greatest probability of occurring are handled first, and risks with lower probability of occurrence and lower loss are handled in descending order. In practice the process of assessing overall risk can be difficult, and balancing resources used to mitigate between risks with a high probability of occurrence but lower loss versus a risk with high loss but lower probability of occurrence can often be mishandled.

Intangible risk management identifies a new type of a risk that has a 100% probability of occurring but is ignored by the organisation due to a lack of identification ability. For example, when deficient knowledge is applied to a situation, a knowledge risk materializes. Relationship risk appears when ineffective collaboration occurs. Process-engagement risk may be an issue when ineffective operational procedures are applied. These risks directly reduce the productivity of knowledge workers, decrease cost-effectiveness, profitability, service, quality, reputation, brand value, and earnings quality. Intangible risk management allows risk management to create immediate value from the identification and reduction of risks that reduce productivity.

Risk management also faces difficulties in allocating resources. This is the idea of opportunity cost. Resources spent on risk management could have been spent on more profitable activities. Again, ideal risk management minimizes spending (or manpower or other resources) and also minimizes the negative effects of risks.

Method

For the most part, these methods consist of the following elements, performed, more or less, in the following order.

1. identify, characterize threats
2. assess the vulnerability of critical assets to specific threats
3. determine the risk (i.e. the expected likelihood and consequences of specific types of attacks on specific assets)
4. identify ways to reduce those risks
5. prioritize risk reduction measures based on a strategy

Principles of Risk Management

The International Organisation for Standardization (ISO) identifies the following principles of risk management:

Risk management should:

- create value – resources expended to mitigate risk should be less than the consequence of inaction, or (as in value engineering), the gain should exceed the pain
- be an integral part of organisational processes
- be part of decision making process
- explicitly address uncertainty and assumptions
- be systematic and structured process
- be based on the best available information
- be tailorable
- take human factors into account
- be transparent and inclusive
- be dynamic, iterative and responsive to change
- be capable of continual improvement and enhancement
- be continually or periodically re-assessed

Process

According to the standard ISO 31000 "Risk management – Principles and guidelines on implementation," the process of risk management consists of several steps as follows:

Establishing the Context

This involves:

1. identification of risk in a selected domain of interest
2. planning the remainder of the process
3. mapping out the following:
   - o the social scope of risk management
   - o the identity and objectives of stakeholders
   - o the basis upon which risks will be evaluated, constraints.
4. defining a framework for the activity and an agenda for identification
5. developing an analysis of risks involved in the process
6. mitigation or solution of risks using available technological, human and organisational resources.

Identification

After establishing the context, the next step in the process of managing risk is to identify potential risks. Risks are about events that, when triggered, cause problems or benefits. Hence, risk identification can start with the source of our problems and those of our competitors (benefit), or with the problem itself.

- Source analysis - Risk sources may be internal or external to the system that is the target of risk management (use mitigation instead of management since by its own definition risk deals with factors of decision-making that cannot be managed).

Examples of risk sources are: stakeholders of a project, employees of a company or the weather over an airport.

- Problem analysis - Risks are related to identified threats. For example: the threat of losing money, the threat of abuse of confidential information or the threat of human errors, accidents and casualties. The threats may exist with various entities, most important with shareholders, customers and legislative bodies such as the government.

When either source or problem is known, the events that a source may trigger or the events that can lead to a problem can be investigated. For example: stakeholders withdrawing during a project may endanger funding of the project; confidential information may be stolen by employees even within a closed network; lightning striking an aircraft during takeoff may make all people on board immediate casualties.

The chosen method of identifying risks may depend on culture, industry practice and compliance. The identification methods are formed by templates or the development of templates for identifying source, problem or event. Common risk identification methods are:

- Objectives-based risk identification - Organisations and project teams have objectives. Any event that may endanger achieving an objective partly or completely is identified as risk.
- Scenario-based risk identification - In scenario analysis different scenarios are created. The scenarios may be the alternative ways to achieve an objective, or an analysis of the interaction of forces in, for example, a market or battle. Any event that triggers an undesired scenario alternative is identified as risk.
- Taxonomy-based risk identification - The taxonomy in taxonomy-based risk identification is a breakdown of possible risk sources. Based on the taxonomy and knowledge of best practices, a questionnaire is compiled. The answers to the questions reveal risks.

- Common-risk checking - In several industries, lists with known risks are available. Each risk in the list can be checked for application to a particular situation.
- Risk charting - This method combines the above approaches by listing resources at risk, threats to those resources, modifying factors which may increase or decrease the risk and consequences it is wished to avoid. Creating a matrix under these headings enables a variety of approaches. One can begin with resources and consider the threats they are exposed to and the consequences of each. Alternatively one can start with the threats and examine which resources they would affect, or one can begin with the consequences and determine which combination of threats and resources would be involved to bring them about.

Composite Risk Index

The above formula can also be re-written in terms of a Composite Risk Index, as follows:

Composite Risk Index = Impact of Risk event x Probability of Occurrence

The impact of the risk event is commonly assessed on a scale of 1 to 5, where 1 and 5 represent the minimum and maximum possible impact of an occurrence of a risk (usually in terms of financial losses). However, the 1 to 5 scale can be arbitrary and need not be on a linear scale.

The probability of occurrence is likewise commonly assessed on a scale from 1 to 5, where 1 represents a very low probability of the risk event actually occurring while 5 represents a very high probability of occurrence. This axis may be expressed in either mathematical terms (event occurs once a year, once in ten years, once in 100 years etc.) or may be expressed in "plain English" (event has occurred here very often; event has been known to occur here; event has been known to occur in the industry etc.). Again, the 1 to 5 scale can be arbitrary or non-linear depending on decisions by subject-matter experts.

The Composite Index thus can take values ranging (typically) from 1 through 25, and this range is usually arbitrarily divided into three sub-ranges. The overall risk assessment is then Low, Medium or High, depending on the sub-range containing the calculated value of the Composite Index. For instance, the three sub-ranges could be defined as 1 to 8, 9 to 16 and 17 to 25.

Note that the probability of risk occurrence is difficult to estimate, since the past data on frequencies are not readily available, as mentioned above. After all, probability does not imply certainty.

Likewise, the impact of the risk is not easy to estimate since it is often difficult to estimate the potential loss in the event of risk occurrence.

Further, both the above factors can change in magnitude depending on the adequacy of risk avoidance and prevention measures taken and due to changes in the external business environment. Hence it is absolutely necessary to periodically re-assess risks and intensify/relax mitigation measures, or as necessary. Changes in procedures, technology, schedules, budgets, market conditions, political environment, or other factors typically require re-assessment of risks.

Risk Options

Risk mitigation measures are usually formulated according to one or more of the following major risk options, which are:

1. Design a new business process with adequate built-in risk control and containment measures from the start.
2. Periodically re-assess risks that are accepted in ongoing processes as a normal feature of business operations and modify mitigation measures.
3. Transfer risks to an external agency (e.g. an insurance company)
4. Avoid risks altogether (e.g. by closing down a particular high-risk business area)

Later research has shown that the financial benefits of risk management are less dependent on the formula used but are more dependent on the frequency and how risk assessment is performed.

In business it is imperative to be able to present the findings of risk assessments in financial, market, or schedule terms. Robert Courtney Jr. (IBM, 1970) proposed a formula for presenting risks in financial terms. The Courtney formula was accepted as the official risk analysis method for the US governmental agencies. The formula proposes calculation of ALE (annualised loss expectancy) and compares the expected loss value to the security control implementation costs (cost-benefit analysis).

Potential Risk Treatments

Once risks have been identified and assessed, all techniques to manage the risk fall into one or more of these four major categories:

- Avoidance (eliminate, withdraw from or not become involved)
- Reduction (optimize – mitigate)
- Sharing (transfer – outsource or insure)
- Retention (accept and budget)

Ideal use of these strategies may not be possible. Some of them may involve trade-offs that are not acceptable to the organisation or person making the risk management decisions. Another source, from the US Department of Defence, Defence Acquisition University, calls these categories ACAT, for Avoid, Control, Accept, or Transfer. This use of the ACAT acronym is reminiscent of another ACAT (for Acquisition Category) used in US Defence industry procurements, in which Risk Management figures prominently in decision making and planning.

Risk Avoidance

This includes not performing an activity that could carry risk. An example would be not buying a property or business in order to not take on the legal liability that comes with it. Another would be not flying in order not to take the risk that the airplane were to be hijacked. Avoidance may seem the answer to all risks, but avoiding risks also means losing out on the potential gain that accepting (retaining) the risk may have allowed. Not entering a business to avoid the risk of loss also avoids the possibility of earning profits. Increasing risk regulation in hospitals has led to avoidance of treating higher risk conditions, in favour of patients presenting with lower risk.

Hazard Prevention

Hazard prevention refers to the prevention of risks in an emergency. The first and most effective stage of hazard prevention is the elimination of hazards. If this takes too long, is too costly, or is otherwise impractical, the second stage is mitigation.

Risk Reduction

Risk reduction or "optimization" involves reducing the severity of the loss or the likelihood of the loss from occurring. For example, sprinklers are designed to put out a fire to reduce the risk of loss by fire. This method may cause a greater loss by water damage and therefore may not be suitable. Halon fire suppression systems may mitigate that risk, but the cost may be prohibitive as a strategy.

Acknowledging that risks can be positive or negative, optimizing risks means finding a balance between negative risk and the benefit of the operation or activity; and between risk reduction and effort applied. By an offshore drilling contractor effectively applying HSE Management in its organisation, it can optimize risk to achieve levels of residual risk that are tolerable.

Modern software development methodologies reduce risk by developing and delivering software incrementally. Early methodologies suffered from the fact that they only delivered software in the final phase of development; any problems encountered in earlier phases meant costly rework and often jeopardized the whole project. By developing in iterations, software projects can limit effort wasted to a single iteration.

Outsourcing could be an example of risk reduction if the outsourcer can demonstrate higher capability at managing or reducing risks. For example, a company may outsource only its software development, the manufacturing of hard goods, or customer support needs to another company, while handling the business management itself. This way, the company can concentrate more on business development without having to worry as much about the manufacturing process, managing the development team, or finding a physical location for a call centre.

Risk Sharing

Briefly defined as "sharing with another party the burden of loss or the benefit of gain, from a risk, and the measures to reduce a risk."

The term of 'risk transfer' is often used in place of risk sharing in the mistaken belief that you can transfer a risk to a third party through insurance or outsourcing. In practice if the insurance company or contractor go bankrupt or end up in court, the original risk is likely to still revert to the first party. As such in the terminology of practitioners and scholars alike, the purchase of an insurance contract is often described as a "transfer of risk." However, technically speaking, the buyer of the contract generally retains legal responsibility for the losses "transferred", meaning that insurance may be described more accurately as a post-event compensatory mechanism. For example, a personal injuries insurance policy does not transfer the risk of a car accident to the insurance company. The risk still lies with the policy holder namely the person who has been in the accident. The insurance policy simply provides that if an accident (the event) occurs involving the policy holder then some compensation may be payable to the policy holder that is commensurate to the suffering/damage.

Some ways of managing risk fall into multiple categories. Risk retention pools are technically retaining the risk for the group, but spreading it over the whole group involves transfer among individual members of the group. This is different from traditional insurance, in that no premium is exchanged between members of the group up front, but instead losses are assessed to all members of the group.

Risk Retention

Involves accepting the loss, or benefit of gain, from a risk when it occurs. True self insurance falls in this category. Risk retention is a viable strategy for small risks where the cost of insuring against the risk would be greater over time than the total losses sustained. All risks that are not avoided or transferred are retained by default. This includes risks that are so large or catastrophic that they either cannot be insured against or the premiums would be infeasible. War is an example since most property and risks are not insured against war, so the loss attributed by war is retained by the insured. Also any amounts of potential loss (risk) over the amount insured is retained risk. This may also be acceptable if the chance of a very large loss is small or if the cost to insure for greater coverage amounts is so great it would hinder the goals of the organisation too much.

Limitations

Prioritizing the *risk management processes* too highly could keep an organisation from ever completing a project or even getting started. This is especially true if other work is suspended until the risk management process is considered complete.

It is also important to keep in mind the distinction between risk and uncertainty. Risk can be measured by impacts x probability.

If risks are improperly assessed and prioritized, time can be wasted in dealing with risk of losses that are not likely to occur. Spending too much time assessing and managing unlikely risks can divert resources that could be used more profitably. Unlikely events do occur but if the risk is unlikely enough to occur it may be better to simply retain the risk and deal with the result if the loss does in fact occur. Qualitative risk assessment is subjective and lacks consistency. The primary justification for a formal risk assessment process is legal and bureaucratic.

Areas of Risk Management

As applied to corporate finance, *risk management* is the technique for measuring, monitoring and controlling the financial or operational risk on a firm's balance sheet.

The Basel II framework breaks risks into market risk (price risk), credit risk and operational risk and also specifies methods for calculating capital requirements for each of these components.

Enterprise Risk Management

In enterprise risk management, a risk is defined as a possible event or circumstance that can have negative influences on the enterprise in question. Its impact can be on the very existence, the resources (human and capital), the products and services, or the customers of the enterprise, as well as external impacts on society, markets, or the environment. In a financial institution, enterprise risk management is normally thought of as the combination of credit risk, interest rate risk or asset liability management, liquidity risk, market risk, and operational risk.

In the more general case, every probable risk can have a pre-formulated plan to deal with its possible consequences (to ensure *contingency* if the risk becomes a *liability*).

From the information above and the average cost per employee over time, or cost accrual ratio, a project manager can estimate:

- the cost associated with the risk if it arises, estimated by multiplying employee costs per unit time by the estimated time lost (*cost impact, C* where *C = cost accrual ratio * S*).
- the probable increase in time associated with a risk (*schedule variance due to risk, Rs* where Rs = P * S):
  - o Sorting on this value puts the highest risks to the schedule first. This is intended to cause the greatest risks to the project to be attempted first so that risk is minimized as quickly as possible.
  - o This is slightly misleading as *schedule variances* with a large P and small S and vice versa are not equivalent. (The risk of the RMS *Titanic* sinking vs. the passengers' meals being served at slightly the wrong time).
- the probable increase in cost associated with a risk (*cost variance due to risk, Rc* where Rc = P*C = P*CAR*S = P*S*CAR)
  - o sorting on this value puts the highest risks to the budget first.

Risk in a project or process can be due either to Special Cause Variation or Common Cause Variation and requires appropriate treatment. That is to re-iterate the concern about extremal cases not being equivalent in the list immediately above.

Medical Device Risk Management

For medical devices, risk management is a process for identifying, evaluating and mitigating risks associated with harm to people and damage to property or the environment. Risk management is an integral part of medical device design and development, production processes and evaluation of field experience, and is applicable to all types of medical devices. The evidence of its application is required by most regulatory bodies such as FDA. The management of risks for medical devices is described by the International Organisation for Standardization (ISO) in ISO 14971:2007, Medical Devices—The application of risk management to medical devices, a product safety standard. The standard provides a process framework and associated requirements for management responsibilities, risk analysis and evaluation, risk controls and lifecycle risk management.

The European version of the risk management standard was updated in 2009 and again in 2012 to refer to the Medical Devices Directive (MDD) and Active Implantable Medical Device Directive (AIMDD) revision in 2007, as well as the In Vitro Medical Device Directive (IVDD). The requirements of EN 14971:2012 are nearly identical to ISO 14971:2007. The differences include an Annex that refers to the new MDD and AIMDD, the requirement for risks to be reduced *as low as possible*, and the requirement that risks be mitigated by design and not by labelling on the medical device (i.e., labelling can no longer be used to mitigate risk).

Typical risk analysis and evaluation techniques adopted by the medical device industry include hazard analysis, fault tree analysis (FTA), failure mode and effect analysis (FMEA), hazard and operability study (HAZOP), and risk traceability analysis for ensuring risk controls are implemented and effective (i.e. tracking risks identified to product requirements, design specifications, verification and validation results etc.)

FTA analysis requires diagramming software. FMEA analysis can be done using a spreadsheet program. There are also integrated medical device risk management solutions.

Through a draft guidance, FDA has introduced another method named "Safety Assurance Case" for medical device safety assurance analysis. The safety assurance case is structured argument reasoning about systems appropriate for scientists and engineers, supported by a body of evidence, that provides a compelling, comprehensible and valid case that a system is safe for a given application in a given environment. With the guidance, a safety assurance case is expected for safety critical devices (e.g. infusion devices) as part of the pre-market clearance submission, e.g. 510(k). In 2013, FDA introduced another draft guidance expecting medical device manufacturers to submit cybersecurity risk analysis information.

Risk Management Activities as Applied to Project Management

In project management, risk management includes the following activities:

- Planning how risk will be managed in the particular project. Plans should include risk management tasks, responsibilities, activities and budget.
- Assigning a risk officer – a team member other than a project manager who is responsible for foreseeing potential project problems. Typical characteristic of risk officer is a healthy skepticism.
- Maintaining live project risk database. Each risk should have the following attributes: opening date, title, short description, probability and importance. Optionally a risk may have an assigned person responsible for its resolution and a date by which the risk must be resolved.
- Creating anonymous risk reporting channel. Each team member should have the possibility to report risks that he/she foresees in the project.
- Preparing mitigation plans for risks that are chosen to be mitigated. The purpose of the mitigation plan is to describe how this particular risk will be handled – what, when, by whom and how will it be done to avoid it or minimize consequences if it becomes a liability.
- Summarizing planned and faced risks, effectiveness of mitigation activities, and effort spent for the risk management.

Risk Management for Megaprojects (Infrastructure)

Megaprojects (sometimes also called "major programs") are extremely large-scale investment projects, typically costing more than US$1 billion per project. Megaprojects include bridges, tunnels, highways, railways, airports, seaports, power plants, dams, wastewater projects, coastal flood protection schemes, oil and natural gas extraction projects, public buildings, information technology systems, aerospace projects, and defence systems. Megaprojects have been shown to be particularly risky in terms of finance, safety, and social and environmental impacts. Risk management is therefore particularly pertinent for megaprojects and special methods and special education have been developed for such risk management.

Risk Management Regarding Natural Disasters

It is important to assess risk in regard to natural disasters like floods, earthquakes, and so on. Outcomes of natural disaster risk assessment are valuable when considering future repair costs, business interruption losses and other downtime, effects on the environment, insurance costs, and the proposed costs of reducing the risk. There are regular conferences in Davos to deal with integral risk management.

Risk Management of Information Technology

Information technology is increasingly pervasive in modern life in every sector.

IT risk is a risk related to information technology. This is a relatively new term due to an increasing awareness that information security is simply one facet of a multitude of risks that are relevant to IT and the real world processes it supports.

A number of methodologies have been developed to deal with this kind of risk.

ISACA's *Risk IT* framework ties IT risk to enterprise risk management.

Risk Management Techniques in Petroleum and Natural Gas

For the offshore oil and gas industry, operational risk management is regulated by the safety case regime in many countries. Hazard identification and risk assessment tools and techniques are described in the international standard ISO 17776:2000, and organisations such as the IADC (International Association of Drilling Contractors) publish guidelines for HSE Case development which are based on the ISO standard. Further, diagrammatic representations of hazardous events are often expected by governmental regulators as part of risk management in safety case submissions; these are known as bow-tie diagrams. The technique is also used by organisations and regulators in mining, aviation, health, defence, industrial and finance.

Risk Management as Applied to the Pharmaceutical Sector

The principles and tools for quality risk management are increasingly being applied to different aspects of pharmaceutical quality systems. These aspects include development, manufacturing, distribution, inspection, and submission/review processes throughout the lifecycle of drug substances, drug products, biological and biotechnological products (including the use of raw materials, solvents, excipients, packaging and labelling materials in drug products, biological and biotechnological products). Risk management is also applied to the assessment of microbiological contamination in relation to pharmaceutical products and cleanroom manufacturing environments.

Positive Risk Management

Positive Risk Management is an approach that recognises the importance of the human factor and of individual differences in propensity for risk taking. It draws from the work of a number of academics and professionals who have expressed concerns about scientific rigor of the wider risk management debate, or who have made a contribution emphasizing the human dimension of risk.

Firstly, it recognises that any object or situation can be rendered hazardous by the involvement of someone with an inappropriate disposition towards risk; whether too risk taking or too risk averse.

Secondly, it recognises that risk is an inevitable and ever present element throughout life: from conception through to the point at the end of life when we finally lose our personal battle with life-threatening risk.

Thirdly, it recognises that every individual has a particular orientation towards risk; while at one extreme people may by nature be timid, anxious and fearful, others will be adventurous, impulsive and almost oblivious to danger. These differences are evident in the way we drive our cars, in our diets, in our relationships, in our careers.

Finally, Positive Risk Management recognises that risk taking is essential to all enterprise, creativity, heroism, education, scientific advance – in fact to any activity and all the initiatives that have contributed to our evolutionary success and civilization. It is worth noting how many enjoyable activities involve fear and willingly embrace risk taking.

Within the entire Risk Management literature you will find little or no reference to the human part of the risk equation other than what might be implied by the term 'compliant'. This illustrates the narrow focus that is a hall mark of much current risk management practice. This situation arises from the basic premises of traditional risk management and the practices associated with health and safety within the working environment. There is a basic logic to the idea that any accident must reflect some kind of oversight or situational predisposition that, if identified, can be rectified. But, largely due to an almost institutionalised neglect of the human factor, this situationally focused paradigm has grown tendrils that reach into every corner of modern life and into situations where the unintended negative consequences threaten to outweigh the benefits.

Positive Risk Management views both risk taking and risk aversion as complementary and of equal value and importance within the appropriate context. As such, it is seen as complementary to the traditional risk management paradigm. It introduces a much needed balance to risk management practices and puts greater onus on management skills and decision making. It is the dynamic approach of the football manager who appreciates the offencive and defencive talents within the available pool of players. Every organisation has roles better suited to risk takers and roles better suited to the risk averse. The task of management is to ensure that the right people are placed in each job.

Positive Risk Management relies on the ability to identify individual differences in propensity for risk taking. The science in this area has been developing rapidly over the past decade within the domain of personality assessment. Once an area of almost tribal allegiance to different schools of thought, today there is widespread consensus about the structure of personality assessment and its status within the framework of the cross disciplinary progress being made in our understanding of Human Nature. The Five Factor Model (FFM) of personality has been shown to have relevance across many different cultures, to remain consistent over adult working life and to be significantly heritable. Within this framework there are many strands which have a clear relationship to risk tolerance and risk taking. For example, Eysenck (1973) reports that personality influences whether we focus on what might go wrong or on potential benefits; Nicholson et al. (2005) report that higher extroversion is related to greater risk tolerance; McCrae and Costa (1997) link personality to tolerance of uncertainty, innovation and willingness to think outside the box; Kowert, 1997) links personality to adventurousness, imagination, the search for new experiences and actively seeking out risk. Building from these foundations of well validated assessment practices, more specialised assessments have been developed, including assessment of Risk Type.

Criticisms

However, researchers at the University of Oxford and King's College London found that the notion of complementarity may be a concept that does not work in practice. In a four-year organisational study of risk management in a leading healthcare organisation, Fischer & Ferlie (2013) found major contradictions between rules-based risk management required by managers, and ethics-based self-regulation favoured by staff and clients. This produced tensions that led neither to complementarity nor to hybrid forms, but produced instead a heated and intractable conflict which escalated, resulting in crisis and organisational collapse.

The graveyard of former greats is littered with examples where the balance of risk went seriously awry; the ENRON and RBS stories have become iconic references in the pantheon of corporate governance and corporate mortality. Eastman Kodak might be a nominee for the opposite pole – the corporately risk averse.

Risk Management and Business Continuity

Risk management is simply a practice of systematically selecting cost-effective approaches for minimising the effect of threat realisation to the organisation. All risks can never be fully avoided or mitigated simply because of financial and practical limitations. Therefore, all organisations have to accept some level of residual risks.

Whereas risk management tends to be preemptive, business continuity planning (BCP) was invented to deal with the consequences of realised residual risks. The necessity to have BCP in place arises because even very unlikely events will occur if given enough time. Risk management and BCP are often mistakenly seen as rivals or overlapping practices. In fact, these processes are so tightly tied together that such separation seems artificial. For example, the risk management process creates important inputs for the BCP (e.g., assets, impact assessments, cost estimates). Risk management also proposes applicable controls for the observed risks. Therefore, risk management covers several areas that are vital for the BCP process. However, the BCP process goes beyond risk management's preemptive approach and assumes that the disaster will happen at some point.

Risk Communication

Risk communication is a complex cross-disciplinary academic field. Problems for risk communicators involve how to reach the intended audience, to make the risk comprehensible and relatable to other risks, how to pay appropriate respect to the audience's values related to the risk, how to predict the audience's response to the communication, etc. A main goal of risk communication is to improve collective and individual decision making. Risk communication is somewhat related to crisis communication.

Seven Cardinal Rules for the Practice of Risk Communication

(as expressed by the U.S. Environmental Protection Agency and several of the field's founders)

- Accept and involve the public/other consumers as legitimate partners (e.g. stakeholders).
- Plan carefully and evaluate your efforts with a focus on your strengths, weaknesses, opportunities, and threats (SWOT).
- Listen to the stakeholders specific concerns.
- Be honest, frank, and open.
- Coordinate and collaborate with other credible sources.
- Meet the needs of the media.
- Speak clearly and with compassion.

Risk Management Plan

A Risk Management Plan is a document that a project manager prepares to foresee risks, estimate impacts, and define responses to issues. It also contains a risk assessment matrix.

A risk is "an uncertain event or condition that, if it occurs, has a positive or negative effect on a project's objectives." Risk is inherent with any project, and project managers should assess risks continually and develop plans to address them. The risk management plan contains an analysis of likely risks with both high and low impact, as well as mitigation strategies to help the project avoid being derailed should common problems arise. Risk management plans should be periodically reviewed by the project team to avoid having the analysis become stale and not reflective of actual potential project risks.

Most critically, risk management plans include a risk strategy. Broadly, there are four potential strategies, with numerous variations. Projects may choose to:

- Avoid risk — Change plans to circumvent the problem;
- Control/Mitigate risk; — Reduces impact or likelihood (or both) through intermediate steps;
- Accept risk — Take the chance of negative impact (or *auto-insurance*), eventually *budget* the cost (e.g. via a contingency budget line);
- Transfer risk — Outsource risk (or a portion of the risk - S*hare risk*) to third party/ies that can manage the outcome. This is done e.g. financially through insurance contracts or hedging transactions, or operationally through outsourcing an activity.

(Mnemonic: SARA for Share Avoid Reduce Accept, or A-CAT for "Avoid, Control, Accept, or Transfer")

Risk Management Plans often Include Matrices

The United States Department of Defence, as part of acquisition, uses risk management planning that may have a Risk Management Plan document for the specific project. The general intent of the RMP in this context is to define the scope of risks to be tracked and means of documenting reports. It is also desired that there would be an integrated relationship to other processes. An example of this would be explaining which developmental tests verify risks of the design type were minimized are stated as part of the Test and Evaluation Master Plan. A further example would be instructions from 5000. 2D that for programs that are part of a System of systems the risk management strategy shall specifically address integration and interoperability as a risk area. The RMP specific process and templates shift over time (e.g. the disappearance of 2002 documents Defence Finance and Accounting Service / System Risk Management Plan, and the SPAWAR Risk Management Process).

Risk–Return Spectrum

The risk–return spectrum also called the *risk–return tradeoff*) is the relationship between the amount of return gained on an investment and the amount of risk undertaken in that investment. The more return sought, the more risk that must be undertaken.

The Progression

There are various classes of possible investments, each with their own positions on the overall risk-return spectrum. The general progression is: short-term debt; long-term debt; property; high-yield debt; equity. There is considerable overlap of the ranges for each investment class. All this can be visualised by plotting expected return on the vertical axis against risk (represented by standard deviation upon that expected return) on the horizontal axis. This line starts at the risk-free rate and rises as risk rises. The line will tend to be straight, and will be straight at equilibrium.

For any particular investment type, the line drawn from the risk-free rate on the vertical axis to the risk-return point for that investment has a slope called the Sharpe ratio.

Short-term Loans to Good Government Bodies

On the lowest end is short-dated loans to government and government-guaranteed entities (usually semi-independent government departments). The lowest of all is the risk-free rate of return. The risk-free rate has zero risk (most modern major governments will inflate and monetise their debts rather than default upon them), but the return is positive because there is still both the time-preference and inflation premium components of minimum expected rates of return that must be met or exceeded if the funding is to be forthcoming from providers. The risk-free rate is commonly approximated by the return paid upon 30-day or their equivalent, but in reality that rate has more to do with the monetary policy of that country's central bank than the market supply conditions for credit.

Mid- and Long-term Loans to Good Government Bodies

The next types of investment is longer-term loans to government, such as 3-year bonds. The range width is larger, and follows the influence of increasing risk premium required as the maturity of that debt grows longer. Nevertheless, because it is debt of good government the highest end of the range is still comparatively low compared to the ranges of other investment types discussed below.

Also, if the government in question is not at the highest jurisdiction (i.e., is a state or municipal government), or the smaller that government is, the more along the risk-return spectrum that government's securities will be.

Short-term Loans to Blue-Chip Corporations

Following the lowest-risk investments are short-dated bills of exchange from major blue-chip corporations with the highest credit ratings. The further away from perfect the credit rating, the higher up the risk-return spectrum that particular investment will be.

Mid- and Long-term Loans to Blue-Chip Corporations

Overlapping the range for short-term debt is the longer term debt from those same well-rated corporations. These are higher up the range because the maturity has increased. The overlap occurs of the mid-term debt of the best rated corporations with the short-term debt of the nearly perfectly, but not perfectly rated corporations.

In this arena, the debts are called investment grade by the rating agencies. The lower the credit rating, the higher the yield and thus the expected return.

Rental Property

A commercial property that the investor rents out is comparable in risk or return to a low-investment grade. Industrial property has higher risk and returns, followed by residential (with the possible exception of the investor's own home).

High-Yield Debt

After the returns upon all classes of investment-grade debt come the returns on speculative-grade high-yield debt (also known derisively as junk bonds). These may come from mid and low rated corporations, and less politically stable governments.

Equity

Equity returns are the profits earned by businesses after interest and tax. Even the equity returns on the highest rated corporations are notably risky. Small-cap stocks are generally riskier than large-cap; companies that primarily service governments, or provide basic consumer goods such as food or utilities, tend to be less volatile than those in other industries. Note that since stocks tend to rise when corporate bonds fall and vice-versa, a portfolio containing a small percentage of stocks can be less risky than one containing only debts.

Options and Futures

Option and futures contracts often provide leverage on underlying stocks, bonds or commodities; this increases the returns but also the risks. Note that in some cases, derivatives can be used to hedge, decreasing the overall risk of the portfolio due to negative correlation with other investments.

Why the Progression?

The existence of risk causes the need to incur a number of expenses. For example, the more risky the investment the more time and effort is usually required to obtain information about it and monitor its progress. For another, the importance of a loss of X amount of value is greater than the importance of a gain of X amount of value, so a riskier investment will attract a higher risk premium even if the forecast return is the same as upon a less risky investment. Risk is therefore something that must be compensated for, and the more risk the more compensation required.

If an investment had a high return with low risk, eventually everyone would want to invest there. That action would drive down the actual rate of return achieved, until it reached the rate of return the market deems commensurate with the level of risk. Similarly, if an investment had a low return with high risk, all the present investors would want to leave that investment, which would then increase the actual return until again it reached the rate of return the market deems commensurate with the level of risk. That part of total returns which sets this appropriate level is called the risk premium.

Leverage Extends the Spectrum

The use of leverage can extend the progression out even further. Examples of this include borrowing funds to invest in equities, or use of derivatives.

If leverage is used then there are two lines instead of one. This is because although one can invest at the risk-free rate, one can only borrow at an interest rate according to one's own credit-rating. This is visualised by the new line starting at the point of the riskiest unleveraged investment (equities) and rising at a lower slope than the original line. If this new line were traced back to the vertical axis of zero risk, it will cross it at the borrowing rate.

Domination

All investment types compete against each other, even though they are on different positions on the risk-return spectrum. Any of the mid-range investments can have their performances simulated by a portfolio consisting of a risk-free component and the highest-risk component. This principle, called the separation property, is a crucial feature of modern portfolio theory. The line is then called the capital market line.

If at any time there is an investment that has a higher Sharpe ratio than another then that return is said to dominate. When there are two or more investments above the spectrum line, then the one with the highest Sharpe ratio is the most dominant one, even if the risk and return on that particular investment is lower than another. If every mid-range return falls below the spectrum line, this means that the highest-risk investment has the highest Sharpe Ratio and so dominates over all others.

If at any time there is an investment that dominates then funds will tend to be withdrawn from all others and be redirected to that dominating investment. This action will lower the return on that investment and raise it on others. The withdrawal and redirection of capital ceases when all returns are at the levels appropriate for the degrees of risk and commensurate with the opportunity cost arising from competition with the other investment types on the spectrum, which means they all tend to end up having the same Sharpe Ratio.

Risk Premium

Risk premium is the minimum amount of money by which the expected return on a risky asset must exceed the known return on a risk-free asset, or the expected return on a less risky asset, in order to induce an individual to hold the risky asset rather than the risk-free asset. (Note that risk premia may be negative.) Thus it is the minimum willingness to accept compensation for the risk.

The certainty equivalent, a related concept, is the guaranteed amount of money that an individual would view as equally desirable as a risky asset.

Formal Definitions

Let an individual's increasing, concave von Neumann-Morgenstern utility function be u, let r_f be the return on the risk-free asset, and let r be the random return on the risky asset. Write r as the sum of its hypothetical expected return $r_f + \pi$ and its zero-mean risky component x. Then the risk premium π is defined by

$$u(r) = Eu(r_f + \pi + x).$$

Thus the risk premium is the amount by which the risky asset's expected return must in fact exceed the risk-free return in order to make the risky and risk-free assets equally attractive.

Further, the certainty equivalent C is defined by

$$u(C) = Eu(r);$$

thus the certainty equivalent is the certain value which is equally attractive as the risky asset; due to risk aversion the certainty equivalent will be less than the expected return on the risky asset.

Example

Suppose a game show participant may choose one of two doors, one that hides $1,000 and one that hides $0. Further suppose that the host also allows the contestant to take $500 instead of choosing a door. The two options (choosing between door 1 and door 2, or taking $500) have the same expected value of $500, so no risk premium is being offered for choosing the doors rather than the guaranteed $500.

A contestant unconcerned about risk is indifferent between these choices. A risk-averse contestant will choose no door and accept the guaranteed $500, while a risk-loving contestant will derive utility from the uncertainty and will therefore choose a door.

If too many contestants are risk averse, the game show may encourage selection of the riskier choice (gambling on one of the doors) by offering a positive risk premium. If the game show offers $1,600 behind the good door, increasing to $800 the expected value of choosing between doors 1 and 2, the risk premium becomes $300 (i.e., $800 expected value minus $500 guaranteed amount). Contestants requiring a minimum risk compensation of less than $300 will choose a door instead of accepting the guaranteed $500.

Finance

In finance, the risk premium refers to the amount by which an asset's expected rate of return exceeds the risk-free interest rate. When measuring risk, a common approach is to compare the risk-free return on T-bills and the risky return on other investments (using the *ex post* return as a proxy for the *ex ante* expected return). The difference between these two returns can be interpreted as a measure of the excess expected return on the risky asset. This excess expected return is known as the risk premium.

- Equity: In the stock market the risk premium is the expected return of a company stock, a group of company stocks, or a portfolio of all stock market company stocks, minus the risk-free rate. The return from equity is the sum of the dividend yield and capital gains. The risk premium for equities is also called the equity premium. Note that this is an unobservable quantity since no one knows for sure what the expected rate of return on equities is. Nonetheless, most people believe that there is a risk premium built into equities, and this is what encourages investors to place at least some of their money in equities.
- Debt: In the context of bonds, the term "risk premium" is often used imprecisely to refer to the credit spread (the difference between the bond interest rate and the risk-free rate). To see why this is inconsistent with the given definition, imagine that the risk free rate is 3% and XYZ corporate bonds are yielding 10%. Does that mean that the expected return in excess of the risk free rate is 7%? Almost certainly not; after all, there is surely a positive probability of a default, as well as a positive probability of positive or negative capital gains due to fluctuations in the market prices of bonds. In reality, the risk premium (as defined above) is likely to be significantly less than the credit spread; it could even be negative, if the bond's default scenarios are negatively correlated with most other bonds' default scenarios.

Diversification (Finance)

In finance, diversification means reducing non-systematic risk by investing in a variety of assets. If the asset values do not move up and down in perfect synchrony, a diversified portfolio will have less risk than the weighted average risk of its constituent assets, and often less risk than the least risky of its constituent.

Diversification is one of two general techniques for reducing investment risk. The other is hedging. Diversification relies on the lack of a tight positive relationship among the assets' returns, and works even when correlations are near zero or somewhat positive. Hedging relies on negative correlation among assets, or shorting assets with positive correlation.

Examples

The simplest example of diversification is provided by the proverb "Don't put all your eggs in one basket". Dropping the basket will break all the eggs. Placing each egg in a different basket is more diversified. There is more risk of losing one egg, but less risk of losing all of them.

In finance, an example of an undiversified portfolio is to hold only one stock. This is risky; it is not unusual for a single stock to go down 50% in one year. It is much less common for a portfolio of 20 stocks to go down that much, especially if they are selected at random. If the stocks are selected from a variety of industries, company sizes and types (such as some growth stocks and some value stocks) it is still less likely.

Since the mid-1970s, it has also been argued that geographic diversification would generate superior risk-adjusted returns for large institutional investors by reducing overall portfolio risk while capturing some of the higher rates of return offered by the emerging markets of Asia and Latin America.

Return Expectations While Diversifying

If the prior expectations of the returns on all assets in the portfolio are identical, the expected return on a diversified portfolio will be identical to that on an undiversified portfolio. *Ex post*, some assets will do better than others; but since one does not know in advance which assets will perform better, this fact cannot be exploited in advance. The *ex post* return on a diversified portfolio can never exceed that of the top-performing investment, and indeed will always be lower than the highest return (unless all returns are *ex post* identical). Conversely, the diversified portfolio's return will always be higher than that of the worst-performing investment. So by diversifying, one loses the chance of having invested solely in the single asset that comes out best, but one also avoids having invested solely in the asset that comes out worst. That is the role of diversification: it narrows the range of possible outcomes. Diversification need not either help or hurt expected returns, unless the alternative non-diversified portfolio has a higher expected return.

Maximum Diversification

Given the advantages of diversification, many experts recommend maximum diversification, also known as "buying the market portfolio." Unfortunately, identifying that portfolio is not straightforward. The earliest definition comes from the capital asset pricing model which argues the maximum diversification comes from buying a *pro rata* share of all available assets. This is the idea underlying index funds.

Diversification has no maximum. Every equally weighted, uncorrelated asset added to a portfolio can add to that portfolios measured diversification. When assets are not uniformly uncorrelated, a weighting approach that puts assets in proportion to their relative correlation can maximize the available diversification.

"Risk parity" is an alternative idea. This weights assets in inverse proportion to risk, so the portfolio has equal risk in all asset classes. This is justified both on theoretical grounds, and with the pragmatic argument that future risk is much easier to forecast than either future market value or future economic footprint. "Correlation parity" is an extension of risk parity, and is the solution whereby each asset in a portfolio has an equal correlation with the portfolio, and is therefore the "most diversified portfolio". Risk parity is the special case of correlation parity when all pair-wise correlations are equal.

Effect of Diversification on Variance

One simple measure of financial risk is variance. Diversification can lower the variance of a portfolio's return below what it would be if the entire portfolio were invested in the asset with the lowest variance of return, even if the assets' returns are uncorrelated. For example, let asset X have stochastic return x and asset Y have stochastic return y, with respective return variances σ_x^2 and σ_y^2. If the fraction q of a one-unit (e.g. one-million-dollar) portfolio is placed in asset X and the fraction $1-q$ is placed in Y, the stochastic portfolio return is $qx+(1-q)y$. If and are uncorrelated, the variance of portfolio return is $var(qx+(1-q)y)=q^2\sigma_x^2+(1-q)^2\sigma_y^2$. The variance-minimizing value of is q, which is strictly between and . Using this value of in the expression for the variance of portfolio return gives the latter as $q=\sigma_y^2/[\sigma_x^2+\sigma_y^2]$, which is less than what it would be at either of the undiversified values $q=1$ and $q=0$ (which respectively give portfolio return variance of σ_x^2 and σ_y^2). Note that the favourable effect of diversification on portfolio variance would be enhanced if x and y were negatively correlated but diminished (though not necessarily eliminated) if they were positively correlated.

In general, the presence of more assets in a portfolio leads to greater diversification benefits, as can be seen by considering portfolio variance as a function of n, the number of assets. For example, if all assets' returns are mutually uncorrelated and have identical variances σ_x^2, portfolio variance is minimized by holding all assets in the equal proportions $1/n$. Then the portfolio return's variance equals $var[(1/n)x_1 + (1/n)x_2 + ... + (1/n)x_n] = n(1/n^2)\sigma_x^2 = \sigma_x^2/n$, which is monotonically decreasing in n.

The latter analysis can be adapted to show why *adding* uncorrelated risky assets to a portfolio, thereby increasing the portfolio's size, is not diversification, which involves subdividing the portfolio among many smaller investments. In the case of adding investments, the portfolio's return is $x_1 + x_2 + \ldots + x_n$ instead of $(1/n)x_1 + (1/n)x_2 + ... + (1/n)x_n$, and the variance of the portfolio return if the assets are uncorrelated is $var[x_1 + x_2 + \ldots + x_n] = \sigma_x^2 + \sigma_x^2 + \ldots + \sigma_x^2 = n\sigma_x^2$, which is *increasing* in n rather than decreasing. Thus, for example, when an insurance company adds more and more uncorrelated policies to its portfolio, this expansion does not itself represent diversification—the diversification occurs in the spreading of the insurance company's risks over a large number of part-owners of the company.

Diversifiable and Non-Diversifiable Risk

The capital asset pricing model introduced the concepts of diversifiable and non-diversifiable risk. Synonyms for diversifiable risk are idiosyncratic risk, unsystematic risk, and security-specific risk. Synonyms for non-diversifiable risk are systematic risk, beta risk and market risk.

If one buys all the stocks in the S&P 500 one is obviously exposed only to movements in that index. If one buys a single stock in the S&P 500, one is exposed both to index movements and movements in the stock based on its underlying company. The first risk is called "non-diversifiable," because it exists however many S&P 500 stocks are bought. The second risk is called "diversifiable," because it can be reduced by diversifying among stocks.

Note that there is also the risk of overdiversifying to the point that your performance will suffer and you will end up paying mostly for fees.

The capital asset pricing model argues that investors should only be compensated for non-diversifiable risk. Other financial models allow for multiple sources of non-diversifiable risk, but also insist that diversifiable risk should not carry any extra expected return. Still other models do not accept this contention.

An Empirical Example Relating Diversification to Risk Reduction

In 1977 Elton and Gruber worked out an empirical example of the gains from diversification. Their approach was to consider a population of 3290 securities available for possible inclusion in a portfolio, and to consider the average risk over all possible randomly chosen n-asset portfolios with equal amounts held in each included asset, for various values of n. Their results are summarized in the following table. It can be seen that most of the gains from diversification come for $n \leq 30$.

Number of Stocks in Portfolio	*Average Standard Deviation of Annual Portfolio Returns*	*Ratio of Portfolio Standard Deviation to Standard Deviation of a Single Stock*
1	49.24%	1.00
2	37.36	0.76
4	29.69	0.60
6	26.64	0.54
8	24.98	0.51
10	23.93	0.49
20	21.68	0.44
30	20.87	0.42
40	20.46	0.42
50	20.20	0.41
400	19.29	0.39
500	19.27	0.39
1000	19.21	0.39

Corporate Diversification Strategies

In corporate portfolio models, diversification is thought of as being vertical or horizontal. Horizontal diversification is thought of as expanding a product line or acquiring related companies. Vertical diversification is synonymous with integrating the supply chain or amalgamating distributions channels.

Non-incremental diversification is a strategy followed by conglomerates, where the individual business lines have little to do with one another, yet the company is attaining diversification from exogenous risk factors to stabilize and provide opportunity for active management of diverse resources.

History

Diversification is mentioned in the Bible, in the book of Ecclesiastes which was written in approximately 935 B.C.:

But divide your investments among many places, for you do not know what risks might lie ahead. Diversification is also mentioned in the Talmud. The formula given there is to split one's assets into thirds: one third in business (buying and selling things), one third kept liquid (e.g. gold coins), and one third in land (real estate).

Diversification is mentioned in Shakespeare (*Merchant of Venice*):

- My ventures are not in one bottom trusted,
- Nor to one place; nor is my whole estate
- Upon the fortune of this present year:
- Therefore, my merchandise makes me not sad.

The modern understanding of diversification dates back to the work of Harry Markowitz in the 1950s.

Diversification with an Equally Weighted Portfolio

The expected return on a portfolio is a weighted average of the expected returns on each individual asset:

$$\mathbb{E}[R_P] = \sum_{i=1}^{n} x_i \mathbb{E}[R_i]$$

where x_i is the proportion of the investor's total invested wealth in asset i.

The variance of the portfolio return is given by:

$$\underbrace{\text{Var}(R_P)}_{\equiv \sigma_P^2} = \mathbb{E}[R_P - \mathbb{E}[R_P]]^2$$

Inserting in the expression for $\mathbb{E}[R_P]$:

$$\sigma_P^2 = \mathbb{E}\left[\sum_{i=1}^{n} x_i R_i - \sum_{i=1}^{n} x_i \mathbb{E}[R_i]\right]^2$$

Rearranging:

$$\sigma_P^2 = \mathbb{E}\left[\sum_{i=1}^{n} x_i (R_i - \mathbb{E}[R_i])\right]^2$$

$$\sigma_P^2 = \mathbb{E}\left[\sum_{i=1}^{n}\sum_{j=1}^{n} x_i x_j (R_i - \mathbb{E}[R_i])(R_j - \mathbb{E}[R_j])\right]$$

$$\sigma_P^2 = \mathbb{E}\left[\sum_{i=1}^{n} x_i^2 (R_i - \mathbb{E}[R_i])^2 + \sum_{i=1}^{n}\sum_{j=1, i\neq j}^{n} x_i x_j (R_i - \mathbb{E}[R_i])(R_j - \mathbb{E}[R_j])\right]$$

$$\sigma_P^2 = \sum_{i=1}^{n} x_i^2 \underbrace{\mathbb{E}\left[R_i - \mathbb{E}[R_i]\right]^2}_{\equiv \sigma_i^2} + \sum_{i=1}^{n} \sum_{j=1, i\neq j}^{n} x_i x_j \underbrace{\mathbb{E}\left[(R_i - \mathbb{E}[R_i])(R_j - \mathbb{E}[R_j])\right]}_{\equiv \sigma_{ij}}$$

$$\sigma_P^2 = \sum_{i=1}^{n} x_i^2 \sigma_i^2 + \sum_{i=1}^{n} \sum_{j=1, i\neq j}^{n} x_i x_j \sigma_{ij}$$

where σ_i^2 is the variance on asset i and σ_{ij} is the covariance between assets i and j. In an equally weighted portfolio, $x_i = x_j = \frac{1}{n}, \forall i, j$.

The portfolio variance then becomes:

$$\sigma_P^2 = n\frac{1}{n^2}\sigma_i^2 + n(n-1)\frac{1}{n}\frac{1}{n}\bar{\sigma}_{ij}$$

Where $\bar{\sigma}_{ij}$ is the average of the covariances σ_{ij} for $i \neq j$. Simplifying we obtain

$$\sigma_P^2 = \frac{1}{n}\sigma_i^2 + \frac{n-1}{n}\bar{\sigma}_{ij}$$

As the number of assets grows we get the asymptotic formula:

$$\lim_{n\to\infty} \sigma_P^2 = \bar{\sigma}_{ij}$$

Thus, in an equally weighted portfolio, the portfolio variance tends to the average of covariances between securities as the number of securities becomes arbitrarily large.

Time Value of Money

A time value of money calculation is one which solves for one of several variables in a financial problem. In a typical case, the variables might be: a balance (the real or nominal value of a debt or a financial asset in terms of monetary units); a periodic rate of interest; the number of periods; and a series of cash flows (in the case of a debt, these are payments against principal and interest; in the case of a financial asset, these are contributions to or withdrawals from the balance). More generally, the cash flows may not be periodic but may be specified individually. Any of the variables may be the independent variable (the sought-for answer) in a given problem. For example, one may know that: the interest is 0.5% per period (per month, say); the number of periods is 60 (months); the initial balance (of the debt, in this case) is 25,000 units; and the final balance is 0 units. The unknown variable may be the monthly payment that the borrower will need to pay.

For example, £100 invested for one year, earning 5% interest, will be worth £105 after one year; therefore, £100 paid now *and* £105 paid exactly one year later *both* have the same value to a recipient who expects 5% interest. That is, £100 invested for one year at 5% interest has a *future value* of £105. This notion dates back at least to Martín de Azpilcueta (1491–1586) of the School of Salamanca.

This principle allows for the valuation of a likely stream of income in the future, in such a way that annual incomes are discounted and then added together, thus providing a lump-sum "present value" of the entire income stream; all of the standard calculations for time value of money derive from the most basic algebraic expression for the present value of a future sum, "discounted" to the present by an amount equal to the time value of money. For example, the future value sum FV to be received in one year is discounted at the rate of interest r to give the present value sum PV :

$$PV = \frac{FV}{(1+r)}$$

Some Standard Calculations Based on the Time Value of Money are

- Present value: The current worth of a future sum of money or stream of cash flows, given a specified rate of return. Future cash flows are "discounted" at the *discount rate;* the higher the discount rate, the lower the present value of the future cash flows. Determining the appropriate discount rate is the key to valuing future cash flows properly, whether they be earnings or obligations.
- Present value of an annuity: An annuity is a series of equal payments or receipts that occur at evenly spaced intervals. Leases and rental payments are examples. The payments or receipts occur at the end of each period for an ordinary annuity while they occur at the beginning of each period for an annuity due.

Present value of a perpetuity is an infinite and constant stream of identical cash flows.

- Future value: The value of an asset or cash at a specified date in the future, based on the value of that asset in the present.
- Future value of an annuity (FVA): The future value of a stream of payments (annuity), assuming the payments are invested at a given rate of interest.

Calculations

There are several basic equations that represent the equalities listed above. The solutions may be found using (in most cases) the formulas, a financial calculator or a spreadsheet. The formulas are programmed into most financial calculators and several spreadsheet functions (such as PV, FV, RATE, NPER, and PMT). For any of the equations below, the formula may also be rearranged to determine one of the other unknowns. In the case of the standard annuity formula, however, there is no closed-form algebraic solution for the interest rate (although financial calculators and spreadsheet programs can readily determine solutions through rapid trial and error algorithms).

These equations are frequently combined for particular uses. For example, bonds can be readily priced using these equations. A typical coupon bond is composed of two types of payments: a stream of coupon payments similar to an annuity, and a lump-sum return of capital at the end of the bond's maturity - that is, a future payment. The two formulas can be combined to determine the present value of the bond.

An important note is that the interest rate i is the interest rate for the relevant period. For an annuity that makes one payment per year, i will be the annual interest rate. For an income or payment stream with a different payment schedule, the interest rate must be converted into the relevant periodic interest rate. For example, a monthly rate for a mortgage with monthly payments requires that the interest rate be divided by 12. The rate of return in the calculations can be either the variable solved for, or a predefined variable that measures a discount rate, interest, inflation, rate of return, cost of equity, cost of debt or any number of other analogous concepts. The choice of the appropriate rate is critical to the exercise, and the use of an incorrect discount rate will make the results meaningless.

For calculations involving annuities, you must decide whether the payments are made at the end of each period (known as an ordinary annuity), or at the beginning of each period (known as an annuity due). If you are using a financial calculator or a spreadsheet, you can usually set it for either calculation. The following formulas are for an ordinary annuity. If you want the answer for the Present Value of an annuity due simply multiply the PV of an ordinary annuity by $(1 + i)$.

Formula

The following formula use these common variables:

- PV is the value at time=0 (present value)
- FV is the value at time=n (future value)
- A is the value of the individual payments in each compounding period

- n is the number of periods (not necessarily an integer)
- i is the discount rate, or the interest rate at which the amount will be compounded each period
- g is the growing rate of payments over each time period

Future value of a present sum:

The future value (FV) formula is similar and uses the same variables.

$$FV = PV \cdot (1+i)^n$$

Present Value of a Future Sum

The present value formula is the core formula for the time value of money; each of the other formulae is derived from this formula. For example, the annuity formula is the sum of a series of present value calculations.

The present value (PV) formula has four variables, each of which can be solved for:

$$PV = \frac{FV}{(1+i)^n}$$

The cumulative present value of future cash flows can be calculated by summing the contributions of FV_t, the value of cash flow at time t

$$PV = \sum_{t=1}^{n} \frac{FV_t}{(1+i)^t}$$

Note that this series can be summed for a given value of n, or when n is ". This is a very general formula, which leads to several important special cases given below.

Present Value of an Annuity for n Payment Periods

In this case the cash flow values remain the same throughout the n periods. The present value of an annuity (PVA) formula has four variables, each of which can be solved for:

$$PV(A) = \frac{A}{i} \cdot \left[1 - \frac{1}{(1+i)^n}\right]$$

To get the PV of an annuity due, multiply the above equation by $(1 + i)$.

Present Value of a Growing Annuity

In this case each cash flow grows by a factor of (1+g). Similar to the formula for an annuity, the present value of a growing annuity (PVGA) uses the same variables with the addition of g as the rate of growth of the annuity (A is the annuity payment in the first period). This is a calculation that is rarely provided for on financial calculators.

Where i ≠ g :

$$PV = \frac{A}{(i-g)}\left[1-\left(\frac{1+g}{1+i}\right)^{n}\right]$$

Where i = g :

$$PV = \frac{A \times n}{1+i}$$

To get the PV of a growing annuity due, multiply the above equation by (1 + *i*).

Present Value of a Perpetuity

A perpetuity is payments of a set amount of money that occur on a routine basis and continues forever. When $n \to \infty$, the *PV* of a perpetuity (a perpetual annuity) formula becomes simple division.

$$PV(P) = \frac{A}{i}$$

Present Value of Int Factor Annuity

$$A = P(1 + r / n)^{nt}$$

Example:

Investment $P = \$1000$

Interest $i = 6.90\%$ Compounded Qtrly (4 Times in Year)

Tenure Years $n = 5$

$$= 1000 \times (1 + .069 / 4)^{(5\ yrs \times 4\ qtrs\ in\ a\ year)}$$

$$= 1000 \times (1 + 0.069 / 4)^{20} \approx 1407.84$$

Present Value of a Growing Perpetuity

When the perpetual annuity payment grows at a fixed rate (g) the value is theoretically determined according to the following formula. In practice, there are few securities with precise characteristics, and the application of this valuation approach is subject to various qualifications and modifications. Most importantly, it is rare to find a growing perpetual annuity with fixed rates of growth and true perpetual cash flow generation. Despite these qualifications, the general approach may be used in valuations of real estate, equities, and other assets.

This is the well known Gordon Growth model used for stock valuation.

Future Value of an Annuity

The future value of an annuity (FVA) formula has four variables, each of which can be solved for:

$$FV(A)=A\cdot\frac{(1+i)^n-1}{i}$$

To get the FV of an annuity due, multiply the above equation by (1 + i).

Future Value of a Growing Annuity

The future value of a growing annuity (FVA) formula has five variables, each of which can be solved for:

Where $i \neq g$:

$$FV(A)=A\cdot\frac{(1+i)^n-(1+g)^n}{i-g}$$

Where $i = g$:

$$FV(A)=A\cdot n(1+i)^{n-1}$$

Formula Table

The following table summarizes the different formulas commonly used in calculating the time value of money.

Find	*Given*	*Formula*
Future value (F)	Present value (P)	$F=P\cdot(1+i)^n$
Present value (P)	Future value (F)	$P=F\cdot(1+i)^{-n}$
Repeating payment (A)	Future value (F)	$A=F\cdot\frac{i}{(1+i)^n-1}$
Repeating payment (A)	Present value (P)	$A=P\cdot\frac{i(1+i)^n}{(1+i)^n-1}$
Future value (F)	Repeating payment (A)	$F=A\cdot\frac{(1+i)^n-1}{i}$
Present value (P)	Repeating payment (A)	$P=A\cdot\frac{(1+i)^n-1}{i(1+i)^n}$
Future value (F)	Gradient payment (G)	$F=G\cdot\frac{(1+i)^n-in-1}{i^2}$
Present value (P)	Gradient payment (G)	$P=G\cdot\frac{(1+i)^n-in-1}{i^2(1+i)^n}$
Fixed payment (A)	Gradient payment (G)	$A=G\cdot\left[\frac{1}{i}-\frac{n}{(1+i)^n-1}\right]$
Future value (F)	Exponentially increasing payment (D) Increasing percentage (g)	$F=D\cdot\frac{(1+g)^n-(1+i)^n}{g-i}$ (for i ≠ g) $F=D\cdot\frac{n(1+i)^n}{1+g}$ (for i = g)
Present value (P)	Exponentially increasing payment (D) Increasing percentage (g)	$P=D\cdot\frac{\left(\frac{1+g}{1+i}\right)^n-1}{g-i}$ (for i ≠ g) $P=D\cdot\frac{n}{1+g}$ (for i = g)

Notes:

- A is a fixed payment amount, every period
- G is a steadily increasing payment amount, that starts at G and increases by G for each subsequent period.
- D is an exponentially or geometrically increasing payment amount, that starts at D and increases by a factor of (1+g) each subsequent period.

Derivations

Annuity Derivation

The formula for the present value of a regular stream of future payments (an annuity) is derived from a sum of the formula for future value of a single future payment, as below, where C is the payment amount and n the period.

A single payment C at future time m has the following future value at future time n:

$$FV = C(1+i)^{n-m}$$

Summing over all payments from time 1 to time n, then reversing t

$$FVA = \sum_{m=1}^{n} C(1+i)^{n-m} = \sum_{k=0}^{n-1} C(1+i)^{k}$$

Note that this is a geometric series, with the initial value being $a = C$, the multiplicative factor being $1 + i$, with n terms. Applying the formula for geometric series, we get

$$FVA = \frac{C(1-(1+i)^n)}{1-(1+i)} = \frac{C(1-(1+i)^n)}{-i}$$

The present value of the annuity (PVA) is obtained by simply dividing by $(1+i)^n$:

$$PVA = \frac{FVA}{(1+i)^n} = \frac{C}{i}\left(1 - \frac{1}{(1+i)^n}\right)$$

Another simple and intuitive way to derive the future value of an annuity is to consider an endowment, whose interest is paid as the annuity, and whose principal remains constant. The principal of this hypothetical endowment can be computed as that whose interest equals the annuity payment amount:

$$\text{Principal} \times i = C$$

$$\text{Principal} = C / i + goal$$

Note that no money enters or leaves the combined system of endowment principal + accumulated annuity payments, and thus the future value of this system can be computed simply via the future value formula:

$$FV = PV(1+i)^n$$

Initially, before any payments, the present value of the system is just the endowment principal ($PV = C / i$). At the end, the future value is the endowment principal (which is the same) plus the future value of the total annuity payments ($FV = C / i + FVA$). Plugging this back into the equation:

$$\frac{C}{i} + FVA = \frac{C}{i}(1+i)^n$$

$$FVA = \frac{C}{i}\left[(1+i)^n - 1\right]$$

Perpetuity Derivation

Without showing the formal derivation here, the perpetuity formula is derived from the annuity formula. Specifically, the term:

$$\left(1 - \frac{1}{(1+i)^n}\right)$$

can be seen to approach the value of 1 as n grows larger. At infinity, it is equal to 1, leaving $\frac{C}{i}$ as the only term remaining.

Examples

Example 1: Present Value

One hundred euros to be paid 1 year from now, where the expected rate of return is 5% per year, is worth in today's money:

$$P = F \times (P / F) = F \times \frac{1}{(1+i)^n} = \frac{100}{1.05} = 95.24$$

So the present value of €100 one year from now at 5% is €95.24.

Example 2: Present Value of an Annuity — Solving for the Payment Amount

Consider a 10-year mortgage where the principal amount P is \$200,000 and the annual interest rate is 6%.

The number of monthly payments is

$$n = 10 \text{ years} \times 12 \text{ months per year} = 120 \text{ months}$$

and the monthly interest rate is

$$i = \frac{6\% \text{ per year}}{12 \text{ months per year}} = 0.5\% \text{ per month}$$

The annuity formula for (*A*/*P*) calculates the monthly payment:

$$A = P \times \left(A / P\right) = P \times \frac{i(1+i)^n}{(1+i)^n - 1} = \$200{,}000 \times \frac{0.005(1.005)^{120}}{(1.005)^{120} - 1}$$

$$\approx \$200{,}000 \times 0.01110205 \approx \$2{,}220.41 \text{ per month}$$

This is considering an interest rate compounding monthly. If the interest were only to compound yearly at 6%, the monthly payment would be significantly different.

An Approximate Solution

For those who only want a rough idea of the mortgage payment there is a much less intimidating approximate formula here. For the numbers given above we simply compute an approximate annual repayment of 200,000*(1/n + (2/3)*i) where n=10 yrs, i=0.06. So 200,000*(1/10 + (2/3)*0.06) = 200,000*(0.1+0.04) = 200,000*0.14 = $28,000 per year, roughly, via mental arithmetic alone. Note, as this is an approximation we may ignore the subtleties of monthly compounding. Now $28,000 per year is about 28,000/12 = $2,333 per month which approximates the true answer to within about 5% but has required only mental arithmetic.

Example 3: Solving for the Period Needed to Double Money

Consider a deposit of £100 placed at 10% (annual). How many years are needed for the value of the deposit to double to £200?

Using the algrebric identity that if:

$$x = b^y$$

then

$$y = \frac{\log(x)}{\log(b)}$$

The present value formula can be rearranged such that:

$$y = \frac{\log(\frac{FV}{PV})}{\log(1+i)} = \frac{\log(\frac{200}{100})}{\log(1.10)} = 7.27(years)$$

This same method can be used to determine the length of time needed to increase a deposit to any particular sum, as long as the interest rate is known. For the period of time needed to double an investment, the Rule of 72 is a useful short-cut that gives a reasonable approximation of the period needed.

Example 4: What Return is Needed to Double Money?

Similarly, the present value formula can be rearranged to determine what rate of return is needed to accumulate a given amount from an investment. For example, £100 is invested today and £200 return is expected in five years; what rate of return (interest rate) does this represent?

The present value formula restated in terms of the interest rate is:

$$i = \left(\frac{FV}{PV}\right)^{\frac{1}{n}} - 1 = \left(\frac{200}{100}\right)^{\frac{1}{5}} - 1 = 2^{0.20} - 1 = 0.15 = 15\%$$

Example 5: Calculate the Value of a Regular Savings Deposit in the Future.

To calculate the future value of a stream of savings deposit in the future requires two steps, or, alternatively, combining the two steps into one large formula. First, calculate the present value of a stream of deposits of \$1,000 every year for 20 years earning 7% interest:

$$PVA = A \cdot \frac{1 - \frac{1}{(1+i)^n}}{i} = 1000 \cdot \frac{1 - \frac{1}{(1+.07)^{20}}}{.07} = 1000 \cdot \frac{1 - 0.258}{.07} = 1000 \times 10.594 \approx \$10,594$$

This does not sound like very much, but remember - this is *future money* discounted back to its value *today*; it is understandably lower. To calculate the future value (at the end of the twenty-year period):

$$FV = PV(1+i)^n = \$10,594 \times (1+.07)^{20} \approx \$10,594 \times 3.87 = \$40,995$$

These steps can be combined into a single formula:

$$FV = A \cdot \frac{1 - \frac{1}{(1+i)^n}}{i} \cdot (1+i)^n = A \cdot \frac{(1+i)^n - 1}{i}$$

Example 6: Price/Earnings (P/E) Ratio

It is often mentioned that perpetuities, or securities with an indefinitely long maturity, are rare or unrealistic, and particularly those with a growing payment. In fact, many types of assets have characteristics that are similar to perpetuities. Examples might include income-oriented real estate, preferred shares, and even most forms of publicly traded stocks. Frequently, the terminology may be slightly different, but are based on the fundamentals of time value of money calculations. The application of this methodology is subject to various qualifications or modifications, such as the Gordon growth model.

For example, stocks are commonly noted as trading at a certain P/E ratio. The P/E ratio is easily recognised as a variation on the perpetuity or growing perpetuity formulae - save that the P/E ratio is usually cited as the *inverse* of the "rate" in the perpetuity formula.

If we substitute for the time being: the *price* of the stock for the present value; the earnings per share of the stock for the cash annuity; and, the discount rate of the stock for the interest rate, we can see that:

$$\frac{P}{E}=\frac{1}{i}=\frac{PV}{A}$$

And in fact, the P/E ratio is analogous to the inverse of the interest rate (or discount rate).

$$\frac{1}{P/E}=i$$

Of course, stocks may have increasing earnings. The formulation above does not allow for growth in earnings, but to incorporate growth, the formula can be restated as follows:

$$\frac{P}{E}=\frac{1}{(i-g)}$$

If we wish to determine the implied rate of growth (if we are given the discount rate), we may solve for g:

$$g=i-\frac{E}{P}$$

Continuous Compounding

Rates are sometimes converted into the continuous compound interest rate equivalent because the continuous equivalent is more convenient (for example, more easily differentiated). Each of the formulæ above may be restated in their continuous equivalents. For example, the present value at time 0 of a future payment at time t can be restated in the following way, where e is the base of the natural logarithm and r is the continuously compounded rate:

$$\text{PV}=\text{FV}\cdot e^{-rt}$$

This can be generalized to discount rates that vary over time: instead of a constant discount rate r, one uses a function of time $r(t)$. In that case the discount factor, and thus the present value, of a cash flow at time T is given by the integral of the continuously compounded rate $r(t)$:

$$\text{PV} = \text{FV}\cdot\exp\left(-\int_0^T r(t)dt\right)$$

Indeed, a key reason for using continuous compounding is to simplify the analysis of varying discount rates and to allow one to use the tools of calculus. Further, for interest accrued and capitalized overnight (hence compounded daily), continuous compounding is a close approximation for the actual daily compounding. More sophisticated analysis includes the use of differential equations, as detailed below.

Examples

Using continuous compounding yields the following formulas for various instruments:

Annuity

$$PV = \frac{A(1-e^{-rt})}{e^r - 1}$$

Perpetuity

$$PV = \frac{A}{e^r - 1}$$

Growing annuity

$$PV = \frac{Ae^{-g}(1-e^{-(r-g)t})}{e^{(r-g)} - 1}$$

Growing perpetuity

$$PV = \frac{Ae^{-g}}{e^{(r-g)} - 1}$$

Annuity with continuous payments

$$PV = \frac{1-e^{(-rt)}}{r}$$

These formulas assume that payment A is made in the first payment period and annuity ends at time t.

Differential Equations

Ordinary and partial differential equations (ODEs and PDEs) – equations involving derivatives and one (respectively, multiple) variables are ubiquitous in more advanced treatments of financial mathematics. While time value of money can be understood without using the framework of differential equations, the added sophistication sheds additional light on time value, and provides a simple introduction before considering more complicated and less familiar situations. This exposition follows (Carr & Flesaker 2006, pp. 6–7).

The fundamental change that the differential equation perspective brings is that, rather than computing a *number* (the present value *now*), one computes a *function* (the present value now or at any point in *future*). This function may then be analyzed – how does its value change over time – or compared with other functions.

Formally, the statement that "value decreases over time" is given by defining the linear differential operator $\mathcal{L}$ as:

$$\mathcal{L} := -\partial_t + r(t).$$

This states that values decreases (–) over time (∂_t) at the discount rate ($r(t)$). Applied to a function it yields:

$$\mathcal{L}f = -\partial_t f(t) + r(t)f(t).$$

For an instrument whose payment stream is described by $f(t)$, the value $V(t)$ satisfies the inhomogeneous first-order ODE $\mathcal{L}V = f$ ("inhomogeneous" is because one has f rather than 0, and "first-order" is because one has first derivatives but no higher derivatives) – this encodes the fact that when any cash flow occurs, the value of the instrument changes by the value of the cash flow (if you receive a £10 coupon, the remaining value decreases by exactly £10).

The standard technique tool in the analysis of ODEs is the use of Green's functions, from which other solutions can be built. In terms of time value of money, the Green's function (for the time value ODE) is the value of a bond paying £1 at a single point in time u – the value of any other stream of cash flows can then be obtained by taking combinations of this basic cash flow. In mathematical terms, this instantaneous cash flow is modelled as a Dirac delta function $\delta_u(t) := \delta(t-u)$.

The Green's function for the value at time t of a £1 cash flow at time u is

$$b(t;u) := H(u-t)\cdot\exp\left(-\int_t^u r(v)dv\right)$$

where H is the Heaviside step function – the notation "$;u$" is to emphasize that u is a *parameter* (fixed in any instance – the time when the cash flow will occur), while t is a *variable* (time). In other words, future cash flows are exponentially discounted (exp) by the sum (integral, $\int$) of the future discount rates ($\int_t^u$ for future, $r(v)$ for discount rates), while past cash flows are worth 0 ($H(u-t)=1$ if $t<u, 0$ if $t>u$), because they have already occurred. Note that the value *at* the moment of a cash flow is not well-defined – there is a discontinuity at that point, and one can use a convention (assume cash flows have already occurred, or not already occurred), or simply not define the value at that point.

In case the discount rate is constant, $r(v) \equiv r$, this simplifies to

$$b(t;u) = H(u-t)\cdot e^{-(u-t)r} = \begin{cases} e^{-(u-t)r} & t<u \\ 0 & t>u, \end{cases}$$

where $(u-t)$ is "time remaining until cash flow".

Thus for a stream of cash flows $f(u)$ ending by time T (which can be set to $T=+\infty$ for no time horizon) the value at time t, $V(t;T)$ is given by combining the values of these individual cash flows:

$$V(t;T) = \int_t^T f(u)b(t;u)du.$$

This formalizes time value of money to future values of cash flows with varying discount rates, and is the basis of many formulas in financial mathematics, such as the Black–Scholes formula with varying interest rates.

Bond Valuation

Bond valuation is the determination of the fair price of a bond. As with any security or capital investment, the theoretical fair value of a bond is the present value of the stream of cash flows it is expected to generate. Hence, the value of a bond is obtained by discounting the bond's expected cash flows to the present using an appropriate discount rate. In practice, this discount rate is often determined by reference to similar instruments, provided that such instruments exist. Various related yield-measures are then calculated for the given price.

If the bond includes embedded options, the valuation is more difficult and combines option pricing with discounting. Depending on the type of option, the option price as calculated is either added to or subtracted from the price of the "straight" portion.

Bond Valuation

As above, the fair price of a "straight bond" (a bond with no embedded options; Features) is usually determined by discounting its expected cash flows at the appropriate discount rate. The formula commonly applied is discussed initially. Although this present value relationship reflects the theoretical approach to determining the value of a bond, in practice its price is (usually) determined with reference to other, more liquid instruments. The two main approaches here, Relative pricing and Arbitrage-free pricing, are discussed next. Finally, where it is important to recognise that future interest rates are uncertain and that the discount rate is not adequately represented by a single fixed number - for example when an option is written on the bond in question - stochastic calculus may be employed.

Where the market price of bond is less than its face value (par value), the bond is selling at a discount. Conversely, if the market price of bond is greater than its face value, the bond is selling at a premium.

Present Value Approach

Below is the formula for calculating a bond's price, which uses the basic present value (PV) formula for a given discount rate: (This formula assumes that a coupon payment has just been made.)

$$P=\left(\frac{C}{1+i}+\frac{C}{(1+i)^2}+\ldots+\frac{C}{(1+i)^N}\right)+\frac{M}{(1+i)^N}=\left(\sum_{n=1}^{N}\frac{C}{(1+i)^n}\right)+\frac{M}{(1+i)^N}=C\left(\frac{1-(1+i)^{-N}}{i}\right)+M(1+i)^{-N}$$

where:

F = face values

i_F = contractual interest rate

$C = F * i_F$ = coupon payment (periodic interest payment)

N = number of payments

i = market interest rate, or required yield, or observed / appropriate yield to maturity

M = value at maturity, usually equals face value

P = market price of bond.

Relative Price Approach

Under this approach — an extension of the above — the bond will be priced relative to a benchmark, usually a government security. Here, the yield to maturity on the bond is determined based on the bond's Credit rating relative to a government security with similar maturity or duration. The better the quality of the bond, the smaller the spread between its required return and the YTM of the benchmark. This required return is then used to discount the bond cash flows, replacing i in the formula above, to obtain the price.

Arbitrage-Free Pricing Approach

As distinct from the two related approaches above, a bond may be thought of as a "package of cash flows" — coupon or face — with each cash flow viewed as a zero-coupon instrument maturing on the date it will be received. Thus, rather than using a single discount rate, one should use multiple discount rates, discounting each cash flow at its own rate. Here, each cash flow is separately discounted at the same rate as a zero-coupon bond corresponding to the coupon date, and of equivalent credit worthiness (if possible, from the same issuer as the bond being valued, or if not, with the appropriate credit spread).

Under this approach, the bond price should reflect its "arbitrage-free" price, as any deviation from this price will be exploited and the bond will then quickly reprice to its correct level. Here, we apply the rational pricing logic relating to "Assets with identical cash flows". In detail: (1) the bond's coupon dates and coupon amounts are known with certainty. Therefore (2) some multiple (or fraction) of zero-coupon bonds, each corresponding to the bond's coupon dates, can be specified so as to produce identical cash flows to the bond. Thus (3) the bond price today must be equal to the sum of each of its cash flows discounted at the discount rate implied by the value of the corresponding ZCB. Were this not the case, (4) the arbitrageur could finance his purchase of whichever of the bond or the sum of the various ZCBs was cheaper, by short selling the other, and meeting his cash flow commitments using the coupons or maturing zeroes as appropriate. Then (5) her "risk free", arbitrage profit would be the difference between the two values.

Stochastic Calculus Approach

When modelling a bond option, or other interest rate derivative (IRD), it is important to recognise that future interest rates are uncertain, and therefore, the discount rate(s) referred to above, under all three cases - i.e. whether for all coupons or for each individual coupon - is not adequately represented by a fixed (deterministic) number. In such cases, stochastic calculus is employed.

The following is a partial differential equation (PDE) in stochastic calculus which is satisfied by any zero-coupon bond.

$$\frac{1}{2}\sigma(r)^2\frac{\partial^2 P}{\partial r^2}+[a(r)+\sigma(r)+\varphi(r,t)]\frac{\partial P}{\partial r}+\frac{\partial P}{\partial t}-rP=0$$

The solution to the PDE - given in - is:

$$P[t,T,r(t)]=E_t^*[e^{-R(t,T)}]$$

where E_t^* is the expectation with respect to risk-neutral probabilities, and $R(t,T)$ is a random variable representing the discount rate.

To actually determine the bond price, the analyst must choose the specific short rate model to be employed. The approaches commonly used are:

- the CIR model
- the Black-Derman-Toy model
- the Hull-White model
- the HJM framework
- the Chen model.

Note that depending on the model selected, a closed-form solution may not be available, and a lattice- or simulation-based implementation of the model in question is then employed.

Clean and Dirty Price

When the bond is not valued precisely on a coupon date, the calculated price, using the methods above, will incorporate accrued interest: i.e. any interest due to the owner of the bond since the previous coupon date. The price of a bond which includes this accrued interest is known as the "dirty price" (or "full price" or "all in price" or "Cash price"). The "clean price" is the price excluding any interest that has accrued. Clean prices are generally more stable over time than dirty prices. This is because the dirty price will drop suddenly when the bond goes "ex interest" and the purchaser is no longer entitled to receive the next coupon payment. In many markets, it is market practice to quote bonds on a clean-price basis. When a purchase is settled, the accrued interest is added to the quoted clean price to arrive at the actual amount to be paid.

Yield and Price Relationships

Once the price or value has been calculated, various yields relating the price of the bond to its coupons can then be determined.

Yield to Maturity

The yield to maturity (YTM) is the discount rate which returns the market price of a bond without embedded optionality; it is identical to i(required return) in the above equation. YTM is thus the internal rate of return of an investment in the bond made at the observed price. Since YTM can be used to price a bond, bond prices are often quoted in terms of YTM.

To achieve a return equal to YTM, i.e. where it is the required return on the bond, the bond owner must:

- buy the bond at price P_0,
- hold the bond until maturity, and
- redeem the bond at par.

Coupon Yield

The coupon yield is simply the coupon payment C as a percentage of the face value F.

$$\text{Coupon yield} = \frac{C}{F}$$

Coupon yield is also called nominal yield.

Current Yield

The current yield is simply the coupon payment C as a percentage of the (*current*) bond price .

$$\text{Current yield} = \frac{C}{P_0}.$$

Relationship

The concept of current yield is closely related to other bond concepts, including yield to maturity, and coupon yield. The relationship between yield to maturity and the coupon rate is as follows:

- When a bond sells at a discount, YTM > current yield > coupon yield.
- When a bond sells at a premium, coupon yield > current yield > YTM.
- When a bond sells at par, YTM = current yield = coupon yield

Price Sensitivity

The sensitivity of a bond's market price to interest rate (i.e. yield) movements is measured by its duration, and, additionally, by its convexity.

Duration is a linear measure of how the price of a bond changes in response to interest rate changes. It is approximately equal to the percentage change in price for a given change in yield, and may be thought of as the elasticity of the bond's price with respect to discount rates. For example, for small interest rate changes, the duration is the approximate percentage by which the value of the bond will fall for a

1% per annum increase in market interest rate. So the market price of a 17-year bond with a duration of 7 would fall about 7% if the market interest rate (or more precisely the corresponding force of interest) increased by 1% per annum.

Convexity is a measure of the "curvature" of price changes. It is needed because the price is not a linear function of the discount rate, but rather a convex function of the discount rate. Specifically, duration can be formulated as the first derivative of the price with respect to the interest rate, and convexity as the second derivative (see: Bond duration closed-form formula; Bond convexity closed-form formula; Taylor series). Continuing the above example, for a more accurate estimate of sensitivity, the convexity score would be multiplied by the square of the change in interest rate, and the result added to the value derived by the above linear formula.

Accounting Treatment

In accounting for liabilities, any bond discount or premium must be amortized over the life of the bond. A number of methods may be used for this depending on applicable accounting rules. One possibility is that amortization amount in each period is calculated from the following formula:

$n \in \{0,1,\ldots,N-1\}$

a_{n+1} = amortization amount in period number "n+1"

$a_{n+1} = |iP - C|(1+i)^n$

Bond Discount or Bond Premium $= |F - P| = a_1 + a_2 + \ldots + a_N$

Bond Discount or Bond Premium $= F\,|i - i_F|\,(\frac{1-(1+i)^{-N}}{i})$

Chapter 4

Capital Budgeting

Budgeting

Organisations develop specific plans for saving and spending income and these plans, or budgets, are essential for developing spending and saving priorities. Properly preparing a budget also serves as a reference to check how well money is being managed during a period by allowing managers to see actual revenues and expenses compared to budgeted revenues and expenses. Corrective action can be taken earlier in a period when revenue shortfalls or expense excesses are identified.

The term "budget" can be dated back to medieval England, where it meant "leather purse" or "wallet." A budget allows businesses to meet specific goals by creating a system of saving and spending money efficiently. Simply defined, a budget is a plan for using corporate funds in a way that best meets the firm's wants and needs. The plan includes a recorded entry of expected income, expenses, and savings over a defined period of time.

A wide range of budgeting techniques exist, and although the fundamental purposes are similar, the specifics among various organisations are often different. One important aspect of budgeting is how organisations increase cash to finance ongoing operations and new opportunities. Large corporations, for example, may have the option of increasing cash by selling treasury stock (previously authorized shares of ownership that have never been offered for sale on the stock market). The liquidity of equity (stock) markets allows managers to implement these equity decisions fairly quickly to budget for projected needs. In addition, the debt-paying ability of large corporations is rated by several independent organisations. This creates a market for corporate debt, more commonly referred to as bonds. Corporations with favourable debt ratings have the ability to borrow money; that is, issue bonds, at lower interest rates than those with unfavourable debt ratings. Small businesses, in contrast, often do not have publicly traded shares of stock. Although these businesses can sell stock to investors, the process is more uncertain because the market for this type of stock is less liquid. Venture capital is also an option, but the number of small businesses seeking venture capital nearly always exceeds the amount of venture capital available. Also, debt-rating agencies do not rate the debt-paying ability of many small businesses, limiting the extent to which these businesses can raise cash through bond issues. Without a ready market for debt, small businesses must often turn to the less liquid forms of debt financing such as bank loans, in some cases at higher interest rates than would be available from established credit markets available to larger corporations.

Budgets allow businesses to better utilise the financial resources available to them. To begin with, budgets help businesses operate within their means; that is, over the long term, budgets assist businesses in spending less money than they earn. Next, budgets help businesses achieve their financial goals by planning for the future and organising money into categories such as income, expenses, and savings. In short, budgets help a business avoid credit problems, better prepare for financial emergencies, and build better money management skills by creating a structured plan.

There are several steps that should be followed to successfully implement a budget. These include setting financial goals, planning budget categories, maintaining financial records, and balancing and adjusting the budget. Setting financial goals is the starting point in the budgeting process. Questions managers should asked include: "What do we want accomplished within one month, one year, or ten years?" "What new products or services do we want to offer in the short- and long-term and how can we finance these?" "Will my operating expenses increase with inflation, and how will we increase revenue to meet these additional expenses?" Clearly, there are dozens of questions managers should ask to cover all the categories of revenue, expense, and debt and equity financing in addition to these, but these questions provide a starting point to spur additional questions. The answers to these questions should help determine how income should be spent and saved, but in general, budgeting questions should revolve around estimates of income and expenses. Categories include fixed expenses such as rent, insurance premiums, and taxes; estimates of variable expenses such as utilities and wages; and estimates that allow for uncertainties.

One way to budget is by comparing estimated financial figures created before a budgeting period with actual experience at the end of the budgeting period. The initial estimates are called pro forma financial statements. The three primary types of financial statements are a balance sheet, income statement, and statement of cash flows. The balance sheet shows assets owned, liabilities owed, and owners' equity (owners' financial stake in the businesses). The income statement details profit and loss for a given period. The statement of cash flows helps managers see where cash came from and where it went. By comparing pro forma financial statements to end-of-period financial statements, managers can judge whether or not their budgets are in line with estimates. Adjustments can then be made for future budgeting periods.

A budget must meet certain characteristics to successfully manage money. The budgeting should be specific enough to provide the needed information. It should be realistic as well as flexible. When unexpected expenses arise, the spending plan should be able to handle these costs. A budget is not a permanent plan and should be realigned when circumstances occur that alter budget categories. The budget should be carefully planned and organised, yet clear enough to be communicated to organisational stakeholders such as lenders and owners.

Companies create budgets for a mixture of reasons. They can serve a variety of functions, and thus many techniques can be implemented to develop them. Budgets can be used as a means of forecasting and planning for the future. Their creation can also be used as a motivational tool. The plan can be used as a means of evaluation and control as well as a resource for information and decision-making. Many different approaches to the budgeting process in addition to preparation or pro forma financial statements and comparison to actual financial statements can be used depending on the desired function of the company. Breakeven analysis, for instance, estimates the amount of sales required to cover a new product's or new service's expenses. Payback periods are similar, but add to breakeven analysis' focus on needed sales by adding the length of time needed to achieve those sales. This tells managers how long it will take to recoup initial expenses. Another type of budgeting is capital budgeting, in which large the estimated revenue from capital projects such as purchase of property, plants, and equipment is projected. Additional techniques include such as parametric, partial, zero-based, and equity budgeting. Each of these may be applied to organisations' financial situations depending on the needs of the individual businesses.

Whatever technique managers use, the important thing is that budgeting is essential. Businesses without budgets can quickly find themselves short of cash not only for new products and services, growth and expansion, and improvements in capital projects, but also in simply meeting short-term needs such as payroll, insurance, and tax expenses. Budgeting is thus a key element in all business planning.

Zero-based Budgeting

The budgeting process is an essential component of management control systems and has been an effective system by which management can successfully plan, coordinate, and control. The process involves the creation and implementation of the broad objectives of an organisation, the detailed objectives, and a short-term and long-term financial plan. The philosophy and procedures used to implement zero-base budgeting in industry and government settings are quite similar, only slightly differing with the mechanics to fit the specific needs of each organisation.

The basic process of zero-based budgeting is to justify budget requests every budgeting cycle, regardless of prior period budgets. The following sections address the specifics including the history, implementation, drawbacks and solutions, and behavioural impacts of zero-based budgeting.

History of Zero-based Budgeting

Government budgeting was established in Great Britain in the late 17th century. The enactment of the 1689 Bill of Rights gave taxing authority to Parliament as opposed to the King. Parliament gradually established spending programs and by the 1820s published detailed annual financial statements showing revenues and expenditures and a projected surplus or deficit. The usage of budgets by the United States government did not begin until 1800 when a law was passed for the Secretary of the Treasury to submit an annual financial report to Congress. This action was not taken by the Treasury department, and instead, federal government agencies developed their own reports and submitted them to the Treasury.

Several attempts were made in the early 1900s to implement federal budgeting and financial management, but each failed, even though 44 individual states had already passed laws concerning budgets. Congress passed the Budgeting and Accounting Act in 1921 along with the creation of a centralized Bureau of the Budget. Although created in 1921, it was not until the mid-1940s that the federal budget included identification of the major goals and program objectives, a systematic analysis of supplies and needs for both military and civilian purposes, and a long-range plan of projects. In the 1960s, the Planning-Programming-Budgeting System (PPBS) was adopted by President Lyndon B. Johnson to be implemented throughout the federal government.

The PPBS was short-lived, however. In the 1970s, every federal department except for the Defence Department abandoned the system. The concept of zero-based budgeting gained notoriety in 1977 when President Jimmy Carter announced he was introducing zero-based budgeting into the federal budgeting process. The term, "zero-based budgeting," and the techniques for carrying out these budgeting processes had been previously introduced in an article written by Peter A. Pyhrr in the Harvard Business Review in 1970, but former President Carter adopted this method at the federal level, zero-based budgeting began to spread more rapidly.

President Carter, while still governor of Georgia in 1973, contracted with Pyhrr to implement the system for the entire executive budget recommendations for the state of Georgia. However, when the system was applied to governmental budgeting, it failed due to the great amount of effort and time required development and implementation. With further refinement, however, zero-based budgeting was largely hailed as a success when introduced to Congress in 1977.

Early business budgets focused on controlling costs and little emphasis on measuring effectiveness. In the early 1900s, the use of budgets increased due to the necessity for industries to implement more careful factory planning. A systematic plan of budgeting arose from two areas: industrial engineering and cost accounting. Scientific methods were used by industrial engineers to arrive at production standards, which could then be used to estimate future operations and performance standards. Cost accountants used budgeting to establish standard costs and to estimate future expected costs in a budgetary form. Also at this time, texts on budgeting and managerial accounting began to emerge.

As zero-based budgeting gained traction in the 1970s among public budgeting constituents, it also gained popularity among private enterprises, and during this time a number of organisations modified and implemented the system. An example of an organisation successfully implementing this system is the Florida Power and Light Company. In 1977 zero-based budgeting became required for all Florida

Power and Light general office staff departments. Ben Dady, the company's director of management control, favoured the system because when managers develop the zero-based budget, they begin with nothing in terms of budgeted dollars, and have to justify or prove why they need to spend money on each activity or project for all the dollars they expect to spend. New and old problems are treated equally. Every managerial activity is properly identified and then evaluated by analyzing more efficient ways and alternative levels of performing the same activity. These alternatives are then ranked and relative priorities are established.

The publicity in the 1970s surrounding zero-based budgeting gave the impression that the system was a relatively new technique, although the system was not new at all. Zero-based budgeting is quite similar to the Planning-Programming-Budgeting system, implemented in the 1960s. Both systems involve evaluating the inputs and outputs for specific activities, as opposed to the traditional line-item format.

Implementation of Zero-based Budgeting

The zero-based budgeting system puts the burden of proof on the manager, and demands that each manager justify the entire budget in detail and prove why he or she should spend the organisation's money in the manner proposed. A "decision package" must be developed by each manager for every project or activity, which includes an analysis of cost, purpose, alternative courses of action, measures of performance, consequences of not performing the activity, and the benefits.

This approach is different than traditional budgeting techniques due to the analysis of alternatives. Managers must identify alternative methods of performing each activity first, such as evaluating the costs and benefits of making a project or outsourcing it, or centralizing versus decentralizing operations. In addition, managers must identify different levels for performing each alternative method of the proposed activity. This means establishing a minimum level of spending, often 75 percent of the current operating level, and then developing separate decision packages that include the costs and benefits of additional levels of spending for that particular activity. The different levels allow managers to consider and evaluate a level of spending lower than the current operating level, giving decision-makers the choice of eliminating an activity or the ability to choose from a selection of levels of effort including tradeoffs and shifts in expenditure levels among organisational units.

The decision packages must be ranked in order of importance once they have been created. This allows each manager to identify priorities, combine decision packages for old and new projects into one ranking, and allows top management to evaluate and compare the needs of individual units or divisions to make funding allocations. In this respect, zero-based budgeting is quite different than traditional rolling budgets. Rolling budgets often appeal to people who prepare budgets because they make budget development much easier. Managers can add an inflation factor to the previous year's budget and then include any adjustments for major changes. Rolling budgets also give management a concrete number to help make comparisons from year to year. However, traditional rolling budgets have a tendency to create conflict; they can create an incentive to spend money carelessly in order to justify the next year's budget. They can also create inefficient operations due to the fact that individual departments or units do not have to justify expenditures based on operations, but only on the prior year's expenditures.

Zero-based budgeting addresses such problems that can occur with traditional rolling budgets. In zero-based budgeting, each dollar spent by management must be justified with a detailed account of what will be purchased, how many labour hours are needed, what problems will be faced, and so forth. This allows management an opportunity to review operations in depth and make recommendations for changes to if necessary. The zero-based budgeting process helps managers identify redundancies and duplications among different departments, concentrating on the dollars needed for proposed programs as opposed to percentage increases or decreases form the previous year. Specific priorities of departments and divisions are identified more easily in zero-based budgeting. The process also allows for the comparability of different departments as to the respective priorities funded. Zero-base budgeting enables a performance audit to determine whether each project or activity has been performed as efficiently as planned.

Zero-based Budgeting Drawbacks and Solutions

One drawback to zero-based budgeting is cost in terms of managerial time; it takes a considerable amount of time to go through the process of reviewing operations in enough detail to justify costs each budget cycle without relying on past expenditures. One solution to this problem is to create a rolling budget every year and perform a zero-based budget every three to five years, or when a major change occurs within the operation. This allows an organisation to benefit from the advantages of zero-based budgeting without an excessive amount of work. Likewise, traditional rolling budgets should never strictly rely on a prior-year budget plus a percentage; consideration should always be given to past numbers. In some cases, a zero-based budget may rely on some prior numbers where it is overwhelming to create a budget from scratch. Ultimately, the process gives top management the opportunity to judge the performance of managers in terms of allocating resources efficiently and effectively, and gives managers more responsibility in developing their budgets.

An organisation should not feel that all budgets must be developed in entirely the same manner. Some departments can utilise an in-depth study of a zero-based budget while others can use a rolling budget. This is a way to spread the extensive work over a number of years instead of concentrating on one certain year. Many organisations have implemented the system in some form or another and found that it did not work. If properly implemented, however, the process could have a considerable improvement over traditional rolling budgets. The number and nature of decision packages varies from organisation to organisation; it is not uncommon for large organisations to identify several thousand packages. Furthermore, it is often hard or even impossible for top executives to have the necessary knowledge or time to develop and rank priorities for thousands of packages.

To alleviate this problem, managers, after ranking their own packages, can have their top executives rank the packages of all the managers that report to them. This approach is used by one of zero-based budgeting's pioneers, Texas Instruments. Another solution is for each level of management to rank a certain percentage of packages within its own area of responsibility. In this solution, the first level of management may rank 40 percent of the proposed packages; the next level may rank the next 40 percent of packages, while top management may concentrate on the remainder of the budget.

Behavioural Impacts of Zero-based Budgeting

The impact of budgeting on organisations was probably first studied by Argyris in the 1950s. These studies show some of the behavioural effects resulting from the way budgets are used in organisations. The results of his research showed that the particular process used could cause dysfunctional behaviour in subordinates, regardless of the degree of technical refinement of the budgetary system. In the 1970s, Hopwood's studies inquired into the effects of budgets on human behaviour. These studies showed that the use by a superior of a budget-constrained style of evaluation gave rise to significant levels of job-related tension; had adverse effects on peer and subordinate-superior relationships, and was implicated in manipulative behaviour on subordinates. A long line of studies have been performed since then to uncover an array of variables that govern the effects of reliance on budgets on behavioural outcomes, including managerial performance. Examples of these variables include budgetary participation, task uncertainty, environmental uncertainty, strategy, and culture.

Zero-based budgeting may require an extensive amount of time, money, and paper work; but it does provide a systematic method of addressing an organisation's financial concerns, in turn enabling an organisation to better allocate its resources. A combination of zero-based budgets with rolling budgets or some other form of budgeting that spreads the work of justifying new budgets each cycle is one way to incorporate zero-based budgeting without undo stress at the same time for all managers with budgetary responsibility.

Capital Budgeting

Capital budgeting, or investment appraisal, is the planning process used to determine whether an organisation's long term investments such as new machinery, replacement machinery, new plants, new products, and research development projects are worth the funding of cash through the firm's capitalization structure (debt, equity or retained earnings). It is the process of allocating resources for major capital, or investment, expenditures. One of the primary goals of capital budgeting investments is to increase the value of the firm to the shareholders.

Capital Budgeting Definition

Capital budgeting is the planning of long-term corporate financial projects relating to investments funded through and affecting the firm's capital structure. Management must allocate the firm's limited resources between competing opportunities (projects), which is one of the main focuses of capital budgeting. Capital budgeting is also concerned with the setting of criteria about which projects should receive investment funding to increase the value of the firm, and whether to finance that investment with equity or debt capital. Investments should be made on the basis of value-added to the future of the corporation. Capital budgeting projects may include a wide variety of different types of investments, including but not limited to, expansion policies, or mergers and acquisitions. When no such value can be added through the capital budgeting process and excess cash surplus exists and is not needed, then management is expected to pay out some or all of those surplus earnings in the form of cash dividends or to repurchase the company's stock through a share buyback program.

Choosing between capital budgeting projects may be based upon several inter-related criteria. (1) Corporate management seeks to maximize the value of the firm by investing in projects which yield a positive net present value when valued using an appropriate discount rate in consideration of risk. (2) These projects must also be financed appropriately. (3) If no positive NPV projects exist and excess cash surplus is not needed to the firm, then financial theory suggests that management should return some or all of the excess cash to shareholders (i.e., distribution via dividends).

Capital budgeting involves allocating the firm's capital resources between competing project and investments. Each potential project's value should be estimated using a discounted cash flow (DCF) valuation, to find its net present value (NPV). (First applied to Corporate Finance by Joel Dean in 1951.) This valuation requires estimating the size and timing of all the incremental cash flows from the project. (These future cash highest NPV(GE).) The NPV is greatly affected by the discount rate, so selecting the proper rate—sometimes called the *hurdle rate*—is critical to making the right decision. The hurdle rate is the Minimum acceptable rate of return on an investment. This should reflect the riskiness of the investment, typically measured by the volatility of cash flows, and must take into account the financing mix. Managers may use models such as the CAPM or the APT to estimate a discount rate appropriate for each particular project, and use the weighted average cost of capital (*WACC*) to reflect the financing mix selected. A common practice in choosing a discount rate for a project is to apply a WACC that applies to the entire firm, but a higher discount rate may be more appropriate when a project's risk is higher than the risk of the firm as a whole.

Ideally, businesses should pursue all projects and opportunities that enhance shareholder value. However, because the amount of capital available at any given time for new projects is limited, management needs to use capital budgeting techniques to determine which projects will yield the most return over an applicable period of time.

Popular methods of capital budgeting include net present value (NPV), internal rate of return (IRR), discounted cash flow (DCF) and payback period.

Factors Influencing Capital Budgeting

- Availability of funds
- Structure of capital
- Taxation Policy
- Government Policy

- Lending Policies of Financial Institutions
- Immediate need of the Project
- Earnings
- Capital Return
- Economic Value of the Project
- Working Capital
- Accounting Practice
- Trend of Earning
- Size of Business
- Risk of the business
- Forecast of the market
- Political unrest
- Geographical Condition
- Exchange Rate of Currency

Internal Rate of Return

The internal rate of return (IRR) is defined as the discount rate that gives a net present value (NPV) of zero. It is a commonly used measure of investment efficiency.

The IRR method will result in the same decision as the NPV method for (non-mutually exclusive) projects in an unconstrained environment, in the usual cases where a negative cash flow occurs at the start of the project, followed by all positive cash flows. In most realistic cases, all independent projects that have an IRR higher than the hurdle rate should be accepted. Nevertheless, for mutually exclusive projects, the decision rule of taking the project with the highest IRR - which is often used - may select a project with a lower NPV.

In some cases, several zero NPV discount rates may exist, so there is no unique IRR. The IRR exists and is unique if one or more years of net investment (negative cash flow) are followed by years of net revenues. But if the signs of the cash flows change more than once, there may be several IRRs. The IRR equation generally cannot be solved analytically but only via iterations.

One shortcoming of the IRR method is that it is commonly misunderstood to convey the actual annual profitability of an investment. However, this is not the case because intermediate cash flows are almost never reinvested at the project's IRR; and, therefore, the actual rate of return is almost certainly going to be lower. Accordingly, a measure called Modified Internal Rate of Return (MIRR) is often used. Despite a strong academic preference for NPV, surveys indicate that executives prefer IRR over NPV, although they should be used in concert. In a budget-constrained environment, efficiency measures should be used to maximize the overall NPV of the firm. Some managers find it intuitively more appealing to evaluate investments in terms of percentage rates of return than dollars of NPV.

Equivalent Annuity Method

The *equivalent annuity* method expresses the NPV as an annualized cash flow by dividing it by the present value of the annuity factor. It is often used when assessing only the costs of specific projects that have the same cash inflows. In this form it is known as the *equivalent annual cost* (EAC) method and is the cost per year of owning and operating an asset over its entire lifespan.

It is often used when comparing investment projects of unequal lifespans. For example if project A has an expected lifetime of 7 years, and project B has an expected lifetime of 11 years it would be improper to simply compare the net present values (NPVs) of the two projects, unless the projects could not be repeated. The use of the EAC method implies that the project will be replaced by an identical project.

Alternatively the *chain method* can be used with the NPV method under the assumption that the projects will be replaced with the same cash flows each time. To compare projects of unequal length, say 3 years and 4 years, the projects are *chained together*, i.e. four repetitions of the 3 year project are compare to three repetitions of the 4 year project. The chain method and the EAC method give mathematically equivalent answers.

The assumption of the same cash flows for each link in the chain is essentially an assumption of zero inflation, so a real interest rate rather than a nominal interest rate is commonly used in the calculations.

Real Options

Real options analysis has become important since the 1970s as option pricing models have gotten more sophisticated. The discounted cash flow methods essentially value projects as if they were risky bonds, with the promised cash flows known. But managers will have many choices of how to increase future cash inflows, or to decrease future cash outflows. In other words, managers get to manage the projects - not simply accept or reject them. Real options analysis try to value the choices - the option value - that the managers will have in the future and adds these values to the NPV.

Ranked Projects

The real value of capital budgeting is to rank projects. Most organisations have many projects that could potentially be financially rewarding. Once it has been determined that a particular project has exceeded its hurdle, then it should be ranked against peer projects (e.g. - highest Profitability index to lowest Profitability index). The highest ranking projects should be implemented until the budgeted capital has been expended.

Funding Sources

Capital budgeting investments and projects must be funded through excess cash provided through the raising of debt capital, equity capital, or the use of retained earnings. Debt capital is borrowed cash, usually in the form of bank loans, or bonds issued to creditors. Equity capital are investments made by shareholders, who purchase shares in the company's stock. Retained earnings are excess cash surplus from the company's present and past earnings.

Need for Capital Budgeting

1. As large sum of money is involved which influences the profitability of the firm making capital budgeting an important task.
2. Long term investment once made can not be reversed without significance loss of invested capital. The investment becomes sunk and mistakes, rather than being readily rectified, must often be borne until the firm can be withdrawn through depreciation charges or liquidation. It influences the whole conduct of the business for the years to come.
3. Investment decision are the base on which the profit will be earned and probably measured through the return on the capital. A proper mix of capital investment is quite important to ensure adequate rate of return on investment, calling for the need of capital budgeting.
4. The implication of long term investment decisions are more extensive than those of short run decisions because of time factor involved, capital budgeting decisions are subject to the higher degree of risk and uncertainty than short run decision.

Net Present Value

In finance, the net present value (NPV) or net present worth (NPW) of a time series of cash flows, both incoming and outgoing, is defined as the sum of the present values (PVs) of the individual cash flows of the same entity. In the case when all future cash flows are incoming (such as coupons and principal of a bond) and the only outflow of cash is the purchase price, the NPV is simply the PV of future cash flows minus the purchase price (which is its own PV). NPV is a central tool in discounted cash flow (DCF) analysis and is a standard method for using the time value of money to appraise long-term projects. Used for capital budgeting and widely used throughout economics, finance, and accounting, it measures the excess or shortfall of cash flows, in present value terms, above the cost of funds.

NPV can be described as the "difference amount" between the sums of discounted: cash inflows and cash outflows. It compares the present value of money today to the present value of money in the future, taking inflation and returns into account. The NPV of a sequence of cash flows takes as input the cash flows and a discount rate or discount curve and outputs a price; the converse process in DCF analysis — taking a sequence of cash flows and a price as input and inferring as output a discount rate (the discount rate which would yield the given price as NPV) — is called the yield and is more widely used in bond trading.

Formula

Each cash inflow/outflow is discounted back to its present value (PV). Then they are summed. Therefore NPV is the sum of all terms,

$$\frac{R_t}{(1+i)^t}$$

where

t– the time of the cash flow

i– the discount rate (the rate of return that could be earned on an investment in the financial markets with similar risk.); the opportunity cost of capital

R_t – the net cash flow i.e. cash inflow – cash outflow, at time t. For educational purposes, R_0 is commonly placed to the left of the sum to emphasize its role as (minus) the investment.

The result of this formula is multiplied with the Annual Net cash inflows and reduced by Initial Cash outlay the present value but in cases where the cash flows are not equal in amount, then the previous formula will be used to determine the present value of each cash flow separately. Any cash flow within 12 months will not be discounted for NPV purpose, nevertheless the usual initial investments during the first year R_0 are summed up a negative cash flow.

Given the (period, cash flow) pairs (t, R_t) where N is the total number of periods, the net present value NPV is given by:

$$\text{NPV}(i, N) = \sum_{t=0}^{N} \frac{R_t}{(1+i)^t}$$

The Discount Rate

The rate used to discount future cash flows to the present value is a key variable of this process.

A firm's weighted average cost of capital (after tax) is often used, but many people believe that it is appropriate to use higher discount rates to adjust for risk, opportunity cost, or other factors. A variable discount rate with higher rates applied to cash flows occurring further along the time span might be used to reflect the yield curve premium for long-term debt.

Another approach to choosing the discount rate factor is to decide the rate which the capital needed for the project could return if invested in an alternative venture. If, for example, the capital required for Project A can earn 5% elsewhere, use this discount rate in the NPV calculation to allow a direct comparison to be made between Project A and the alternative. Related to this concept is to use the firm's reinvestment rate. Reinvestment rate can be defined as the rate of return for the firm's investments on average. When analyzing projects in a capital constrained environment, it may be appropriate to use the reinvestment rate rather than the firm's weighted average cost of capital as the discount factor. It reflects opportunity cost of investment, rather than the possibly lower cost of capital.

An NPV calculated using variable discount rates (if they are known for the duration of the investment) may better reflect the situation than one calculated from a constant discount rate for the entire investment duration.

For some professional investors, their investment funds are committed to target a specified rate of return. In such cases, that rate of return should be selected as the discount rate for the NPV calculation. In this way, a direct comparison can be made between the profitability of the project and the desired rate of return.

To some extent, the selection of the discount rate is dependent on the use to which it will be put. If the intent is simply to determine whether a project will add value to the company, using the firm's weighted average cost of capital may be appropriate. If trying to decide between alternative investments in order to maximize the value of the firm, the corporate reinvestment rate would probably be a better choice.

Using variable rates over time, or discounting "guaranteed" cash flows differently from "at risk" cash flows, may be a superior methodology but is seldom used in practice. Using the discount rate to adjust for risk is often difficult to do in practice (especially internationally) and is difficult to do well. An alternative to using discount factor to adjust for risk is to explicitly correct the cash flows for the risk elements using rNPV or a similar method, then discount at the firm's rate.

Use in Decision Making

NPV is an indicator of how much value an investment or project adds to the firm. With a particular project, if R_t is a positive value, the project is in the status of positive cash inflow in the time of t. If R_t is a negative value, the project is in the status of discounted cash outflow in the time of t. Appropriately risked projects with a positive NPV could be accepted. This does not necessarily mean that they should be undertaken since NPV at the cost of capital may not account for opportunity cost, *i.e.*, comparison with other available investments. In financial theory, if there is a choice between two mutually exclusive alternatives, the one yielding the higher NPV should be selected.

If...	*It means...*	*Then...*
NPV > 0	the investment would add value to the firm	the project may be accepted
NPV < 0	the investment would subtract value from the firm	the project should be rejected
NPV = 0	the investment would neither gain nor lose value for the firm	We should be indifferent in the decision whether to accept or reject the project. This project adds no monetary value. Decision should be based on other criteria, e.g., strategic positioning or other factors not explicitly included in the calculation.

Interpretation as Integral Transform

The time-discrete formula of the net present value

$$\text{NPV}(i) = \sum_{t=0}^{N} \frac{R_t}{(1+i)^t}$$

can also be written in a continuous variation

$$\text{NPV}(i) = \int_{t=0}^{\infty} (1+i)^{-t} \cdot r(t)\,dt$$

where

$r(t)$ is the rate of flowing cash given in money per time, and $r(t) = 0$ when the investment is over.

Net present value can be regarded as Laplace- respectively Z-transformed cash flow with the integral operator including the complex number s which resembles to the interest rate i from the real number space or more precisely $s = \ln(1 + i)$.

$$F(s) = \{\mathcal{L}f\}(s) = \int_0^{\infty} e^{-st} f(t)dt$$

From this follow simplifications known from cybernetics, control theory and system dynamics. Imaginary parts of the complex number s describe the oscillating behaviour (compare with the pork cycle, cobweb theorem, and phase shift between commodity price and supply offer) whereas real parts are responsible for representing the effect of compound interest (compare with damping).

Example

A corporation must decide whether to introduce a new product line. The new product will have start-up expenditures, operational expenditures, and then it will have associated incoming cash receipts (sales) and disbursements (Cash paid for materials, supplies, direct labour, maintenance, repairs, and direct overhead) over 12 years. This project will have an immediate ($t = 0$) cash outflow of 100,000 (which might include all cash paid for the machinery, transportation-in and set-up expenditures, and initial employee training disbursements.) The annual net cash flow (receipts less disbursements) from this new line for years 1–12 is forecast as follows: –54672, –39161, 3054, 7128, 25927, 28838, 46088, 77076, 46726, 76852, 132332, 166047, reflecting two years of running deficits as experience and sales are built up, with net cash receipts forecast positive after that. At the end of the 12 years it's estimated that the entire line becomes obsolete and its scrap value just covers all the removal and disposal expenditures. All values are after-tax, and the required rate of return is given to be 10%. (This also makes the simplifying assumption that the net cash received or paid is lumped into a single transaction occurring *on the last day* of each year.)

The Present Value (PV) can be Calculated for Each Year

Year	*Cash flow*	*Present value*
$T = 0$		–100,000
$T = 1$		–49701.8182
$T = 2$		–32364.46281
$T = 3$		2294.515402
$T = 4$		4868.51991
$T = 5$		16098.62714

Contd...

Year	*Cash flow*	*Present value*
$T = 6$		16278.29919
$T = 7$		23650.43135
$T = 8$		35956.52284
$T = 9$		19816.38532
$T = 10$	$\frac{76852}{(1+0.10)^{10}}$	29629.77288
$T = 11$	$\frac{132332}{(1+0.10)^{11}}$	46381.55871
$T = 12$	$\frac{166047}{(1+0.10)^{12}}$	52907.69139

The sum of all these present values is the net present value, which equals 65,816.04. Since the NPV is greater than zero, it would be better to invest in the project than to do nothing, and the corporation should invest in this project if there is no alternative with a higher NPV. There are a few inherent assumptions in this type of discounted cash flow / net present value type analysis:

1. The *investment horizon* of all possible investment projects considered are equally acceptable to the investor (e.g. a 3-year project is not necessarily preferable vs. a 20 year project.)
2. The 10% discount rate is the appropriate (and stable) rate to discount the expected cash flows from each project being considered. Each project is assumed equally speculative.
3. the shareholders can't get above a 10% return on their money if they were to directly assume an equivalent level of risk. (If the investor could do better elsewhere, no projects should be undertaken by the firm, and the excess capital should be turned over to the shareholder through dividends and stock repurchases.)

More realistic problems would also need to consider other factors, generally including: smaller time buckets, the calculation of taxes (including the cash flow timing), inflation, currency exchange fluctuations, hedged or unhedged commodity costs, risks of technical obsolescence, potential future competitive factors, uneven or unpredictable cash flows, and a more realistic salvage value assumption, as well as many others.

Common Pitfalls

- If, for example, the R_t are generally negative late in the project (*e.g.*, an industrial or mining project might have clean-up and restoration costs), then at that stage the company owes money, so a high discount rate is not cautious but too optimistic. Some people see this as a problem with NPV. A way to avoid this problem is to include explicit provision for financing any losses after the initial investment, that is, explicitly calculate the cost of financing such losses.
- Another common pitfall is to adjust for risk by adding a premium to the discount rate. Whilst a bank might charge a higher rate of interest for a risky project, that does not mean that this is a valid approach to adjusting a net present value for risk, although it can be a reasonable approximation in some specific cases. One reason such an approach may not work well can be seen from the following: if some risk is incurred resulting in some losses, then a discount rate in the NPV will reduce the impact of such losses below their true financial cost. A rigorous approach to risk requires identifying and valuing risks explicitly, *e.g.*, by actuarial or Monte Carlo techniques, and explicitly calculating the cost of financing any losses incurred.
- Yet another issue can result from the compounding of the risk premium. R is a composite of the risk free rate and the risk premium. As a result, future cash flows are discounted by both the risk-free rate as well as the risk premium and this effect is compounded by each subsequent cash flow. This compounding results in a much lower NPV than might be otherwise calculated. The certainty equivalent model can be used to account for the risk premium without compounding its effect on present value.
- Another issue with relying on NPV is that it does not provide an overall picture of the gain or loss of executing a certain project. To see a percentage gain relative to the investments for the project, usually, Internal rate of return or other efficiency measures are used as a complement to NPV.
- Non-specialist users frequently make the error of computing NPV based on cash flows after interest. This is wrong because it double counts the time value of money. Free cash flow should be used as the basis for NPV computations.

Accounting Rate of Return

Accounting rate of return, also known as the Average rate of return, or ARR is a financial ratio used in capital budgeting. The ratio does not take into account the concept of time value of money. ARR calculates the return, generated from net income of the proposed capital investment. The ARR is a percentage return. Say, if ARR = 7%, then it means that the project is expected to earn seven cents out of each dollar invested (yearly). If the ARR is equal to or greater than the required rate of return, the project is acceptable. If it is less than the desired rate, it should be rejected. When comparing investments, the higher the ARR, the more attractive the investment. Over one-half of large firms calculate ARR when appraising projects.

Basic Formulas

- $\text{ARR} = \dfrac{\text{Average return during period}}{\text{Average investment}}$

where

- $\text{Average investment} = \dfrac{\text{Book value at beginning of year 1} + \text{Book value at end of useful life}}{2}$

=Profit/investment equals to ARR.

ARR = Incremental Revenue - Incremental Expenses (Including Depreciation)/Initial Investment

Average Profit = Profit After Tax/Life of Project

Payback Period

Payback period in capital budgeting refers to the period of time required to recoup the funds expended in an investment, or to reach the break-even point. For example, a $1000 investment which returned $500 per year would have a two-year payback period. The time value of money is not taken into account. Payback period intuitively measures how long something takes to "pay for itself." All else being equal, shorter payback periods are preferable to longer payback periods. Payback period is popular due to its ease of use despite the recognised limitations described below.

The term is also widely used in other types of investment areas, often with respect to energy efficiency technologies, maintenance, upgrades, or other changes. For example, a compact fluorescent light bulb may be described as having a payback period of a certain number of years or operating hours, assuming certain costs. Here, the return to the investment consists of reduced operating costs. Although primarily a financial term, the concept of a payback period is occasionally extended to other uses, such as energy payback period (the period of time over which the energy savings of a project equal the amount of energy expended since project inception); these other terms may not be standardized or widely used.

Purpose

Payback period as a tool of analysis is often used because it is easy to apply and easy to understand for most individuals, regardless of academic training or field of endeavor. When used carefully or to compare similar investments, it can be quite useful. As a stand-alone tool to compare an investment to "doing nothing," payback period has no explicit criteria for decision-making (except, perhaps, that the payback period should be less than infinity).

The payback period is considered a method of analysis with serious limitations and qualifications for its use, because it does not account for the time value of money, risk, financing, or other important considerations, such as the opportunity cost. Whilst the time value of money can be rectified by applying a weighted average cost of capital discount, it is generally agreed that this tool for investment decisions should not be used in isolation. Alternative measures of "return" preferred by economists are net present value and internal rate of return. An implicit assumption in the use of payback period is that returns to the investment continue after the payback period. Payback period does not specify any required comparison to other investments or even to not making an investment.

Construction

Payback period is usually expressed in years. Start by calculating Net Cash Flow for each year: Net Cash Flow Year 1 = Cash Inflow Year 1 - Cash Outflow Year 1. Then Cumulative Cash Flow = (Net Cash Flow Year 1 + Net Cash Flow Year 2 + Net Cash Flow Year 3, etc.) Accumulate by year until Cumulative Cash Flow is a positive number: that year is the payback year.

To calculate a more exact payback period: Payback Period = Amount to be Invested/Estimated Annual Net Cash Flow

It can also be calculated using the formula:

$$\text{Payback Period} = (p - n) \div p + n_y$$
$$= 1 + n_y - n \div p \quad \text{(unit:years)}$$

Where

n_y = The number of years after the initial investment at which the last negative value of cumulative cash flow occurs.

n= The value of cumulative cash flow at which the last negative value of cumulative cash flow occurs.

p= The value of cash flow at which the first positive value of cumulative cash flow occurs.

This formula can only be used to calculate the soonest payback period; that is, the first period after which the investment has paid for itself. If the cumulative cash flow drops to a negative value some time after it has reached a positive value, thereby changing the payback period, this formula can't be applied. This formula ignores values that arise after the payback period has been reached.

Additional complexity arises when the cash flow changes sign several times; i.e., it contains outflows in the midst or at the end of the project lifetime. The modified payback period algorithm may be applied then. First, the sum of all of the cash outflows is calculated. Then the cumulative positive cash flows are determined for each period. The modified payback is calculated as the moment in which the cumulative positive cash flow exceeds the total cash outflow.

Internal Rate of Return

The internal rate of return (IRR) or economic rate of return (ERR) is a rate of return used in capital budgeting to measure and compare the profitability of investments. It is also called the discounted cash flow rate of return (DCFROR). In the context of savings and loans the IRR is also called the effective interest rate. The term *internal* refers to the fact that its calculation does not incorporate environmental factors (e.g., the interest rate or inflation).

Definition

The internal rate of return on an investment or project is the "annualized effective compounded return rate" or rate of return that makes the net present value (NPV as NET*1/(1+IRR)^year) of all cash flows (both positive and negative) from a particular investment equal to zero. It can also be defined as the discount rate at which the present value of all future cash flow is equal to the initial investment or in other words the rate at which an investment breaks even.

In more specific terms, the IRR of an investment is the discount rate at which the net present value of costs (negative cash flows) of the investment equals the net present value of the benefits (positive cash flows) of the investment.

IRR calculations are commonly used to evaluate the desirability of investments or projects. The higher a project's IRR, the more desirable it is to undertake the project. Assuming all projects require the same amount of up-front investment, the project with the highest IRR would be considered the best and undertaken first.

A firm (or individual) should, in theory, undertake all projects or investments available with IRRs that exceed the cost of capital. Investment may be limited by availability of funds to the firm and/or by the firm's capacity or ability to manage numerous projects.

Uses of IRR

Because the internal rate of return is a rate quantity, it is an indicator of the efficiency, quality, or yield of an investment. This is in contrast with the net present value, which is an indicator of the value or magnitude of an investment.

An investment is considered acceptable if its internal rate of return is greater than an established minimum acceptable rate of return or cost of capital. In a scenario where an investment is considered by a firm that has shareholders, this minimum rate is the cost of capital of the investment (which may be determined by the risk-adjusted cost of capital of alternative investments). This ensures that the investment is supported by equity holders since, in general, an investment whose IRR exceeds its cost of capital adds value for the company (i.e., it is economically profitable).

One of the uses of IRR is by corporations that wish to compare capital projects. For example, a corporation will evaluate an investment in a new plant versus an extension of an existing plant based on the IRR of each project. In such a case, each new capital project must produce an IRR that is higher than the company's cost of capital. Once this hurdle is surpassed, the project with the highest IRR would be the wiser investment, all other things being equal (including risk).

IRR is also useful for corporations in evaluating stock buyback programs. Clearly, if a company allocates a substantial amount to a stock buyback, the analysis must show that the company's own stock is a better investment (has a higher IRR) than any other use of the funds for other capital projects, or than any acquisition candidate at current market prices.

Calculation

Given a collection of pairs (time, cash flow) involved in a project, the internal rate of return follows from the net present value as a function of the rate of return. A rate of return for which this function is zero is an internal rate of return.

Given the (period, cash flow) pairs (n, C_n) where n is a positive integer, the total number of periods N, and the net present value NPV, the internal rate of return is given by r in:

$$\text{NPV} = \sum_{n=0}^{N} \frac{C_n}{(1+r)^n} = 0$$

The period is usually given in years, but the calculation may be made simpler if r is calculated using the period in which the majority of the problem is defined (e.g., using months if most of the cash flows occur at monthly intervals) and converted to a yearly period thereafter. Any fixed time can be used in place of the present (e.g., the end of one interval of an annuity); the value obtained is zero if and only if the NPV is zero. In the case that the cash flows are random variables, such as in the case of a life annuity, the expected values are put into the above formula.

Often, the value of r cannot be found analytically. In this case, numerical methods or graphical methods must be used.

Example

If an investment may be given by the sequence of cash flows

Year (n)	Cash flow (C_n)
0	-123400
1	36200
2	54800
3	48100

then the IRR r is given by

$$\text{NPV} = -123400 + \frac{36200}{(1+r)^1} + \frac{54800}{(1+r)^2} + \frac{48100}{(1+r)^3} = 0.$$

In this case, the answer is 5.96% (in the calculation, that is, r = .0596).

Numerical Solution

Since the above is a manifestation of the general problem of finding the roots of the equation $\text{NPV}(r) = 0$, there are many numerical methods that can be used to estimate r. For example, using the secant method, r is given by

$$r_{n+1} = r_n - \text{NPV}_n \left(\frac{r_n - r_{n-1}}{\text{NPV}_n - \text{NPV}_{n-1}} \right).$$

where r_n is considered the nth approximation of the IRR.

This r can be found to an arbitrary degree of accuracy. An accuracy of 0.00001% is provided by Microsoft Excel.

The convergence behaviour of by the following:

- If the function $\text{NPV}(i)$ has a single real root r, then the sequence converges reproducibly towards r.
- If the function $\text{NPV}(i)$ has n real roots $r_1, r_2, \ldots, r_n$, then the sequence converges to one of the roots, and changing the values of the initial pairs may change the root to which it converges.
- If function $\text{NPV}(i)$ has no real roots, then the sequence tends towards $+\infty$.

Having $r_1 > r_0$ when $\text{NPV}_0 > 0$ or $r_1 < r_0$ when $\text{NPV}_0 < 0$ may speed up convergence of r_n to r.

Numerical Solution for Single Outflow and Multiple Inflows

Of particular interest is the case where the stream of payments consists of a single outflow, followed by multiple inflows occurring at equal periods. In the above notation, this corresponds to:

$$C_0 < 0, \quad C_n \geq 0 \text{ for } n \geq 1.$$

In this case the NPV of the payment stream is a convex, strictly decreasing function of interest rate. There is always a single unique solution for IRR.

Given two estimates r_1 and r_2 for IRR, the secant method equation with $n = 2$ always produces an improved estimate r_3. This is sometimes referred to as the Hit and Trial (or Trial and Error) method. More accurate interpolation formulas can also be obtained: for instance the secant formula with correction

$$r_{n+1} = r_n - \text{NPV}_n \left(\frac{r_n - r_{n-1}}{\text{NPV}_n - \text{NPV}_{n-1}} \right) \left(1 - 1.4 \frac{\text{NPV}_{n-1}}{\text{NPV}_{n-1} - 3\text{NPV}_n + 2C_0} \right),$$

(which is most accurate when $0 > \text{NPV}_n > \text{NPV}_{n-1}$) has been shown to be almost 10 times more accurate than the secant formula for a wide range of interest rates and initial guesses. For example, using the stream of payments {–4000, 1200, 1410, 1875, 1050} and initial guesses $r_1 = 0.25$ and $r_2 = 0.2$ the secant formula with correction gives an IRR estimate of 14.2% (0.7% error) as compared to IRR = 13.2% (7% error) from the secant method. Other improved formulas may be found in

If applied iteratively, either the secant method or the improved formula always converges to the correct solution.

Both the secant method and the improved formula rely on initial guesses for IRR. The following initial guesses may be used:

$$r_1 = \left(A / |C_0|\right)^{2/(N+1)} - 1$$

$$r_2 = (1 + r_1)^p - 1$$

where

$$A = \text{ sum of inflows } = C_1 + \cdots + C_N$$

$$p = \frac{\log(A / |C_0|)}{\log(A / \text{NPV}_{1,in})}.$$

Here, $\text{NPV}_{1,in}$ refers to the NPV of the inflows only (that is, set C_0=0 and compute NPV).

Decision Criterion

If the IRR is greater than the cost of capital, accept the project.

If the IRR is less than the cost of capital, reject the project.

Problems with Using Internal Rate of Return

As an investment decision tool, the calculated IRR should *not* be used to rate mutually exclusive projects, but only to decide whether a single project is worth investing in.

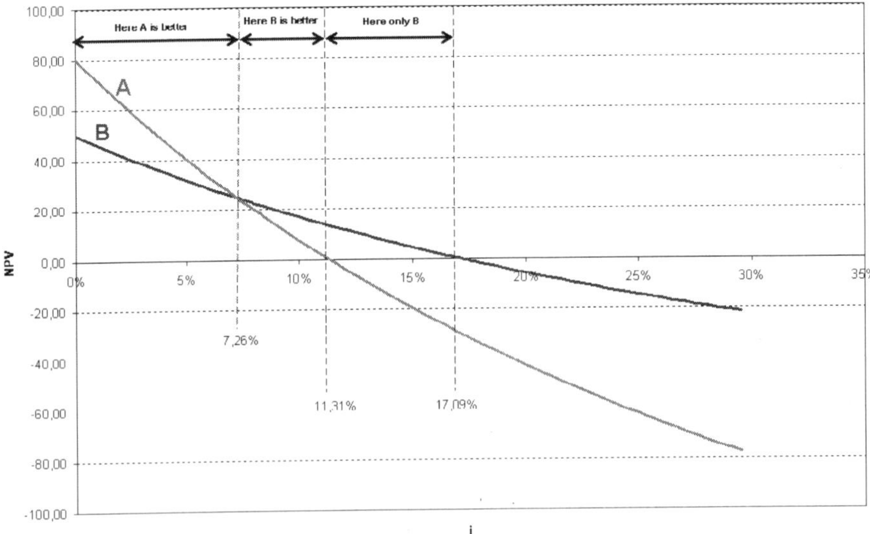

Figure: *NPV vs discount rate comparison for two mutually exclusive projects. Project 'A' has a higher NPV (for certain discount rates), even though its IRR (= x-axis intercept) is lower than for project 'B'*

In cases where one project has a higher initial investment than a second mutually exclusive project, the first project may have a lower IRR (expected return), but a higher NPV (increase in shareholders' wealth) and should thus be accepted over the second project (assuming no capital constraints). IRR should not be used to compare projects of different duration. For example, the net present value added by a project with longer duration but lower IRR could be greater than that of a project of similar size, in terms of total net cash flows, but with shorter duration and higher IRR.

Modified Internal Rate of Return (MIRR) considers cost of capital, and is intended to provide a better indication of a project's probable return.

In the case of positive cash flows followed by negative ones and then by positive ones (for example, + + – – – +) the IRR may have multiple values. In this case a discount rate may be used for the borrowing cash flow and the IRR calculated for the investment cash flow. This applies for example when a customer makes a deposit before a specific machine is built.

In a series of cash flows like (–10, 21, –11), one initially invests money, so a high rate of return is best, but then receives more than one possesses, so then one owes money, so now a low rate of return is best. In this case it is not even clear whether a high or a low IRR is better. There may even be multiple IRRs for a single project, like in the example 0% as well as 10%. Examples of this type of project are strip mines and nuclear power plants, where there is usually a large cash outflow at the end of the project.

In general, the IRR can be calculated by solving a polynomial equation. Sturm's theorem can be used to determine if that equation has a unique real solution. In general the IRR equation cannot be solved analytically but only iteratively.

When a project has multiple IRRs it may be more convenient to compute the IRR of the project with the benefits reinvested. Accordingly, MIRR is used, which has an assumed reinvestment rate, usually equal to the project's cost of capital.

It has been shown that with multiple internal rates of return, the IRR approach can still be interpreted in a way that is consistent with the present value approach provided that the underlying investment stream is correctly identified as net investment or net borrowing.

Despite a strong academic preference for NPV, surveys indicate that executives prefer IRR over NPV. Apparently, managers find it easier to compare investments of different sizes in terms of percentage rates of return than by dollars of NPV. However, NPV remains the "more accurate" reflection of value to the business. IRR, as a measure of investment efficiency may give better insights in capital constrained situations. However, when comparing mutually exclusive projects, NPV is the appropriate measure.

Mathematics

Mathematically, the value of the investment is assumed to undergo exponential growth or decay according to some rate of return (any value greater than "100%), with discontinuities for cash flows, and the IRR of a series of cash flows is defined as any rate of return that results in a net present value of zero (or equivalently, a rate of return that results in the correct value of zero after the last cash flow).

Thus, internal rate(s) of return follow from the net present value as a function of the rate of return. This function is continuous. Towards a rate of return of "100% the net present value approaches infinity with the sign of the last cash flow, and towards a rate of return of positive infinity the net present value approaches the first cash flow (the one at the present). Therefore, if the first and last cash flow have a different sign there exists an internal rate of return. Examples of time series without an IRR:

- Only negative cash flows — the NPV is negative for every rate of return.
- (–1, 1, –1), rather small positive cash flow between two negative cash flows; the NPV is a quadratic function of $1/(1 + r)$, where r is the rate of return, or put differently, a quadratic function of the discount rate $r/(1 + r)$; the highest NPV is –0.75, for $r =$ 100%.

In the case of a series of exclusively negative cash flows followed by a series of exclusively positive ones, the resulting function of the rate of return is continuous and monotonically decreasing from positive infinity (when the rate of return approaches -100%) to the value of the first cash flow (when the rate of return approaches infinity), so there is a unique rate of return for which it is zero. Hence, the IRR is also unique (and equal). Although the NPV-function itself is not necessarily monotonically decreasing on its whole domain, it *is* at the IRR.

Similarly, in the case of a series of exclusively positive cash flows followed by a series of exclusively negative ones the IRR is also unique.

Finally, by Descartes' rule of signs, the number of internal rates of return can never be more than the number of changes in sign of cash flow.

The Reinvestment Misconception

It is often stated that IRR assumes reinvestment of all cash flows until the very end of the project. This is a misconception. There is no hidden reinvestment assumption associated with the calculation of IRR. IRR is simply the solution to the equation in the example shown above. The cash flows are static. The NPV is set at zero. There is only one unknown variable in the equation, namely r.

This misconception likely stems from the modified internal rate of return MIRR concept, which allows for inclusion of a second, subsequent investment. If the reinvestment rate is set at IRR, the MIRR equals the IRR. This is hardly a surprise - compounding cash flows (with the IRR) and then discounting them using the same discount factor (the IRR) is obviously a zero-sum game.

There are many, highly reputable sources arguing that there is a hidden reinvestment assumption in the IRR calculation. There are, however, also many sources disputing the so-called reinvestment assumption.

The Internal Rate of Return in Personal Finance

The IRR can be used to measure the money-weighted performance of financial investments such as an individual investor's 401(k) or brokerage account. For this scenario, an equivalent, more intuitive definition of the IRR is, "The IRR is the annual interest rate of the fixed rate account (like a somewhat idealized savings account) which, when subjected to the same deposits and withdrawals as the actual investment, has the same ending balance as the actual investment." This fixed rate account is also called the *replicating fixed rate account* for the investment. There are examples where the replicating fixed rate account encounters negative balances despite the fact that the actual investment did not. In those cases, the IRR calculation assumes that the same interest rate that is paid on positive balances is charged on negative balances. It has been shown that this way of charging interest is the root cause of the IRR's multiple solutions problem. If the model is modified so that, as is the case in real life, an externally supplied cost of borrowing (possibly varying over time) is charged on negative balances, the multiple solutions issue disappears. The resulting rate is called the *fixed rate equivalent* (*FREQ*).

Unannualized Internal Rate of Return

In the context of investment performance measurement, there is sometimes ambiguity in terminology between the periodic rate of return, such as the internal rate of return as defined above, and a holding period return. The term *internal rate of return* or *IRR* or *Since Inception Internal Rate of Return (SI-IRR)* is in some contexts used to refer to the unannualized return over the period, particularly for periods of less than a year.

Modified Internal Rate of Return

The Modified Internal Rate of Return (MIRR) is a financial measure of an investment's attractiveness. It is used in capital budgeting to rank alternative investments of equal size. As the name implies, MIRR is a modification of the internal rate of return (IRR) and as such aims to resolve some problems with the IRR.

Problems with the IRR

While there are several problems with the IRR, MIRR resolves two of them.

Firstly, IRR is sometime misapplied, under an assumption that interim positive cash flows are reinvested at the same rate of return as that of the project that generated them. This is usually an unrealistic scenario and a more likely situation is that the funds will be reinvested at a rate closer to the firm's cost of capital. The IRR therefore often gives an unduly optimistic picture of the projects under study. Generally for comparing projects more fairly, the weighted average cost of capital should be used for reinvesting the interim cash flows.

Secondly, more than one IRR can be found for projects with alternating positive and negative cash flows, which leads to confusion and ambiguity. MIRR finds only one value.

Calculation of the MIRR

MIRR is calculated as follows:

$$\text{MIRR} = \sqrt[n]{\frac{FV(\text{positive cash flows, reinvestment rate})}{-PV(\text{negative cash flows, finance rate})}} - 1,$$

where n is the number of equal periods at the end of which the cash flows occur (not the number of cash flows), *PV* is present value (at the beginning of the first period), *FV* is future value (at the end of the last period).

The formula adds up the negative cash flows after discounting them to time zero using the external cost of capital, adds up the positive cash flows including the proceeds of reinvestment at the external reinvestment rate to the final period, and then works out what rate of return would cause the magnitude of the discounted negative cash flows at time zero to be equivalent to the future value of the positive cash flows at the final time period.

Spreadsheet applications, such as Microsoft Excel, have inbuilt functions to calculate the MIRR. In Microsoft Excel this function is "=MIRR".

Example

If an investment project is described by the sequence of cash flows:

Year	*Cash flow*
0	–1000
1	–4000
2	5000
3	2000

then the IRR r is given by

$$\text{NPV} = -1000 + \frac{-4000}{(1+r)^1} + \frac{5000}{(1+r)^2} + \frac{2000}{(1+r)^3} = 0.$$

In this case, the answer is 25.48% (the other solutions to this equation are -593.16% and -132.32%, but they will not be considered meaningful IRRs).

To calculate the MIRR, we will assume a finance rate of 10% and a reinvestment rate of 12%. First, we calculate the present value of the negative cash flows (discounted at the finance rate):

$$PV(\text{negative cash flows, finance rate}) = -1000 + \frac{-4000}{(1+10\%)^1} = -4636.36.$$

Second, we calculate the future value of the positive cash flows (reinvested at the reinvestment rate):

$$FV(\text{positive cash flows, reinvestment rate}) = 5000 \cdot (1+12\%)^1 + 2000 = 7600.$$

Third, we find the MIRR:

$$\text{MIRR} = \sqrt[3]{\frac{7600}{4636.36}} - 1 = 17.91\%.$$

The calculated MIRR (17.91%) is significantly different from the IRR (25.48%).

Comparing Projects of Different Sizes

Like the internal rate of return, the modified internal rate of return is not valid for ranking projects of different sizes, because a larger project with a smaller modified internal rate of return may have a higher net present value. However, there exist variants of the modified internal rate of return which can be used for such comparisons.

Equivalent Annual Cost

In finance, the equivalent annual cost (EAC) is the cost per year of owning and operating an asset over its entire lifespan.

EAC is often used as a decision making tool in capital budgeting when comparing investment projects of unequal lifespans. For example if project A has an expected lifetime of 7 years, and project B has an expected lifetime of 11 years it would be improper to simply compare the net present values (NPVs) of the two projects, unless neither project could be repeated.

EAC is calculated by dividing the NPV of a project by the *present value of an annuity* factor. Equivalently, the NPV of the project may be multiplied by the *loan repayment factor.*

$$EAC = \frac{NPV}{A_{t,r}}$$

The use of the EAC method implies that the project will be replaced by an identical project.

A Practical Example

A manager must decide on which machine to purchase:

Machine A

Investment cost \$50,000

Expected lifetime 3 years

Annual maintenance \$13,000

Machine B

Investment cost \$150,000

Expected lifetime 8 years

Annual maintenance \$7,500

The cost of capital is 5%.

The EAC for machine A is: (\$50,000/ $A_{3,5}$)+\$13,000=\$31,360

The EAC for machine B is: (\$150,000/ $A_{8,5}$)+\$7,500=\$30,708

The conclusion is to invest in machine B since it has a lower EAC.

Note: The loan repayment factors (A values) are for t years (3 or 8 years) and 5% cost of capital. $A_{3,5}$ is given by $\frac{1-1/(1.05)^3}{0.05} = 2.723$ and

$A_{8,5}$ is given by $\dfrac{1-1/(1.05)^8}{0.05}$ = 6.463. The larger an A value is, the greater the present value is on a succession of future annuity payments, thus contributing to a smaller annual cost.

Alternative method:1

The manager calculates the PV of the machines:

Machine A EAC=$85,400/ $A_{3,5}$ =$31,360

Machine B EAC=$198,474/ $A_{8,5}$ =$30,708

Note: To get the numerators add the present value of the annual maintenance to the purchase price. For example, for Machine A: 50,000 + 13,000/1.05 + 13,000/(1.05)^2 + 13,000/(1.05)^3 = 85,402.

The result is the same, although the first method is easier it is essential that the annual maintenance cost is the same each year.

Alternatively the manager can use the NPV method under the assumption that the machines will be replaced with the same cost of investment each time. This is known as the *chain method* since 8 repetitions of machine A are chained together and 3 repetitions of machine B are chained together. Since the time horizon used in the NPV comparison must be set to 24 years (3*8=24) in order to compare projects of equal length, this method can be slightly more complicated than calculating the EAC. In addition, the assumption of the same cost of investment for each link in the chain is essentially an assumption of zero inflation, so a real interest rate rather than a nominal interest rate is commonly used in the calculations.

Real Options Valuation

Real Options Valuation, also often termed real options analysis, (ROV or ROA) applies option valuation techniques to capital budgeting decisions. A real option itself, is the right — but not the obligation — to undertake certain business initiatives, such as deferring, abandoning, expanding, staging, or contracting a capital investment project. For example, the opportunity to invest in the expansion of a firm's factory, or alternatively to sell the factory, is a real call or put option, respectively. Real options are generally distinguished from conventional financial options in that they are not typically traded as securities, and do not usually involve decisions on an underlying asset that is traded as a financial security. A further distinction is that option holders here, i.e. management, can directly influence the value of the option's underlying project; whereas this is not a consideration as regards the underlying security of a financial option. Real options analysis, as a discipline, extends from its application in corporate finance, to decision making under uncertainty in general, adapting the techniques developed for financial options to "real-life" decisions. For example, R&D managers can use Real Options Valuation to help them allocate their R&D budget among diverse projects; a non business example might be the decision to join the work force, or rather, to forgo several years of income to attend graduate school. It, thus, forces decision makers to be explicit about the assumptions underlying their projections, and for this reason ROV is increasingly employed as a tool in business strategy formulation.

Types of Real Option

Simple Examples: *Investment:* This simple example shows the relevance of the real option to delay investment and wait for further information, and is adapted from "Investment Example"..

Consider a firm that has the option to invest in a new factory. It can invest this year or next year. The question is: when should the firm invest? If the firm invests this year, it has an income stream earlier. But, if it invests next year, the firm obtains further information about the state of the economy, which can prevent it from investing with losses.

The firm knows its discounted cash flows if it invests this year: 5M. If it invests next year, the discounted cash flows are 6M with a 66.7% probability, and 3M€ with a 33.3% probability. Assuming a risk neutral rate of 10%, future discounted cash flows are, in present terms, 5.45M and 2.73M, respectively. The investment cost is 4M. If the firm invests next year, the present value of the investment cost is 3.63M.

Following the net present value rule for investment, the firm should invest this year because the discounted cash flows (5M) are greater than the investment costs (4M) by 1M. Yet, if the firm waits for next year, it only invests if discounted cash flows do not decrease. If discounted cash flows decrease to 3M€, then investment is no longer profitable. If, they grow to 6M, then the firm invests. This implies that the firm invests next year with a 66.7% probability and earns 5.45M - 3.63M if it does invest. Thus the value to invest next year is 1.21M. Given that the value to invest next year exceeds the value to invest this year, the firm should wait for further information to prevent losses. This simple example shows how the net present value may lead the firm to take unnecessary risk, which could be prevented by real options valuation.

Staged Investment

Staged investments are quite often in the pharmaceutical, mineral, and oil industries. In this example, it is studied a staged investment abroad in which a firm decides whether to open one or two stores in a foreign country. This is adapted from "Staged Investment Example"..

The firm does not how well its stores are accepted in a foreign country. If their stores have high demand, the discounted cash flows per store is 10M. If their stores have low demand, the discounted cash flows per store is 5M. Assuming that the probability of both events is 50%, the expected discounted cash flows per store is 7.5M. It is also known that if the store's demand is independent of the store: if one store has high demand, the other also has high demand. The risk neutral rate is 10%. The investment cost per store is 8M.

Should the firm invest in one store, two stores, or not invest? The net present value suggests the firm should not invest: the net present value is -0.5M per store. But is it the best alternative? Following real options valuation, it is not: the firm has the real option to open one store this year, wait a year to know its demand, and invest in the new store next year if demand is high. By opening one store, the firm knows that the probability of high demand is 50%. The potential value gain to expand next year is thus 50%*(10M-8M)/1.1 = 0.91M. The value to open one store this year is 7.5M - 8M = -0.5. Thus the value of the real option to invest in one store, wait a year, and invest next year is 0.41M. Given this, the firm should opt by opening one store. This simple example shows that a negative net present value does not imply that the firm should not invest.

The flexibility available to management – i.e. the actual "real options" – generically, will relate to project size, project timing, and the operation of the project once established. In all cases, any (non-recoverable) upfront expenditure related to this flexibility is the option premium. Real options are also commonly applied to stock valuation. Option pricing approaches - as well as to various other "Applications" referenced below.

Options Relating to Project Size

Where the project's scope is uncertain, flexibility as to the size of the relevant facilities is valuable, and constitutes optionality.

- *Option to expand:* Here the project is built with capacity in excess of the expected level of output so that it can produce at higher rate if needed. Management then has the option (but not the obligation) to expand – i.e. exercise the option – should conditions turn out to be favourable. A project with the option to expand will cost more to establish, the excess being the option premium, but is worth more than the same without the possibility of expansion. This is equivalent to a call option.

- *Option to contract :* The project is engineered such that output can be contracted in future should conditions turn out to be unfavourable. Forgoing these future expenditures constitutes option exercise. This is the equivalent to a put option, and again, the excess upfront expenditure is the option premium.
- *Option to expand or contract:* Here the project is designed such that its operation can be dynamically turned on and off. Management may shut down part or all of the operation when conditions are unfavourable (a put option), and may restart operations when conditions improve (a call option). A flexible manufacturing system (FMS) is a good example of this type of option. This option is also known as a Switching option.

Options Relating to Project Life and Timing

Where there is uncertainty as to when, and how, business or other conditions will eventuate, flexibility as to the timing of the relevant project(s) is valuable, and constitutes optionality. Growth options are perhaps the most generic in this category – these entail the option to exercise only those projects that appear to be profitable at the time of initiation.

- *Initiation or deferment options:* Here management has flexibility as to when to start a project. For example, in natural resource exploration a firm can delay mining a deposit until market conditions are favourable. This constitutes an American styled call option.
- *Option to abandon:* Management may have the option to cease a project during its life, and, possibly, to realise its salvage value. Here, when the present value of the remaining cash flows falls below the liquidation value, the asset may be sold, and this act is effectively the exercising of a put option. This option is also known as a Termination option. Abandonment options are American styled.
- *Sequencing options:* This option is related to the initiation option above, although entails flexibility as to the timing of more than one inter-related projects: the analysis here is as to whether it is advantageous to implement these sequentially or in parallel. Here, observing the outcomes relating to the first project, the firm can resolve some of the uncertainty relating to the venture overall. Once resolved, management has the option to proceed or not with the development of the other projects. If taken in parallel, management would have already spent the resources

and the value of the option not to spend them is lost. The sequencing of projects is an important issue in corporate strategy. Related here is also the notion of Intraproject vs. Interproject options.

Options Relating to Project Operation

Management may have flexibility relating to the product produced and /or the process used in manufacture. This flexibility constitutes optionality.

- *Output mix options:* The option to produce different outputs from the same facility is known as an output mix option or product flexibility. These options are particularly valuable in industries where demand is volatile or where quantities demanded in total for a particular good are typically low, and management would wish to change to a different product quickly if required.
- *Input mix options:* An input mix option – process flexibility – allows management to use different inputs to produce the same output as appropriate. For example, a farmer will value the option to switch between various feed sources, preferring to use the cheapest acceptable alternative. An electric utility, for example, may have the option to switch between various fuel sources to produce electricity, and therefore a flexible plant, although more expensive may actually be more valuable.
- *Operating scale options:* Management may have the option to change the output rate per unit of time or to change the total length of production run time, for example in response to market conditions. These options are also known as Intensity options.

Valuation

Given the above, it is clear that there is an analogy between real options and financial options, and we would therefore expect options-based modelling and analysis to be applied here. At the same time, it is nevertheless important to understand why the more standard valuation techniques may not be applicable for ROV.

Applicability of Standard Techniques

ROV is often contrasted with more standard techniques of capital budgeting, such as discounted cash flow (DCF) analysis / net present value (NPV). Under this "standard" NPV approach, future expected cash flows are present valued under the empirical probability measure at a discount rate that reflects the embedded risk in the project. Here, only the expected cash flows are considered, and the "flexibility" to alter corporate strategy in view of actual market realisations is "ignored". The NPV framework (implicitly) assumes that management is "passive" with regard to their Capital Investment once committed. Some analysts account for this uncertainty by adjusting the discount rate, e.g. by increasing the cost of capital, or the cash flows, e.g. using certainty equivalents, or applying (subjective) "haircuts" to the forecast numbers, or via probability-weighting as in rNPV. Even when employed, however, these latter methods do not normally properly account for changes in risk over the project's lifecycle and hence fail to appropriately adapt the risk adjustment.

By contrast, ROV assumes that management is "active" and can "continuously" respond to market changes. Real options consider each and every scenario and indicate the best corporate action in any of these contingent events. Because management adapts to each negative outcome by decreasing its exposure and to positive scenarios by scaling up, the firm benefits from uncertainty in the underlying market, achieving a lower variability of profits than under the commitment/NPV stance. The contingent nature of future profits in real option models is captured by employing the techniques developed for financial options in the literature on contingent claims analysis. Here the approach, known as risk-neutral valuation, consists in adjusting the probability distribution for risk consideration, while discounting at the risk-free rate. This technique is also known as the certainty-equivalent or martingale approach, and uses a risk-neutral measure.

Given these different treatments, the real options value of a project is typically higher than the NPV – and the difference will be most marked in projects with major flexibility, contingency, and volatility. (As for financial options higher volatility of the underlying leads to higher value).

Options Based Valuation

Although there is much similarity between the modelling of real options and financial options, ROV is distinguished from the latter, in that it takes into account uncertainty about the future evolution of the parameters that determine the value of the project, *coupled with* management's ability to respond to the evolution of these parameters. It is the combined effect of these that makes ROV technically more challenging than its alternatives.

First, you must figure out the full range of possible values for the underlying asset.... This involves estimating what the asset's value would be if it existed today and forecasting to see the full set of possible future values... [These] calculations provide you with numbers for all the possible future values of the option at the various points where a decision is needed on whether to continue with the project...

When valuing the real option, the analyst must therefore consider the inputs to the valuation, the valuation method employed, and whether any technical limitations may apply.

Valuation Inputs

Given the similarity in valuation approach, the inputs required for modelling the real option correspond, generically, to those required for a financial option valuation. The specific application, though, is as follows:

- The option's underlying is the project in question – it is modelled in terms of:
  - o Spot price: the starting or current value of the project is required: this is usually based on management's "best guess" as to the gross value of the project's cash flows and resultant NPV;
  - o Volatility: a measure for uncertainty as to the change in value over time is required:
    - – the volatility in project value is generally used, usually derived via monte carlo simulation; sometimes the volatility of the first period's cash flows are preferred.
    - – some analysts substitute a listed security as a proxy, using either its price volatility (historical volatility), or, if options exist on this security, their implied volatility.
- o Dividends generated by the underlying asset: As part of a project, the dividend equates to any income which could be derived from real assets and paid to the owner. These reduce the appreciation of the asset.
- Option characteristics:
  - o Strike price: this corresponds to any (non-recoverable) investment outlays, typically the prospective costs of the project. In general, management would proceed (i.e. the option would be in the money) given that the present value of expected cash flows exceeds this amount;
  - o Option term: the time during which management may decide to act, or not act, corresponds to the life of the option. As above, examples include the time to expiry of a patent, or of the mineral rights for a new mine.

- o Option style and option exercise. Management's ability to respond to changes in value is modelled at each decision point as a series of options, as above these may comprise, i.a.:
  - – the option to contract the project (an American styled put option);
  - – the option to abandon the project (also an American put);
  - – the option to expand or extend the project (both American styled call options);
  - – switching options, composite options or rainbow options which may also apply to the project.

Valuation Methods

The valuation methods usually employed, likewise, are adapted from techniques developed for valuing financial options. Note though that, in general, while most "real" problems allow for American style exercise at any point (many points) in the project's life and are impacted by multiple underlying variables, the standard methods are limited either with regard to dimensionality, to early exercise, or to both. In selecting a model, therefore, analysts must make a trade off between these considerations. The model must also be flexible enough to allow for the relevant decision rule to be coded appropriately at each decision point.

- Closed form, Black–Scholes-like solutions are sometimes employed. These are applicable only for European styled options or perpetual American options. Note that this application of Black–Scholes, assumes constant — i.e. deterministic — costs: in cases where the project's costs, like its revenue, are also assumed stochastic, then Margrabe's formula can (should) be applied instead, here valuing the option to "exchange" expenses for revenue.
- The most commonly employed methods are binomial lattices. These are more widely used given that most real options are American styled. Additionally, and particularly, lattice-based models allow for flexibility as to exercise, where the relevant, and differing, rules may be encoded at each node. Note that lattices cannot readily handle high-dimensional problems; treating the project's costs as stochastic would add (at least) one dimension to the lattice, increasing the number of ending-nodes by the square (the exponent here, corresponding to the number of sources of uncertainty).

- Specialised Monte Carlo Methods have also been developed and are increasingly, and especially, applied to high-dimensional problems. Note that for American styled real options, this application is somewhat more complex; although recent research combines a least squares approach with simulation, allowing for the valuation of real options which are both multidimensional and American styled.
- When the Real Option can be modelled using a partial differential equation, then Finite difference methods for option pricing are sometimes applied. Although many of the early ROV articles discussed this method, its use is relatively uncommon today—particularly amongst practitioners—due to the required mathematical sophistication; these too cannot readily be used for high-dimensional problems.

Various other methods, aimed mainly at practitioners, have been developed for real option valuation. These typically use cash-flow scenarios for the projection of the future pay-off distribution, and are not based on restricting assumptions similar to those that underlie the closed form (or even numeric) solutions discussed. The most recent additions include the Datar–Mathews method and the fuzzy pay-off method.

Limitations

The relevance of Real options, even as a thought framework, may be limited due to market, organisational and / or technical considerations. When the framework is employed, therefore, the analyst must first ensure that ROV is relevant to the project in question. These considerations are as below.

Market Characteristics

As discussed above, the market and environment underlying the project must be one where "change is most evident", and the "source, trends and evolution" in product demand and supply, create the "flexibility, contingency, and volatility" which result in optionality. Without this, the NPV framework would be more relevant.

Organisational Considerations

Real options are "particularly important for businesses with a few key characteristics", and may be less relevant otherwise. In overview:

1. Corporate strategy has to be adaptive to contingent events. Some corporations face organisational rigidities and are unable to react to market changes; in this case, the NPV approach is appropriate.

2. Practically, the business must be positioned such that it has appropriate information flow, and opportunities to act. This will often be a market leader and / or a firm enjoying economies of scale and scope.
3. Management must understand options, be able to identify and create them, and appropriately exercise them. (This contrasts with business leaders focused on maintaining the status quo and / or near-term accounting earnings.)
4. The financial position of the business must be such that it has the ability to fund the project as, and when, required (i.e. issue shares, absorb further debt and / or use internally generated cash flow).

Technical Considerations

Limitations as to the use of these models arise due to the contrast between Real Options and financial options, for which these were originally developed. The main difference is that the underlying is often not tradable – e.g. the factory owner cannot easily sell the factory upon which he has the option. Additionally, the real option itself may also not be tradeable – e.g. the factory owner cannot sell the right to extend his factory to another party, only he can make this decision (some real options, however, can be sold, e.g., ownership of a vacant lot of land is a real option to develop that land in the future). Even where a market exists – for the underlying or for the option – in most cases there is limited (or no) market liquidity. Finally, even if the firm can actively adapt to market changes, it remains to determine the right paradigm to discount future claims

The Difficulties

1. As above, data issues arise as far as estimating key model inputs. Here, since the value or price of the underlying cannot be (directly) observed, there will always be some (much) uncertainty as to its value (i.e. spot price) and volatility (further complicated by uncertainty as to management's actions in the future).
2. It is often difficult to capture the rules relating to exercise, and consequent actions by management: Some real options are proprietary (owned or exercisable by a single individual or a company) while others are shared (can be exercised by many parties). Further, a project may have a portfolio of embedded real options, some of which may be mutually exclusive.
3. Theoretical difficulties, which are more serious, may also arise.

- Option pricing models are built on rational pricing logic. Here, essentially: (a) it is presupposed that one can create a "hedged portfolio" comprising one option and "delta" shares of the underlying. (b) Arbitrage arguments then allow for the option's price to be estimated today. (c) When hedging of this sort is possible, since delta hedging and risk neutral pricing are *mathematically* identical, then risk neutral valuation may be applied, as is the case with most option pricing models. (d) Under ROV however, the option and (usually) its underlying are clearly not traded, and forming a hedging portfolio would be difficult, if not impossible.
- Standard option models: (a) Assume that the risk characteristics of the underlying do not change over the life of the option, usually expressed via a constant volatility assumption. (b) Hence a standard, risk free rate may be applied as the discount rate at each decision point, allowing for risk neutral valuation. Under ROV, however: (a) managements' actions actually change the risk characteristics of the project in question, and hence (b) the Required rate of return could differ depending on what state was realised, and a premium over risk free would be required, invalidating (technically) the risk neutrality assumption.

These issues are addressed via several interrelated assumptions:

1. As discussed above, the data issues are usually addressed using a simulation of the project, or a listed proxy. Various new methods – also address these issues.
2. Also as above, specific exercise rules can often be accommodated by coding these in a bespoke binomial tree; see:.
3. The theoretical issues:

- To use standard option pricing models here, despite the difficulties relating to rational pricing, practitioners adopt the "fiction" that the real option and the underlying project are both traded (the so called, Marketed Asset Disclaimer (MAD) approach). Although this is a strong assumption, it is pointed out that, interestingly, a similar fiction in fact underpins standard NPV / DCF valuation (and using simulation as above). See: and.
- To address the fact that changing characteristics invalidate the use of a constant discount rate, some analysts use the "replicating portfolio approach", as opposed to Risk neutral

valuation, and modify their models correspondingly. Under this approach, we "replicate" the cash flows on the option by holding a risk free bond and the underlying in the correct proportions. Then, since the value of the option and the portfolio will be identical in the future, they may be equated today, and *no* discounting is required.

History

Whereas business managers have been making capital investment decisions for centuries, the term "real option" is relatively new, and was coined by Professor Stewart Myers of the MIT Sloan School of Management in 1977. It is interesting to note though, that in 1930, Irving Fisher wrote explicitly of the "options" available to a business owner (*The Theory of Interest*, II.VIII). The description of such opportunities as "real options", however, followed on the development of analytical techniques for financial options, such as Black–Scholes in 1973. As such, the term "real option" is closely tied to these option methods.

Real options are today an active field of academic research. Professor Lenos Trigeorgis has been a leading name for many years, publishing several influential books and academic articles. Other pioneering academics in the field include Professors Eduardo Schwartz, Gonzalo Cortazar, Michael Brennan, Han Smit, Avinash Dixit and Robert Pindyck (the latter two, authoring the pioneering text in the discipline). An academic conference on real options is organised yearly (Annual International Conference on Real Options).

Amongst others, the concept was "popularized" by Michael J. Mauboussin, then chief U.S. investment strategist for Credit Suisse First Boston. He uses real options to explain the gap between how the stock market prices some businesses and the "intrinsic value" for those businesses. Trigeorgis also has broadened exposure to real options through layman articles in publications such as The Wall Street Journal. This popularization is such that ROV is now a standard offering in postgraduate finance degrees, and often, even in MBA curricula at many Business Schools.

Recently, real options have been employed in business strategy, both for valuation purposes and as a conceptual framework. The idea of treating strategic investments as options was popularized by Timothy Luehrman in two HBR articles: "In financial terms, a business strategy is much more like a series of options, than a series of static cash flows". Investment opportunities are plotted in an "option space" with dimensions "volatility" & value-to-cost ("NPVq").

Luehrman also co-authored with William Teichner a Harvard Business School case study, *Arundel Partners: The Sequel Project,* in 1992, which may have been the first business school case study to teach ROV. Interestingly, and reflecting the "mainstreaming" of ROV, Professor Robert C. Merton discussed the essential points of Arundel in his Nobel Prize Lecture in 1997.

Arundel involves a group of investors that is considering acquiring the sequel rights to a portfolio of yet-to-be released feature films. In particular, the investors must determine the value of the sequel rights before any of the first films are produced. Here, the investors face two main choices. They can produce an original movie and sequel at the same time *or* they can wait to decide on a sequel after the original film is released.

The second approach, he states, provides the option *not* to make a sequel in the event the original movie is not successful. This real option has economic worth and can be valued monetarily using an option-pricing model.

Profitability Index

Profitability index (PI), also known as profit investment ratio (PIR) and value investment ratio (VIR), is the ratio of payoff to investment of a proposed project. It is a useful tool for ranking projects because it allows you to quantify the amount of value created per unit of investment.

The ratio is calculated as follows:

- $\text{Profitability index} = \dfrac{\text{PV of future cash flows}}{\text{Initial investment}}$

Assuming that the cash flow calculated does not include the investment made in the project, a profitability index of 1 indicates breakeven. Any value lower than one would indicate that the project's PV is less than the initial investment. As the value of the profitability index increases, so does the financial attractiveness of the proposed project.

Rules for selection or rejection of a project:

- If PI > 1 then accept the project
- If PI < 1 then reject the project

For example:

- Investment = $40,000
- Life of the Machine = 5 Years

CFAT Year	CFAT
1	18000
2	12000
3	10000
4	9000
5	6000

Calculate Net present value at 10% and PI:

Year	CFAT	PV@10%	PV
1	18000	0.909	16362
2	12000	0.827	9924
3	10000	0.752	7520
4	9000	0.683	6147
5	6000	0.621	3726
	Total present value		43679
	(-) Investment		40000
		NPV	3679

PI = 43679/40000 = 1.091 > 1 ⇒ Accept the project

Cost of Capital

In accounting, the cost of capital is the cost of a company's funds (both debt and equity), or, from an investor's point of view "the shareholder's required return on a portfolio company's existing securities". It is used to evaluate new projects of a company. It is the minimum return that investors expect for providing capital to the company, thus setting a benchmark that a new project has to meet.

Summary

For an investment to be worthwhile, the expected return on capital must be greater than the cost of capital. The cost of capital is the rate of return that capital could be expected to earn in an alternative investment of equivalent risk. If a project is of similar risk to a company's average business activities it is reasonable to use the company's average cost of capital as a basis for the evaluation. A company's securities typically include both debt and equity, one must therefore calculate both the cost of debt and the cost of equity to determine a company's cost of capital. However, a rate of return larger than the cost of capital is usually required.

The cost of debt is relatively simple to calculate, as it is composed of the rate of interest paid. In practice, the interest-rate paid by the company can be modelled as the risk-free rate plus a risk component (risk premium), which itself incorporates a probable rate of default (and amount of recovery given default). For companies with similar risk or credit ratings, the interest rate is largely exogenous (not linked to the cost of debt), the cost of equity is broadly defined as the risk-weighted projected return required by investors, where the return is largely unknown. The cost of equity is therefore *inferred* by comparing the investment to other investments (comparable) with similar risk profiles to determine the "market" cost of equity. It is commonly equated using the capital asset pricing model formula (below), although articles such as Stulz 1995 question the validity of using a local CAPM versus an international CAPM- also considering whether markets are fully integrated or segmented (if fully integrated, there would be no need for a local CAPM).

Once cost of debt and cost of equity have been determined, their blend, the weighted-average cost of capital (WACC), can be calculated. This WACC can then be used as a discount rate for a project's projected cash flows.

Cost of Debt

When companies borrow funds from outside or take debt from financial institutions or other resources the interest paid on that amount is called cost of debt. The cost of debt is computed by taking the rate on a risk-free bond whose duration matches the term structure of the corporate debt, then adding a default premium. This default premium will rise as the amount of debt increases (since, all other things being equal, the risk rises as the amount of debt rises). Since in most cases debt expense is a deductible expense, the cost of debt is computed as an after tax cost to make it comparable with the cost of equity (earnings are after-tax as well). Thus, for profitable firms, debt is discounted by the tax rate. The formula can be written as (Rf + credit risk rate)(1-T), where T is the corporate tax rate and Rf is the risk free rate.

Cost of Equity

Cost of equity = Risk free rate of return + Premium expected for risk

Cost of equity = Risk free rate of return + Beta x (market rate of return- risk free rate of return) where Beta= sensitivity to movements in the relevant market

$$E_s = R_f + \beta_s(R_m - R_f).$$

Where:

E_s The expected return for a security

R_f The expected risk-free return in that market (government bond yield)

β_s The sensitivity to market risk for the security

R_M The historical return of the stock market/ equity market

$(R_M - R_f)$ The risk premium of market assets over risk free assets.

The risk free rate is taken from the lowest yielding bonds in the particular market, such as government bonds.

An alternative to the estimation of the required return by the capital asset pricing model as above, is the use of the Fama–French three-factor model.

Expected Return

The expected return (or required rate of return for investors) can be calculated with the "dividend capitalization model", which is

$$K_{cs} = \frac{Dividend_{Payment/Share}(1 + Growth)}{Price_{Market}} + Growth_{rate}.$$

Comments

The models state that investors will expect a return that is the risk-free return plus the security's sensitivity to market risk times the market risk premium.

The risk premium varies over time and place, but in some developed countries during the twentieth century it has averaged around 5%. The equity market real capital gain return has been about the same as annual real GDP growth. The capital gains on the Dow Jones Industrial Average have been 1.6% per year over the period 1910-2005. The dividends have increased the total "real" return on average equity to the double, about 3.2%.

The sensitivity to market risk (β) is unique for each firm and depends on everything from management to its business and capital structure. This value cannot be known "ex ante" (beforehand), but can be estimated from *ex post* (past) returns and past experience with similar firms.

Cost of Retained Earnings/Cost of Internal Equity

Note that retained earnings are a component of equity, and therefore the cost of retained earnings (internal equity) is equal to the cost of equity as explained above. Dividends (earnings that are paid to investors and not retained) are a component of the return on capital to equity holders, and influence the cost of capital through that mechanism.

Cost of internal equity = [(next year's dividend per share/(current market price per share - flotation costs)] + growth rate of dividends)]

Weighted Average Cost of Capital

The Weighted Cost of Capital (WACC) is used in finance to measure a firm's cost of capital.

The total capital for a firm is the value of its equity (for a firm without outstanding warrants and options, this is the same as the company's market capitalization) plus the cost of its debt (the cost of debt should be continually updated as the cost of debt changes as a result of interest rate changes). Notice that the "equity" in the debt to equity ratio is the market value of all equity, not the shareholders' equity on the balance sheet. To calculate the firm's weighted cost of capital, we must first calculate the costs of the individual financing sources: Cost of Debt, Cost of Preference Capital and Cost of Equity Cap.

Calculation of WACC is an iterative procedure which requires estimation of the fair market value of equity capital.

Capital Structure

Because of tax advantages on debt issuance, it will be cheaper to issue debt rather than new equity (this is only true for profitable firms, tax breaks are available only to profitable firms). At some point, however, the cost of issuing new debt will be greater than the cost of issuing new equity. This is because adding debt increases the default risk - and thus the interest rate that the company must pay in order to borrow money. By utilising too much debt in its capital structure, this increased default risk can also drive up the costs for other sources (such as retained earnings and preferred stock) as well. Management must identify the "optimal mix" of financing – the capital structure where the cost of capital is minimized so that the firm's value can be maximized.

The Thomson Financial league tables show that global debt issuance exceeds equity issuance with a 90 to 10 margin.

The structure of capital should be determined considering the weighted average cost of capital.

Modigliani-Miller Theorem

If there were no tax advantages for issuing debt, and equity could be freely issued, Miller and Modigliani showed that, under certain assumptions, the value of a leveraged firm and the value of an unleveraged firm should be the same.

Chapter 5

Financial Models

Financial Modelling

Financial modelling is the task of building an abstract representation (a model) of a real world financial situation. This is a mathematical model designed to represent (a simplified version of) the performance of a financial asset or portfolio of a business, project, or any other investment. Financial modelling is a general term that means different things to different users; the reference usually relates either to accounting and corporate finance applications, or to quantitative finance applications. While there has been some debate in the industry as to the nature of financial modelling—whether it is a tradecraft, such as welding, or a science—the task of financial modelling has been gaining acceptance and rigor over the years. Typically, financial modelling is understood to mean an exercise in either asset pricing or corporate finance, of a quantitative nature. In other words, financial modelling is about translating a set of hypotheses about the behaviour of markets or agents into numerical predictions; for example, a firm's decisions about investments (the firm will invest 20% of assets), or investment returns (returns on "stock A" will, on average, be 10% higher than the market's returns).

Accounting

In corporate finance, investment banking, and the accounting profession *financial modelling* is largely synonymous with financial statement forecasting. This usually involves the preparation of detailed company specific models used for decision making purposes and financial analysis.

Applications include:

- Business valuation, especially discounted cash flow, but including other valuation problems
- Scenario planning and management decision making ("what is"; "what if"; "what has to be done")
- Capital budgeting
- Cost of capital (i.e. WACC) calculations
- Financial statement analysis (including of operating- and finance leases, and R&D)
- Project finance
- Mergers and Acquisitions (i.e. estimating the future performance of combined entities)

To generalize as to the nature of these models: firstly, as they are built around financial statements, calculations and outputs are monthly, quarterly or annual; secondly, the inputs take the form of "assumptions", where the analyst *specifies* the values that will apply in each period for external / global variables (exchange rates, tax percentage, etc...; may be thought of as the model *parameters*), and for internal / company specific *variables* (wages, unit costs, etc....). Correspondingly, both characteristics are reflected (at least implicitly) in the mathematical form of these models: firstly, the models are in discrete time; secondly, they are deterministic.

Modellers are sometimes referred to (tongue in cheek) as "number crunchers", and are often designated "financial analyst". Typically, the modeller will have completed an MBA or MSF with (optional) coursework in "financial modelling". Accounting qualifications and finance certifications such as the CIIA and CFA generally do not provide direct or explicit training in modelling. At the same time, numerous commercial training courses are offered, both through universities and privately.

Although purpose built software does exist, the vast proportion of the market is spreadsheet-based — this is largely since the models are almost always company specific; also, analysts will each have their own criteria and methods for financial modelling. Microsoft Excel now has by far the dominant position, having overtaken Lotus 1-2-3 in the 1990s. Spreadsheet-based modelling can have its own problems, and several standardizations and "best practices" have been proposed. "Spreadsheet risk" is increasingly studied and managed.

One critique here, is that model *outputs*, i.e. line items, often incorporate "unrealistic implicit assumptions" and "internal inconsistencies". (For example, a forecast for growth in revenue but without corresponding increases in working capital, fixed assets and the associated financing, may imbed unrealistic assumptions about asset turnover, leverage and / or equity financing.) What is required, but often lacking, is that all key elements are explicitly and consistently forecasted. Related to this, is that modellers often additionally "fail to identify crucial assumptions" relating to *inputs*, "and to explore what can go wrong". Here, in general, modellers "use point values and simple arithmetic instead of probability distributions and statistical measures" — i.e., as mentioned, the problems are treated as deterministic in nature — and thus calculate a single value for the asset or project, but without providing information on the range, variance and sensitivity of outcomes. Other critiques discuss the lack of adequate spreadsheet design skills, and of basic computer programming concepts. More serious criticism, in fact, relates to the nature of budgeting itself, and its impact on the organisation.

The annual *Modeloff Financial Modelling World Championships* is held in New York annually since 2013.

Quantitative Finance

In quantitative finance, *financial modelling* entails the development of a sophisticated mathematical model. Models here deal with asset prices, market movements, portfolio returns and the like. A key distinction is between models of the financial situation of a large, complex firm or "quantitative financial management", models of the returns of different stocks or "quantitative asset pricing", models of the price or returns of derivative securities or "financial engineering" and models of the firm's financial decisions or "quantitative corporate finance".

Applications include:

- Option pricing and calculation of their "Greeks"
- Other derivatives, especially interest rate derivatives, credit derivatives and exotic derivatives
- Modelling the term structure of interest rates (short rate modelling) and credit spreads
- Credit scoring and provisioning
- Corporate financing activity prediction problems
- Portfolio optimization
- Real options
- Risk modelling (Financial risk modelling) and value at risk
- Dynamic financial analysis (DFA)

These problems are often stochastic and continuous in nature, and models here thus require complex algorithms, entailing computer simulation, advanced numerical methods (such as numerical differential equations, numerical linear algebra, dynamic programming) and/or the development of optimization models. The general nature of these problems is discussed under Mathematical finance, while specific techniques are listed under Outline of finance# Mathematical tools.

Modellers are generally referred to as "quants" (quantitative analysts), and typically have advanced (Ph.D. level) backgrounds in quantitative disciplines such as physics, engineering, computer science, mathematics or operations research. Alternatively, or in addition to their quantitative background, they complete a finance masters with a quantitative orientation, such as the Master of Quantitative Finance, or the more specialised Master of Computational Finance or Master of Financial Engineering; the CQF is increasingly common.

Although spreadsheets are widely used here also (almost always requiring extensive VBA), custom C++ or numerical analysis software such as MATLAB is often preferred, particularly where stability or speed is a concern. MATLAB is the tool of choice for doing economics research because of its intuitive programming, graphical and debugging tools, but C++/Fortran are preferred for conceptually simple but high computational-cost applications where MATLAB is too slow. Additionally, for many (of the standard) derivative and portfolio applications, commercial software is available, and the choice as to whether the model is to be developed in-house, or whether existing products are to be deployed, will depend on the problem in question.

The complexity of these models may result in incorrect pricing or hedging or both. This *Model risk* is the subject of ongoing research by finance academics, and is a topic of great, and growing, interest in the risk management arena.

Criticism of the discipline (often preceding the financial crisis of 2007–08 by several years) emphasizes the differences between the mathematical and physical sciences and finance, and the resultant caution to be applied by modelers, and by traders and risk managers using their models. Notable here are Emanuel Derman and Paul Wilmott, authors of the *Financial Modelers' Manifesto*. Some go further and question whether mathematical- and statistical modelling may be applied to finance at all, at least with the assumptions usually made (for options; for portfolios). In fact, these may go so far as to question the "empirical and scientific validity... of modern financial theory". Notable here are Nassim Taleb and Benoit Mandelbrot.

Valuation of Options

In finance, a price (premium) is paid or received for purchasing or selling options. This price can be split into two components.

These are:

- Intrinsic value
- Time value

Intrinsic Value

The *intrinsic value* is the difference between the underlying price and the strike price, to the extent that this is in favour of the option holder. For a call option, the option is in-the-money if the underlying price is higher than the strike price; then the intrinsic value is the underlying price minus the strike price. For a put option, the option is in-the-money if the *strike* price is higher than the *underlying* price; then the intrinsic value is the strike price minus the underlying price. Otherwise the intrinsic value is zero.

In simple words, it is the value by which is already available in the market. If you are holding NIFTY 5000 Call (Bullish/Long) option and NIFTY is at 5050 level then you already have [1] 50 advantage even if the option expires today. These [1] 50 are the intrinsic value of option.

Conversely if you are holding a put option and NIFTY is below strike price then your option has an intrinsic value equalling the difference between the strike price and NIFTY value. So,

Intrinsic Value

= current stock price – strike price (call option)

= strike price – current stock price (put option)

Time Value

The option premium is always greater than the intrinsic value. This extra money is for the risk which the option writer/seller is undertaking. This is called the Time Value.

Time value is the amount the option trader is paying for a contract above its intrinsic value, with the belief that prior to expiration the contract value will increase because of a favourable change in the price of the underlying asset. Obviously, the longer the amount of time until the expiry of the contract, the greater the time value. So,

Time value = option premium – intrinsic value

There are many factors which determine option premium. These factors affect the premium of the option with varying intensity. Some of these factors are listed here:

- Price of the underlying: Any fluctuation in the price of the underlying (stock/index/commodity) obviously has the largest impact on premium of an option contract. An increase in the underlying price increases the premium of call option and decreases the premium of put option. Reverse is true when underlying price decreases.
- Strike price: How far is the strike price from spot also has an impact on option premium. Say, if NIFTY goes from 5000 to 5100 the premium of 5000 strike and of 5100 strike will change a lot compared to a contract with strike of 5500 or 4700.
- Time till expiry: Lesser the time to expiry, option premium follows the intrinsic value more closely. On the expiry date Time Value approaches zero.
- Volatility of underlying: Underlying security is a constantly changing entity. The degree by which its price fluctuates can be termed as volatility. So a share which fluctuates 5% on either side on daily basis is said to have more volatility than let's say a stable blue chip shares whose fluctuation is more benign at 2–3%. Volatility affects calls and puts alike. Higher volatility increases the option premium because of greater risk it brings to the seller.

Apart from above, other factors like bond yield (or interest rate) also affect the premium. This is due to the fact that the money invested by the seller can earn this risk free income in any case and hence while selling option; he has to earn more than this because of higher risk he is taking.

Pricing Models

Because the values of option contracts depend on a number of different variables in addition to the value of the underlying asset, they are complex to value. There are many pricing models in use, although all essentially incorporate the concepts of rational pricing, moneyness, option time value and put-call parity.

Amongst the Most Common Models are

- Black–Scholes and the Black model
- Binomial options pricing model
- Monte Carlo option model
- Finite difference methods for option pricing

Other Approaches Include

- Heston model

- Heath–Jarrow–Morton framework
- Variance gamma model

Derivative (Finance)

In finance, a derivative is a contract that *derives* its value from the performance of an underlying entity. This underlying entity can be an asset, index, or interest rate, and is often called the "underlying". Derivatives can be used for a number of purposes - including insuring against price movements (hedging), increasing exposure to price movements for speculation or getting access to otherwise hard to trade assets or markets.

Some of the more common derivatives include forwards, futures, options, swaps, and variations of these such as collateralized debt obligations, credit default swaps, and mortgage backed securities. Most derivatives are traded over-the-counter (off-exchange) or on an exchange such as the Chicago Mercantile Exchange, while most insurance contracts have developed into a separate industry. Derivatives are one of the three main categories of financial instruments, the other two being equities (i.e. stocks or shares) and debt (i.e. bonds and mortgages).

Basics

Derivatives are contracts between two parties that specify conditions (especially the dates, resulting values and definitions of the underlying variables, the parties' contractual obligations, and the notional amount) under which payments are to be made between the parties. The most common underlying assets include commodities, stocks, bonds, interest rates and currencies, but they can also be other derivatives, which adds another layer of complexity to proper valuation. The components of a firm's capital structure, e.g. bonds and stock, can also be considered derivatives, more precisely options, with the underlying being the firm's assets, but this is unusual outside of technical contexts.

From the economic point of view, financial derivatives are cash flows, that are conditionally stochastically and discounted to present value. The market risk inherent in the underlying asset is attached to the financial derivative through contractual agreements and hence can be traded separately. The underlying asset does not have to be acquired. Derivatives therefore allow the breakup of ownership and participation in the market value of an asset. This also provides a considerable amount of freedom regarding the contract design. That contractual freedom allows to modify the participation in the performance of the underlying asset almost arbitrarily. Thus, the participation in the market value of the underlying can be effectively weaker, stronger (leverage effect), or implemented as inverse. Hence, specifically the market price risk of the underlying asset can be controlled in almost every situation. There are two groups of derivative contracts: the privately traded over-the-counter (OTC) derivatives such as swaps that do not go through an exchange or other intermediary, and exchange-traded derivatives (ETD) that are traded through specialised derivatives exchanges or other exchanges.

Derivatives are more common in the modern era, but their origins trace back several centuries. One of the oldest derivatives is rice futures, which have been traded on the Dojima Rice Exchange since the eighteenth century. Derivatives are broadly categorized by the relationship between the underlying asset and the derivative (such as forward, option, swap); the type of underlying asset (such as equity derivatives, foreign exchange derivatives, interest rate derivatives, commodity derivatives, or credit derivatives); the market in which they trade (such as exchange-traded or over-the-counter); and their pay-off profile. Derivatives may broadly be categorized as "lock" or "option" products. Lock products (such as swaps, futures, or forwards) obligate the contractual parties to the terms over the life of the contract. Option products (such as interest rate caps) provide the buyer the right, but not the obligation to enter the contract under the terms specified.

Derivatives can be used either for risk management (i.e. to "hedge" by providing offsetting compensation in case of an undesired event, a kind of "insurance") or for speculation (i.e. making a financial "bet"). This distinction is important because the former is a prudent aspect of operations and financial management for many firms across many industries; the latter offers managers and investors a risky opportunity to increase profit, which may not be properly disclosed to stakeholders.

Along with many other financial products and services, derivatives reform is an element of the Dodd–Frank Wall Street Reform and Consumer Protection Act of 2010. The Act delegated many rule-making details of regulatory oversight to the Commodity Futures Trading Commission and those details are not finalized nor fully implemented as of late 2012.

Size of Market

To give an idea of the size of the derivative market, *The Economist* magazine has reported that as of June 2011, the over-the-counter (OTC) derivatives market amounted to approximately $700 trillion, and the size of the market traded on exchanges totaled an additional $83 trillion. However, these are "notional" values, and some economists say that this value greatly exaggerates the market value and the true credit risk faced by the parties involved. For example, in 2010, while the aggregate of OTC derivatives exceeded $600 trillion, the value of the market was estimated much lower, at $21 trillion. The credit risk equivalent of the derivative contracts was estimated at $3.3 trillion.

Still, even these scaled down figures represent huge amounts of money. For perspective, the budget for total expenditure of the United States Government during 2012 was $3.5 trillion, and the total current value of the US stock market is an estimated $23 trillion. The world annual Gross Domestic Product is about $65 trillion.

And for one type of derivative at least, Credit Default Swaps (CDS), for which the inherent risk is considered high, the higher, nominal value, remains relevant. It was this type of derivative that investment magnate Warren Buffet referred to in his famous 2002 speech in which he warned against "weapons of financial mass destruction." CDS notional value in early 2012 amounted to $25.5 trillion, down from $55 trillion in 2008.

Usage

Derivatives are used for the following:

- Hedge or mitigate risk in the underlying, by entering into a derivative contract whose value moves in the opposite direction to their underlying position and cancels part or all of it out
- Create option ability where the value of the derivative is linked to a specific condition or event (e.g. the underlying reaching a specific price level)
- Obtain exposure to the underlying where it is not possible to trade in the underlying (e.g. weather derivatives)
- Provide leverage (or gearing), such that a small movement in the underlying value can cause a large difference in the value of the derivative
- Speculate and make a profit if the value of the underlying asset moves the way they expect (e.g. moves in a given direction, stays in or out of a specified range, reaches a certain level)
- Switch asset allocations between different asset classes without disturbing the underlying assets, as part of transition management

- Avoid paying taxes. For example, an equity swap allows an investor to receive steady payments, e.g. based on LIBOR rate, while avoiding paying capital gains tax and keeping the stock.

Mechanics and Valuation Basics

Lock products are theoretically valued at zero at the time of execution and thus do not typically require an up-front exchange between the parties. Based upon movements in the underlying asset over time, however, the value of the contract will fluctuate, and the derivative may be either an asset (i.e. "in the money") or a liability (i.e. "out of the money") at different points throughout its life. Importantly, either party is therefore exposed to the credit quality of its counterparty and is interested in protecting itself in an event of default.

Option products have immediate value at the outset because they provide specified protection (intrinsic value) over a given time period (time value). One common form of option product familiar to many consumers is insurance for homes and automobiles. The insured would pay more for a policy with greater liability protections (intrinsic value) and one that extends for a year rather than six months (time value). Because of the immediate option value, the option purchaser typically pays an up front premium. Just like for lock products, movements in the underlying asset will cause the option's intrinsic value to change over time while its time value deteriorates steadily until the contract expires. An important difference between a lock product is that, after the initial exchange, the option purchaser has no further liability to its counterparty; upon maturity, the purchaser will execute the option if it has positive value (i.e. if it is "in the money") or expire at no cost (other than to the initial premium) (i.e. if the option is "out of the money").

Hedging

Derivatives allow risk related to the price of the underlying asset to be transferred from one party to another. For example, a wheat farmer and a miller could sign a futures contract to exchange a specified amount of cash for a specified amount of wheat in the future. Both parties have reduced a future risk: for the wheat farmer, the uncertainty of the price, and for the miller, the availability of wheat. However, there is still the risk that no wheat will be available because of events unspecified by the contract, such as the weather, or that one party will renege on the contract. Although a third party, called a clearing house, insures a futures contract, not all derivatives are insured against counter-party risk.

From another perspective, the farmer and the miller both reduce a risk and acquire a risk when they sign the futures contract: the farmer reduces the risk that the price of wheat will fall below the price specified in the contract and acquires the risk that the price of wheat will rise above the price specified in the contract (thereby losing additional income that he could have earned). The miller, on the other hand, acquires the risk that the price of wheat will fall below the price specified in the contract (thereby paying more in the future than he otherwise would have) and reduces the risk that the price of wheat will rise above the price specified in the contract. In this sense, one party is the insurer (risk taker) for one type of risk, and the counter-party is the insurer (risk taker) for another type of risk.

Hedging also occurs when an individual or institution buys an asset (such as a commodity, a bond that has coupon payments, a stock that pays dividends, and so on) and sells it using a futures contract. The individual or institution has access to the asset for a specified amount of time, and can then sell it in the future at a specified price according to the futures contract. Of course, this allows the individual or institution the benefit of holding the asset, while reducing the risk that the future selling price will deviate unexpectedly from the market's current assessment of the future value of the asset.

Derivatives trading of this kind may serve the financial interests of certain particular businesses. For example, a corporation borrows a large sum of money at a specific interest rate. The interest rate on the loan reprices every six months. The corporation is concerned that the rate of interest may be much higher in six months. The corporation could buy a forward rate agreement (FRA), which is a contract to pay a fixed rate of interest six months after purchases on a notional amount of money. If the interest rate after six months is above the contract rate, the seller will pay the difference to the corporation, or FRA buyer. If the rate is lower, the corporation will pay the difference to the seller. The purchase of the FRA serves to reduce the uncertainty concerning the rate increase and stabilize earnings.

Speculation and Arbitrage

Derivatives can be used to acquire risk, rather than to hedge against risk. Thus, some individuals and institutions will enter into a derivative contract to speculate on the value of the underlying asset, betting that the party seeking insurance will be wrong about the future value of the underlying asset. Speculators look to buy an asset in the future at a low price according to a derivative contract when the future market price is high, or to sell an asset in the future at a high price according to a derivative contract when the future market price is less.

Individuals and institutions may also look for arbitrage opportunities, as when the current buying price of an asset falls below the price specified in a futures contract to sell the asset.

Speculative trading in derivatives gained a great deal of notoriety in 1995 when Nick Leeson, a trader at Barings Bank, made poor and unauthorized investments in futures contracts. Through a combination of poor judgment, lack of oversight by the bank's management and regulators, and unfortunate events like the Kobe earthquake, Leeson incurred a US$1.3 billion loss that bankrupted the centuries-old institution.

Proportion Used for Hedging and Speculation

The true proportion of derivatives contracts used for hedging purposes is unknown (and perhaps unknowable), but it appears to be relatively small. Also, derivatives contracts account for only 3–6% of the median firms' total currency and interest rate exposure. Nonetheless, we know that many firms' derivatives activities have at least some speculative component for a variety of reasons.

Types

OTC and Exchange-Traded

In broad terms, there are two groups of derivative contracts, which are distinguished by the way they are traded in the market:

- Over-the-counter (OTC) derivatives are contracts that are traded (and privately negotiated) directly between two parties, without going through an exchange or other intermediary. Products such as swaps, forward rate agreements, exotic options – and other exotic derivatives – are almost always traded in this way. The OTC derivative market is the largest market for derivatives, and is largely unregulated with respect to disclosure of information between the parties, since the OTC market is made up of banks and other highly sophisticated parties, such as hedge funds. Reporting of OTC amounts is difficult because trades can occur in private, without activity being visible on any exchange.

According to the Bank for International Settlements, who first surveyed OTC derivatives in 1995, reported that the "gross market value, which represent the cost of replacing all open contracts at the prevailing market prices, ... increased by 74% since 2004, to $11 trillion at the end of June 2007 (BIS 2007:24)." Positions in the OTC derivatives market increased to $516 trillion at the end of June 2007, 135% higher than the level recorded in 2004. The total outstanding notional amount is US$708 trillion (as of June 2011). Of this total notional amount, 67% are interest rate contracts, 8% are credit default swaps (CDS), 9% are foreign exchange contracts, 2% are commodity contracts, 1% are equity contracts, and 12% are other. Because OTC derivatives are not traded on an exchange, there is no central counter-party. Therefore, they are subject to counterparty risk, like an ordinary contract, since each counter-party relies on the other to perform.

- Exchange-traded derivatives (ETD) are those derivatives instruments that are traded via specialised derivatives exchanges or other exchanges. A derivatives exchange is a market where individuals trade standardized contracts that have been defined by the exchange. A derivatives exchange acts as an intermediary to all related transactions, and takes initial margin from both sides of the trade to act as a guarantee. The world's largest derivatives exchanges (by number of transactions) are the Korea Exchange (which lists KOSPI Index Futures & Options), Eurex (which lists a wide range of European products such as interest rate & index products), and CME Group (made up of the 2007 merger of the Chicago Mercantile Exchange and the Chicago Board of Trade and the 2008 acquisition of the New York Mercantile Exchange). According to BIS, the combined turnover in the world's derivatives exchanges totaled USD 344 trillion during Q4 2005. By December 2007 the Bank for International Settlements reported that "derivatives traded on exchanges surged 27% to a record $681 trillion."

Common Derivative Contract Types

Some of the common variants of derivative contracts are as follows:

1. Forwards: A tailored contract between two parties, where payment takes place at a specific time in the future at today's pre-determined price.
2. Futures: are contracts to buy or sell an asset on or before a future date at a price specified today. A futures contract differs from a forward contract in that the futures contract is a standardized contract written by a clearing house that operates an exchange where the contract can be bought and sold; the forward contract is a non-standardized contract written by the parties themselves.
3. Options are contracts that give the owner the right, but not the obligation, to buy (in the case of a call option) or sell (in the

case of a put option) an asset. The price at which the sale takes place is known as the strike price, and is specified at the time the parties enter into the option. The option contract also specifies a maturity date. In the case of a European option, the owner has the right to require the sale to take place on (but not before) the maturity date; in the case of an American option, the owner can require the sale to take place at any time up to the maturity date. If the owner of the contract exercises this right, the counter-party has the obligation to carry out the transaction. Options are of two types: call option and put option. The buyer of a Call option has a right to buy a certain quantity of the underlying asset, at a specified price on or before a given date in the future, he however has no obligation whatsoever to carry out this right. Similarly, the buyer of a Put option has the right to sell a certain quantity of an underlying asset, at a specified price on or before a given date in the future, he however has no obligation whatsoever to carry out this right.

4. Binary options are contracts that provide the owner with an all-or-nothing profit profile.
5. Warrants: Apart from the commonly used short-dated options which have a maximum maturity period of 1 year, there exists certain long-dated options as well, known as Warrant (finance). These are generally traded over-the-counter.
6. Swaps are contracts to exchange cash (flows) on or before a specified future date based on the underlying value of currencies exchange rates, bonds/interest rates, commodities exchange, stocks or other assets. Another term which is commonly associated to Swap is Swaption which is basically an option on the forward Swap. Similar to a Call and Put option, a Swaption is of two kinds: a receiver Swaption and a payer Swaption. While on one hand, in case of a receiver Swaption there is an option wherein you can receive fixed and pay floating, a payer swaption on the other hand is an option to pay fixed and receive floating.

Swaps can Basically be Categorized into Two Types

- Interest rate swap: These basically necessitate swapping only interest associated cash flows in the same currency, between two parties.
- Currency swap: In this kind of swapping, the cash flow between the two parties includes both principal and interest. Also, the money which is being swapped is in different currency for both parties.

Some common examples of these derivatives are the following:

UNDERLYING	*CONTRACT TYPES*				
	Exchange-traded futures	Exchange-traded options	OTC swap	OTC forward	OTC option
Equity	DJIA Index future Single-stock future	Option on DJIA Index future Single-share option	Equity swap	Back-to-back Repurchase agreement	Stock option Warrant Turbo warrant
Interest rate	Eurodollar future Euribor future	Option on Eurodollar future Option on Euribor future	Interest rate swap	Forward rate agreement	Interest rate cap and floor Swaption Basis swap Bond option
Credit	Bond future	Option on Bond future	Credit default swap Total return swap	Repurchase agreement	Credit default option
Foreign exchange	Currency future	Option on currency future	Currency swap	Currency forward	Currency option
Commodity	WTI crude oil futures	Weather derivative	Commodity swap	Iron ore forward contract	Gold option

Economic Function of the Derivative Market

Some of the salient economic functions of the derivative market include:

1. Prices in a structured derivative market not only replicate the discernment of the market participants about the future but also lead the prices of underlying to the professed future level. On the expiration of the derivative contract, the prices of derivatives congregate with the prices of the underlying. Therefore, derivatives are essential tools to determine both current and future prices.
2. The derivatives market reallocates risk from the people who prefer risk aversion to the people who have an appetite for risk.
3. The intrinsic nature of derivatives market associates them to the underlying Spot market. Due to derivatives there is a considerable increase in trade volumes of the underlying Spot market. The dominant factor behind such an escalation is increased participation by additional players who would not have otherwise participated due to absence of any procedure to transfer risk.
4. As supervision, reconnaissance of the activities of various participants becomes tremendously difficult in assorted markets; the establishment of an organised form of market

becomes all the more imperative. Therefore, in the presence of an organised derivatives market, speculation can be controlled, resulting in a more meticulous environment.

5. Third parties can use publicly available derivative prices as educated predictions of uncertain future outcomes, for example, the likelihood that a corporation will default on its debts.

In a nutshell, there is a substantial increase in savings and investment in the long run due to augmented activities by derivative Market participant.

Valuation

Market and Arbitrage-Free Prices

Two common measures of value are:

- Market price, i.e. the price at which traders are willing to buy or sell the contract
- Arbitrage-free price, meaning that no risk-free profits can be made by trading in these contracts

Determining the Market Price

For exchange-traded derivatives, market price is usually transparent (often published in real time by the exchange, based on all the current bids and offers placed on that particular contract at any one time). Complications can arise with OTC or floor-traded contracts though, as trading is handled manually, making it difficult to automatically broadcast prices. In particular with OTC contracts, there is no central exchange to collate and disseminate prices.

Determining the Arbitrage-Free Price

The arbitrage-free price for a derivatives contract can be complex, and there are many different variables to consider. Arbitrage-free pricing is a central topic of financial mathematics. For futures/forwards the arbitrage free price is relatively straightforward, involving the price of the underlying together with the cost of carry (income received less interest costs), although there can be complexities.

However, for options and more complex derivatives, pricing involves developing a complex pricing model: understanding the stochastic process of the price of the underlying asset is often crucial. A key equation for the theoretical valuation of options is the Black–Scholes formula, which is based on the assumption that the cash flows from a European stock option can be replicated by a continuous buying and selling strategy using only the stock. A simplified version of this valuation technique is the binomial options model.

OTC represents the biggest challenge in using models to price derivatives. Since these contracts are not publicly traded, no market price is available to validate the theoretical valuation. Most of the model's results are input-dependent (meaning the final price depends heavily on how we derive the pricing inputs). Therefore it is common that OTC derivatives are priced by Independent Agents that both counterparties involved in the deal designate upfront (when signing the contract).

Criticisms: Derivatives are often subject to the following criticisms:

Hidden Tail Risk

According to Raghuram Rajan, a former chief economist of the International Monetary Fund (IMF), "... it may well be that the managers of these firms [investment funds] have figured out the correlations between the various instruments they hold and believe they are hedged. Yet as Chan and others (2005) point out, the lessons of summer 1998 following the default on Russian government debt is that correlations that are zero or negative in normal times can turn overnight to one — a phenomenon they term "phase lock-in." A hedged position can become unhedged at the worst times, inflicting substantial losses on those who mistakenly believe they are protected."

Risks

The use of derivatives can result in large losses because of the use of leverage, or borrowing. Derivatives allow investors to earn large returns from small movements in the underlying asset's price. However, investors could lose large amounts if the price of the underlying moves against them significantly. There have been several instances of massive losses in derivative markets, such as the following:

- American International Group (AIG) lost more than US$18 billion through a subsidiary over the preceding three quarters on credit default swaps (CDSs). The United States Federal Reserve Bank announced the creation of a secured credit facility of up to US$85 billion, to prevent the company's collapse by enabling AIG to meet its obligations to deliver additional collateral to its credit default swap trading partners.
- The loss of US$7.2 Billion by Société Générale in January 2008 through mis-use of futures contracts.
- The loss of US$6.4 billion in the failed fund Amaranth Advisors, which was long natural gas in September 2006 when the price plummeted.

- The loss of US$4.6 billion in the failed fund Long-Term Capital Management in 1998.
- The loss of US$1.3 billion equivalent in oil derivatives in 1993 and 1994 by Metallgesellschaft AG.
- The loss of US$1.2 billion equivalent in equity derivatives in 1995 by Barings Bank.
- UBS AG, Switzerland's biggest bank, suffered a $2 billion loss through unauthorized trading discovered in September 2011.

This comes to a staggering $39.5 billion, the majority in the last decade after the Commodity Futures Modernisation Act of 2000 was passed.

Counter Party Risk

Some derivatives (especially swaps) expose investors to counterparty risk, or risk arising from the other party in a financial transaction. Different types of derivatives have different levels of counter party risk. For example, standardized stock options by law require the party at risk to have a certain amount deposited with the exchange, showing that they can pay for any losses; banks that help businesses swap variable for fixed rates on loans may do credit checks on both parties. However, in private agreements between two companies, for example, there may not be benchmarks for performing due diligence and risk analysis.

Large Notional Value

Derivatives typically have a large notional value. As such, there is the danger that their use could result in losses for which the investor would be unable to compensate. The possibility that this could lead to a chain reaction ensuing in an economic crisis was pointed out by famed investor Warren Buffett in Berkshire Hathaway's 2002 annual report. Buffett called them 'financial weapons of mass destruction.' A potential problem with derivatives is that they comprise an increasingly larger notional amount of assets which may lead to distortions in the underlying capital and equities markets themselves. Investors begin to look at the derivatives markets to make a decision to buy or sell securities and so what was originally meant to be a market to transfer risk now becomes a leading indicator.

Financial Reform and Government Regulation

Under US law and the laws of most other developed countries, derivatives have special legal exemptions that make them a particularly attractive legal form to extend credit. The strong creditor protections afforded to derivatives counterparties, in combination with their complexity and lack of transparency however, can cause capital markets to underprice credit risk. This can contribute to credit booms, and increase systemic risks. Indeed, the use of derivatives to conceal credit risk from third parties while protecting derivative counterparties contributed to the financial crisis of 2008 in the United States.

In the context of a 2010 examination of the ICE Trust, an industry self-regulatory body, Gary Gensler, the chairman of the Commodity Futures Trading Commission which regulates most derivatives, was quoted saying that the derivatives marketplace as it functions now "adds up to higher costs to all Americans." More oversight of the banks in this market is needed, he also said. Additionally, the report said, "[t]he Department of Justice is looking into derivatives, too. The department's antitrust unit is actively investigating 'the possibility of anticompetitive practices in the credit derivatives clearing, trading and information services industries,' according to a department spokeswoman."

For legislators and committees responsible for financial reform related to derivatives in the United States and elsewhere, distinguishing between hedging and speculative derivatives activities has been a nontrivial challenge. The distinction is critical because regulation should help to isolate and curtail speculation with derivatives, especially for "systemically significant" institutions whose default could be large enough to threaten the entire financial system. At the same time, the legislation should allow for responsible parties to hedge risk without unduly tying up working capital as collateral that firms may better employ elsewhere in their operations and investment. In this regard, it is important to distinguish between financial (e.g. banks) and non-financial end-users of derivatives (e.g. real estate development companies) because these firms' derivatives usage is inherently different. More importantly, the reasonable collateral that secures these different counterparties can be very different. The distinction between these firms is not always straight forward (e.g. hedge funds or even some private equity firms do not neatly fit either category). Finally, even financial users must be differentiated, as 'large' banks may classified as "systemically significant" whose derivatives activities must be more tightly monitored and restricted than those of smaller, local and regional banks.

Over-the-counter dealing will be less common as the Dodd–Frank Wall Street Reform and Consumer Protection Act comes into effect. The law mandated the clearing of certain swaps at registered exchanges and imposed various restrictions on derivatives. To implement Dodd-

Frank, the CFTC developed new rules in at least 30 areas. The Commission determines which swaps are subject to mandatory clearing and whether a derivatives exchange is eligible to clear a certain type of swap contract.

Nonetheless, the above and other challenges of the rule-making process have delayed full enactment of aspects of the legislation relating to derivatives. The challenges are further complicated by the necessity to orchestrate globalized financial reform among the nations that comprise the world's major financial markets, a primary responsibility of the Financial Stability Board whose progress is ongoing.

In the U.S., by February 2012 the combined effort of the SEC and CFTC had produced over 70 proposed and final derivatives rules. However, both of them had delayed adoption of a number of derivatives regulations because of the burden of other rulemaking, litigation and opposition to the rules, and many core definitions (such as the terms "swap," "security-based swap," "swap dealer," "security-based swap dealer," "major swap participant" and "major security-based swap participant") had still not been adopted. SEC Chairman Mary Schapiro opined: "At the end of the day, it probably does not make sense to harmonize everything [between the SEC and CFTC rules] because some of these products are quite different and certainly the market structures are quite different."

In November 2012, the SEC and regulators from Australia, Brazil, the European Union, Hong Kong, Japan, Ontario, Quebec, Singapore, and Switzerland met to discuss reforming the OTC derivatives market, as had been agreed by leaders at the 2009 G-20 Pittsburgh summit in September 2009. In December 2012, they released a joint statement to the effect that they recognised that the market is a global one and "firmly support the adoption and enforcement of robust and consistent standards in and across jurisdictions", with the goals of mitigating risk, improving transparency, protecting against market abuse, preventing regulatory gaps, reducing the potential for arbitrage opportunities, and fostering a level playing field for market participants. They also agreed on the need to reduce regulatory uncertainty and provide market participants with sufficient clarity on laws and regulations by avoiding, to the extent possible, the application of conflicting rules to the same entities and transactions, and minimizing the application of inconsistent and duplicative rules. At the same time, they noted that "complete harmonization – perfect alignment of rules across jurisdictions" would be difficult, because of jurisdictions' differences in law, policy, markets, implementation timing, and legislative and regulatory processes. On December 20, 2013 the CFTC provided information on its swaps regulation "comparability" determinations. The release addressed the CFTC's cross-border compliance exceptions. Specifically it addressed which entity level and in some cases transaction-level requirements in six jurisdictions (Australia, Canada, the European Union, Hong Kong, Japan, and Switzerland) it found comparable to its own rules, thus permitting non-US swap dealers, major swap participants, and the foreign branches of US Swap Dealers and major swap participants in these jurisdictions to comply with local rules in lieu of Commission rules.

Reporting

Mandatory reporting regulations are being finalized in a number of countries, such as Dodd Frank Act in the US, the European Market Infrastructure Regulations (EMIR) in Europe, as well as regulations in Hong Kong, Japan, Singapore, Canada, and other countries. The OTC Derivatives Regulators Forum (ODRF), a group of over 40 world-wide regulators, provided trade repositories with a set of guidelines regarding data access to regulators, and the Financial Stability Board and CPSS IOSCO also made recommendations in with regard to reporting.

DTCC, through its "Global Trade Repository" (GTR) service, manages global trade repositories for interest rates, and commodities, foreign exchange, credit, and equity derivatives. It makes global trade reports to the CFTC in the U.S., and plans to do the same for ESMA in Europe and for regulators in Hong Kong, Japan, and Singapore. It covers cleared and uncleared OTC derivatives products, whether or not a trade is electronically processed or bespoke.

Value at Risk

In financial mathematics and financial risk management, value at risk (VaR) is a widely used risk measure of the risk of loss on a specific portfolio of financial assets. For a given portfolio, time horizon, and probability p, the $100p\%$ VaR is defined as a threshold loss value, such that the probability that the loss on the portfolio over the given time horizon exceeds this value is p. This assumes mark-to-market pricing, normal markets, and no trading in the portfolio.

For example, if a portfolio of stocks has a one-day 5% VaR of $1 million, there is a 0.05 probability that the portfolio will fall in value by more than $1 million over a one day period if there is no trading. Informally, a loss of $1 million or more on this portfolio is expected on

1 day out of 20 days (because of 5% probability). A loss which exceeds the VaR threshold is termed a "VaR break."

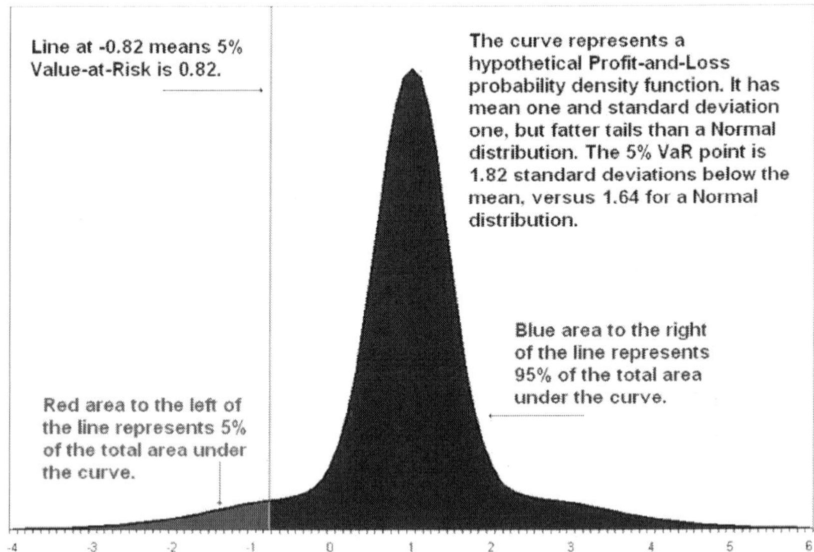

Figure: *The 5% Value at Risk of a hypothetical profit-and-loss probability density function*

VaR has four main uses in finance: risk management, financial control, financial reporting and computing regulatory capital. VaR is sometimes used in non-financial applications as well.

Important related ideas are economic capital, backtesting, stress testing, expected shortfall, and tail conditional expectation.

Details

Common parameters for VaR are 1% and 5% probabilities and one day and two week horizons, although other combinations are in use.

The reason for assuming normal markets and no trading, and to restricting loss to things measured in daily accounts, is to make the loss observable. In some extreme financial events it can be impossible to determine losses, either because market prices are unavailable or because the loss-bearing institution breaks up. Some longer-term consequences of disasters, such as lawsuits, loss of market confidence and employee morale and impairment of brand names can take a long time to play out, and may be hard to allocate among specific prior decisions. VaR marks the boundary between normal days and extreme events. Institutions can lose far more than the VaR amount; all that can be said is that they will not do so very often.

The probability level is about equally often specified as one minus the probability of a VaR break, so that the VaR in the example above would be called a one-day 95% VaR instead of one-day 5% VaR. This generally does not lead to confusion because the probability of VaR breaks is almost always small, certainly less than 0.5.

Although it virtually always represents a loss, VaR is conventionally reported as a positive number. A negative VaR would imply the portfolio has a high probability of making a profit, for example a one-day 5% VaR of negative $1 million implies the portfolio has a 95% chance of making more than $1 million over the next day.

Another inconsistency is that VaR is sometimes taken to refer to profit-and-loss at the end of the period, and sometimes as the maximum loss at any point during the period. The original definition was the latter, but in the early 1990s when VaR was aggregated across trading desks and time zones, end-of-day valuation was the only reliable number so the former became the *de facto* definition. As people began using multiday VaRs in the second half of the 1990s, they almost always estimated the distribution at the end of the period only. It is also easier theoretically to deal with a point-in-time estimate versus a maximum over an interval. Therefore the end-of-period definition is the most common both in theory and practice today.

Varieties of VaR

The definition of VaR is nonconstructive; it specifies a property VaR must have, but not how to compute VaR. Moreover, there is wide scope for interpretation in the definition. This has led to two broad types of VaR, one used primarily in risk management and the other primarily for risk measurement. The distinction is not sharp, however, and hybrid versions are typically used in financial control, financial reporting and computing regulatory capital.

To a risk manager, VaR is a system, not a number. The system is run periodically (usually daily) and the published number is compared to the computed price movement in opening positions over the time horizon. There is never any subsequent adjustment to the published VaR, and there is no distinction between VaR breaks caused by input errors (including Information Technology breakdowns, fraud and rogue trading), computation errors (including failure to produce a VaR on time) and market movements.

A frequentist claim is made, that the long-term frequency of VaR breaks will equal the specified probability, within the limits of sampling error, and that the VaR breaks will be independent in time and independent of the level of VaR. This claim is validated by a backtest, a comparison of published VaRs to actual price movements. In this interpretation, many different systems could produce VaRs with equally good backtests, but wide disagreements on daily VaR values.

For risk measurement a number is needed, not a system. A Bayesian probability claim is made, that given the information and beliefs at the time, the subjective probability of a VaR break was the specified level. VaR is adjusted after the fact to correct errors in inputs and computation, but not to incorporate information unavailable at the time of computation. In this context, "backtest" has a different meaning. Rather than comparing published VaRs to actual market movements over the period of time the system has been in operation, VaR is retroactively computed on scrubbed data over as long a period as data are available and deemed relevant. The same position data and pricing models are used for computing the VaR as determining the price movements.

Although some of the sources listed here treat only one kind of VaR as legitimate, most of the recent ones seem to agree that risk management VaR is superior for making short-term and tactical decisions today, while risk measurement VaR should be used for understanding the past, and making medium term and strategic decisions for the future. When VaR is used for financial control or financial reporting it should incorporate elements of both. For example, if a trading desk is held to a VaR limit, that is both a risk-management rule for deciding what risks to allow today, and an input into the risk measurement computation of the desk's risk-adjusted return at the end of thc reporting period.

VaR in Governance

VaR can also be applied to governance of endowments, trusts, and pension plans. Essentially trustees adopt portfolio Values-at-Risk metrics for the entire pooled account and the diversified parts individually managed. Instead of probability estimates they simply define maximum levels of acceptable loss for each. Doing so provides an easy metric for oversight and adds accountability as managers are then directed to manage, but with the additional constraint to avoid losses within a defined risk parameter. VaR utilised in this manner adds relevance as well as an easy way to monitor risk measurement control far more intuitive than Standard Deviation of Return. Use of VaR in this context, as well as a worthwhile critique on board governance practices as it relates to investment management oversight in general can be found in *Best Practices in Governance.*

Mathematical Definition

Given a confidence level $\alpha \in (0,1)$, the VaR of the portfolio at the confidence level α is given by the smallest number l such that the probability that the loss Lexceeds is at most $(1-\alpha)$. Mathematically, if L is the loss of a portfolio, then $\mathrm{VaR}_\alpha(L)$ is the level α-quantile, i.e.

$$\mathrm{VaR}_\alpha(L) = \inf\{l \in \mathbb{R} : P(L > l) \leq 1-\alpha\} = \inf\{l \in \mathbb{R} : F_L(l) \geq \alpha\}.$$

The left equality is a definition of VaR. The right equality assumes an underlying probability distribution, which makes it true only for parametric VaR. Risk managers typically assume that some fraction of the bad events will have undefined losses, either because markets are closed or illiquid, or because the entity bearing the loss breaks apart or loses the ability to compute accounts. Therefore, they do not accept results based on the assumption of a well-defined probability distribution. Nassim Taleb has labelled this assumption, "charlatanism." On the other hand, many academics prefer to assume a well-defined distribution, albeit usually one with fat tails. This point has probably caused more contention among VaR theorists than any other.

Value of Risks can also be written as a distortion risk measure given by the distortion function $g(x) = \begin{cases} 0 & \text{if } 0 \leq x < 1-\alpha \\ 1 & \text{if } 1-\alpha \leq x \leq 1 \end{cases}$.

Risk Measure and Risk Metric

The term "VaR" is used both for a risk measure and a risk metric. This sometimes leads to confusion. Sources earlier than 1995 usually emphasize the risk measure, later sources are more likely to emphasize the metric.

The VaR risk measure defines risk as mark-to-market loss on a fixed portfolio over a fixed time horizon, assuming normal markets. There are many alternative risk measures in finance. Instead of mark-to-market, which uses market prices to define loss, loss is often defined as change in fundamental value. For example, if an institution holds a loan that declines in market price because interest rates go up, but has no change in cash flows or credit quality, some systems do not recognise a loss. Or we could try to incorporate the economic cost of things not measured in daily financial statements, such as loss of market confidence or employee morale, impairment of brand names or lawsuits.

Rather than assuming a fixed portfolio over a fixed time horizon, some risk measures incorporate the effect of expected trading (such as a stop loss order) and consider the expected holding period of positions. Finally, some risk measures adjust for the possible effects of abnormal markets, rather than excluding them from the computation.

The VaR risk metric summarizes the distribution of possible losses by a quantile, a point with a specified probability of greater losses. Common alternative metrics are standard deviation, mean absolute deviation, expected shortfall and downside risk.

VaR Risk Management

Supporters of VaR-based risk management claim the first and possibly greatest benefit of VaR is the improvement in systems and modelling it forces on an institution. In 1997, Philippe Jorion wrote:

[T]he greatest benefit of VAR lies in the imposition of a structured methodology for critically thinking about risk. Institutions that go through the process of computing their VAR are forced to confront their exposure to financial risks and to set up a proper risk management function. Thus the process of getting to VAR may be as important as the number itself.

Publishing a daily number, on-time and with specified statistical properties holds every part of a trading organisation to a high objective standard. Robust backup systems and default assumptions must be implemented. Positions that are reported, modelled or priced incorrectly stand out, as do data feeds that are inaccurate or late and systems that are too-frequently down. Anything that affects profit and loss that is left out of other reports will show up either in inflated VaR or excessive VaR breaks. "A risk-taking institution that *does not* compute VaR might escape disaster, but an institution that *cannot* compute VaR will not."

The second claimed benefit of VaR is that it separates risk into two regimes. Inside the VaR limit, conventional statistical methods are reliable. Relatively short-term and specific data can be used for analysis. Probability estimates are meaningful, because there are enough data to test them. In a sense, there is no true risk because you have a sum of many independent observations with a left bound on the outcome. A casino doesn't worry about whether red or black will come up on the next roulette spin. Risk managers encourage productive risk-taking in this regime, because there is little true cost. People tend to worry too much about these risks, because they happen frequently, and not enough about what might happen on the worst days.

Outside the VaR limit, all bets are off. Risk should be analyzed with stress testing based on long-term and broad market data. Probability statements are no longer meaningful. Knowing the distribution of losses beyond the VaR point is both impossible and useless. The risk manager should concentrate instead on making sure good plans are in place to limit the loss if possible, and to survive the loss if not.

One specific system uses three regimes.

1. One to three times VaR are normal occurrences. You expect periodic VaR breaks. The loss distribution typically has fat tails, and you might get more than one break in a short period of time. Moreover, markets may be abnormal and trading may exacerbate losses, and you may take losses not measured in daily marks such as lawsuits, loss of employee morale and market confidence and impairment of brand names. So an institution that can't deal with three times VaR losses as routine events probably won't survive long enough to put a VaR system in place.
2. Three to ten times VaR is the range for stress testing. Institutions should be confident they have examined all the foreseeable events that will cause losses in this range, and are prepared to survive them. These events are too rare to estimate probabilities reliably, so risk/return calculations are useless.
3. Foreseeable events should not cause losses beyond ten times VaR. If they do they should be hedged or insured, or the business plan should be changed to avoid them, or VaR should be increased. It's hard to run a business if foreseeable losses are orders of magnitude larger than very large everyday losses. It's hard to plan for these events, because they are out of scale with daily experience. Of course there will be unforeseeable losses more than ten times VaR, but it's pointless to anticipate them, you can't know much about them and it results in needless worrying. Better to hope that the discipline of preparing for all foreseeable three-to-ten times VaR losses will improve chances for surviving the unforeseen and larger losses that inevitably occur.

"A risk manager has two jobs: make people take more risk the 99% of the time it is safe to do so, and survive the other 1% of the time. VaR is the border."

Computation Methods

VaR can be estimated either parametrically (for example, variance-covariance VaR or delta-gamma VaR) or nonparametrically (for examples, historical simulation VaR or resampled VaR). Nonparametric methods of VaR estimation are discussed in Markovich and Novak.

A McKinsey report published in May 2012 estimated that 85% of large banks were using historical simulation. The other 15% used Monte Carlo methods.

History of VaR

The problem of risk measurement is an old one in statistics, economics and finance. Financial risk management has been a concern of regulators and financial executives for a long time as well. Retrospective analysis has found some VaR-like concepts in this history. But VaR did not emerge as a distinct concept until the late 1980s. The triggering event was the stock market crash of 1987. This was the first major financial crisis in which a lot of academically-trained quants were in high enough positions to worry about firm-wide survival.

The crash was so unlikely given standard statistical models, that it called the entire basis of quant finance into question. A reconsideration of history led some quants to decide there were recurring crises, about one or two per decade, that overwhelmed the statistical assumptions embedded in models used for trading, investment management and derivative pricing. These affected many markets at once, including ones that were usually not correlated, and seldom had discernible economic cause or warning (although after-the-fact explanations were plentiful). Much later, they were named "Black Swans" by Nassim Taleb and the concept extended far beyond finance.

If these events were included in quantitative analysis they dominated results and led to strategies that did not work day to day. If these events were excluded, the profits made in between "Black Swans" could be much smaller than the losses suffered in the crisis. Institutions could fail as a result.

VaR was developed as a systematic way to segregate extreme events, which are studied qualitatively over long-term history and broad market events, from everyday price movements, which are studied quantitatively using short-term data in specific markets. It was hoped that "Black Swans" would be preceded by increases in estimated VaR or increased frequency of VaR breaks, in at least some markets. The extent to which this has proven to be true is controversial.

Abnormal markets and trading were excluded from the VaR estimate in order to make it observable. It is not always possible to define loss if, for example, markets are closed as after 9/11, or severely illiquid, as happened several times in 2008. Losses can also be hard to define if the risk-bearing institution fails or breaks up. A measure that depends on traders taking certain actions, and avoiding other actions, can lead to self reference.

This is risk management VaR. It was well established in quantitative trading groups at several financial institutions, notably Bankers Trust, before 1990, although neither the name nor the definition had been standardized. There was no effort to aggregate VaRs across trading desks.

The financial events of the early 1990s found many firms in trouble because the same underlying bet had been made at many places in the firm, in non-obvious ways. Since many trading desks already computed risk management VaR, and it was the only common risk measure that could be both defined for all businesses and aggregated without strong assumptions, it was the natural choice for reporting firmwide risk. J. P. Morgan CEO Dennis Weatherstone famously called for a "4:15 report" that combined all firm risk on one page, available within 15 minutes of the market close.

Risk measurement VaR was developed for this purpose. Development was most extensive at J. P. Morgan, which published the methodology and gave free access to estimates of the necessary underlying parameters in 1994. This was the first time VaR had been exposed beyond a relatively small group of quants. Two years later, the methodology was spun off into an independent for-profit business now part of RiskMetrics Group.

In 1997, the U.S. Securities and Exchange Commission ruled that public corporations must disclose quantitative information about their derivatives activity. Major banks and dealers chose to implement the rule by including VaR information in the notes to their financial statements.

Worldwide adoption of the Basel II Accord, beginning in 1999 and nearing completion today, gave further impetus to the use of VaR. VaR is the preferred measure of market risk, and concepts similar to VaR are used in other parts of the accord.

Criticism

VaR has been controversial since it moved from trading desks into the public eye in 1994. A famous 1997 debate between Nassim Taleb and Philippe Jorion set out some of the major points of contention. Taleb claimed VaR:

1. Ignored 2,500 years of experience in favour of untested models built by non-traders

2. Was charlatanism because it claimed to estimate the risks of rare events, which is impossible
3. Gave false confidence
4. Would be exploited by traders

In 2008 David Einhorn and Aaron Brown debated VaR in Global Association of Risk Professionals Review Einhorn compared VaR to "an airbag that works all the time, except when you have a car accident." He further charged that VaR:

1. Led to excessive risk-taking and leverage at financial institutions
2. Focused on the manageable risks near the centre of the distribution and ignored the tails
3. Created an incentive to take "excessive but remote risks"
4. Was "potentially catastrophic when its use creates a false sense of security among senior executives and watchdogs."

New York Times reporter Joe Nocera wrote an extensive piece Risk Mismanagement on January 4, 2009 discussing the role VaR played in the Financial crisis of 2007-2008. After interviewing risk managers (including several of the ones cited above) the article suggests that VaR was very useful to risk experts, but nevertheless exacerbated the crisis by giving false security to bank executives and regulators. A powerful tool for professional risk managers, VaR is portrayed as both easy to misunderstand, and dangerous when misunderstood.

Taleb, in 2009, testified in Congress asking for the banning of VaR on two arguments, the first that "tail risks are non-measurable" scientifically and the second is that for anchoring reasons VaR for leading to higher risk taking.

A common complaint among academics is that VaR is not subadditive. That means the VaR of a combined portfolio can be larger than the sum of the VaRs of its components. To a practising risk manager this makes sense. For example, the average bank branch in the United States is robbed about once every ten years. A single-branch bank has about 0.0004% chance of being robbed on a specific day, so the risk of robbery would not figure into one-day 1% VaR. It would not even be within an order of magnitude of that, so it is in the range where the institution should not worry about it, it should insure against it and take advice from insurers on precautions. The whole point of insurance is to aggregate risks that are beyond individual VaR limits, and bring them into a large enough portfolio to get statistical predictability. It does not pay for a one-branch bank to have a security expert on staff. As institutions get more branches, the risk of a robbery on a specific day rises to within an order of magnitude of VaR. At that point it makes sense for the institution to run internal stress tests and analyze the risk itself. It will spend less on insurance and more on in-house expertise. For a very large banking institution, robberies are a routine daily occurrence. Losses are part of the daily VaR calculation, and tracked statistically rather than case-by-case. A sizable in-house security department is in charge of prevention and control, the general risk manager just tracks the loss like any other cost of doing business.

As portfolios or institutions get larger, specific risks change from low-probability/low-predictability/high-impact to statistically predictable losses of low individual impact. That means they move from the range of far outside VaR, to be insured, to near outside VaR, to be analyzed case-by-case, to inside VaR, to be treated statistically.

Even VaR supporters generally agree there are common abuses of VaR:

1. Referring to VaR as a "worst-case" or "maximum tolerable" loss. In fact, you expect two or three losses per year that exceed one-day 1% VaR.
2. Making VaR control or VaR reduction the central concern of risk management. It is far more important to worry about what happens when losses exceed VaR.
3. Assuming plausible losses will be less than some multiple, often three, of VaR. The entire point of VaR is that losses can be extremely large, and sometimes impossible to define, once you get beyond the VaR point. To a risk manager, VaR is the level of losses at which you stop trying to guess what will happen next, and start preparing for anything.
4. Reporting a VaR that has not passed a backtest. Regardless of how VaR is computed, it should have produced the correct number of breaks (within sampling error) in the past. A common specific violation of this is to report a VaR based on the unverified assumption that everything follows a multivariate normal distribution.

VaR, CVaR and EvaR

The VaR is not a coherent risk measure since it violates the sub-additivity property, which is

$$\text{If } X, Y \in \mathbf{L}, \text{ then } \rho(X+Y) \leq \rho(X) + \rho(Y).$$

However, it can be bounded by coherent risk measures like Conditional Value-at-Risk (CVaR) or entropic value at risk (EVaR). In fact, for $X \in \mathbf{L}_{M^+}$ (with $\mathbf{L}_{M^+}$ the set of all Borel measurable functions whose moment-generating function exists for all positive real values) we have

$$\mathrm{VaR}_{1-\alpha}(X) \le \mathrm{CVaR}_{1-\alpha}(X) \le \mathrm{EVaR}_{1-\alpha}(X),$$

where

$$\mathrm{VaR}_{1-\alpha}(X) := \inf_{t \in \mathbf{R}} \{t : \Pr(X \le t) \ge 1-\alpha\},$$

$$\mathrm{CVaR}_{1-\alpha}(X) := \frac{1}{\alpha} \int_0^\alpha \mathrm{VaR}_{1-\gamma}(X) d\gamma,$$

$$\mathrm{EVaR}_{1-\alpha}(X) := \inf_{z>0} \{z^{-1} \ln(M_X(z)/\alpha)\},$$

in which $M_X(z)$ is the moment-generating function of X at z. In the above equations the variable denotes the financial loss, rather than wealth as is typically the case.

Dynamic Financial Analysis

Dynamic financial analysis (DFA) is a simulation approach that looks at an insurance enterprise's risks holistically as opposed to traditional actuarial analysis, which analyzes risks individually. Specifically, DFA reveals the dependencies of hazards and their impacts on the insurance company's financial well being such as business mix, reinsurance, asset allocation, profitability, solvency, and compliance.

In addition to projecting stochastic future economic scenarios through using scenario generators such as interest rate, underwriting cycle and jurisdictional risk models, DFA also links the scenarios with the financial models of the targeted insurance company that is being analyzed. Such models not only reveal the operation and the business structure of the company, but also uncover the dependencies among its business practices. Because DFA tries to account for every aspect of the company, it produces a vast amount of data. As a result, analyzing and presenting the outputs effectively is of great importance.

Objectives

DFA is used primarily by financial practitioners to manage profitability and financial stability (the risk control function of DFA) Not only do DFA users seek to maximize shareholder values, but they also try to maintain customer values. Furthermore, outputs from DFA could help managers identify strengths and weaknesses of the following areas.

- Business mix: estimates relative and absolute value of each line of business (e.g. premium and commission level) compared to the company's financial.
- Reinsurance: uncovers the structure of the company's line of businesses such as contract types, interrelation among contracts, and cost of reinsurance.
- Asset allocation: determines whether a company is taking on too much investment risk, which could be minimized through diversification of investments.
- Profitability: measures the profitability of the company's each line of business.
- Solvency: reveals liquidity problems, which are mismatches of cash flows that a company might experience if it did not have enough cash to immediately meet financial obligations.
- Compliance: assesses the likelihood of insurance regulators intervening the company's business due to change in regulations or deteriorating business operations.
- Sensitivity: explores the company's reaction to a change in strategies and economic conditions in the future.
- Dependency: uncovers dependencies of all kinds of risks that are hard to understand without a holistic modelling and analysis tool.

Elements

DFA consists of the following 3 parts:

- Scenarios, generating expected and extreme economic scenarios to assess the company's reaction to changes
- Business Models, quantifying the company's business models and uncovering the dependencies among them
- Analysis Presentation, presenting the analysis to the executives who make strategic decisions

Careful calibration is required to ensure the accuracy of the scenarios and the correlations among business models.

Scenario

The scenario generator must meet the following criteria:

- Generate individual risks while keeping track of their dependencies with one another and with time (e.g., an increase in the price of gasoline might lead to less driving mileages of automobile policy holders, thus leading to fewer car accidents).

- Produce both normal and abnormal behaviour of the risk factors (e.g., a 1% change in S&P index is normal; a 40% change is extreme).
- Simulate stochastic scenarios, meaning that scenarios are not the same every time you run the analysis.
- Assign mathematical models that best imitate the behaviours of the risk factors. Such models could be found in, though not exclusively, actuarial science, finance and economic disciplines.
- Track the incurred losses and the development of the losses, specifically the cash flows of the company's operation. This may help managers recognise the need to implement better asset liability management strategies.

Interest Rate Generator

The interest rate generator is the core fundamental of DFA. Many sophisticated interest rate models were created in the effort to best imitate the real world interest rate behaviour. Although none of the existing models are perfect, they have their own advantages and disadvantages. The following is a simple interest rate model used in a publicly access DFA model.

Cox, Ingersoll, and Ross (CIR) Interest Rate Generator

The CIR interest rate model characterizes the short term interest rate as a mean-reverting stochastic projection. Although CIR was first used to project continuous changes in the interest rates, it is also acceptable to use it to project discrete changes from one time period to another. Below is the formula.

$$dr_t = a(b - r_t)dt + \sigma\sqrt{r_t}\,dW_t$$

where

- b = the long-run mean to which the interest rate reverts; the expected interest rate in the long run
- a = the speed of reversion of the interest rate to its long-run mean (e.g., a = 2 means the interest is expected to return to its long term mean within half a year, and a = 1/5 means it would take 5 years).
- r_t = the current short-term interest rate
- σ= the volatility of the interest rate process expressed as the standard deviation of historical or projected interest rate changes.

The CIR model has two components: a deterministic $a(b - r_t)$ and a stochastic part $\sigma\sqrt{r_t}$. The deterministic part will go in the reverse direction of what the current short term rate is heading. In other words, the further the current interest rate is from the long term expected rate, the harder the deterministic part tries to reverse it back to the long term mean.

The stochastic part is purely random; it can either help the current interest rate deviate from its long term mean or the reverse. Because this part is multiplied by the square root of the current interest rate, when the current interest rate is low, its impact is minimum, thus leading to the unlikelihood of the interest rate going below zero, and the interest rate cannot be negative. However, the reverse is true if the current rate is high.

Jurisdictional Risk Generator

In the United States, each state has its own regulatory, jurisdictional and legislative bodies, and there are advantages and disadvantages for an insurance company conducting businesses in different states. For example, some states have restrictions on how much rate increase that an insurance company can charge for the risks on which it takes. Such risk can severely hamper the insurance entity's profitability and operation.

In DFA, jurisdiction risk is reflected in two ways.

1. "Acceptable" rate changes: each state has its own limit for how much rate increase in percentage proportional to the existing rate an insurance company can charge without attracting regulators' scrutiny. Under the scenarios, if DFA indicates that the insurance company needs to charge more than the state's maximum limit for the risks, that should raise a red flag to the executives overseeing the insurance business in that region.
2. Lag in implementing indicated rate changes: insurance companies often do not immediately implement the approved rate changes, and in fact there is often a lag of 3 to 6 months. The lag, shown in the model in terms of years, is longer in states with harsh rate regulation.

Underwriting Cycles Generator

The number of policies an insurance company can sell depends on the macroeconomic environment of the insurance industry. The DFA scenario accounts for this risk factor to best simulate the nature of insurance business.

Below are four underwriting cycles that an insurance company may experience.

- *Mature Hard:* Rates can be increased and may still sell more policies
- *Mature Soft:* Rates need to be decrease in order to sell more policies
- *Immature Hard:* Transition state from mature soft to mature hard
- *Immature Soft:* Transition state from mature hard to mature soft

Company and Strategy Modelling

To estimate the impacts that the scenarios have on an insurance company, the company's business practices needed to be quantified and linked to the scenario factors such as interest rate and underwriting cycles.

Types of Models

- *Cash Flow Oriented Model*: Such model tries to imitate the cash flows of the insurance company's assets and liabilities. Also it assess the impacts on the company's financial statement.
  - o Advantages: It might not be difficult to project cash flows linked to economic factors for the company's assets.
  - o Disadvantages: Liabilities are often unknown for an insurance company, and thus it is hard to generate outgoing cash flows for claims.
- *Simple Model*: Such model only account for part of the economic factors of the scenarios
  - o Advantages: The model is mathematically tractable, and accuracy can be achieved.
  - o Disadvantages: It defeats the purpose of implementing a DFA, which is to analyze potential impacts that changes in economic factors can have on the insurance company's financial performance.
- *Complex Model*: Such model not only tries to account for all the economic factors that the scenarios generate, but also the dependencies among the company's lines of business. It involves sophisticated mathematical models and parameter to achieve its goal.
  - o Advantages: This approach helps executives truly understand the dependencies among its business models and the external impacts on the company's profitability.

- o Disadvantages: Such model is very unlikely to be mathematically tractable. In other words, the model can be totally wrong because no one may know the exact dependencies among the business models and the impacts that economic risks can pose to the company.

Analysis and Presentation

Without effective analysis and presentation, managers can hardly make any sense out of the vast amount of data that DFA produces. The goal of DFA is to help the managers to find out whether the company's current strategies are in line with its financial goals. Below are some tricks of conducting and presenting DFA analysis.

1. Keep communication concise and focused.
2. Eliminate, if needed, part of the DFA's outputs that are irrelevant to the company's financial objectives.
3. Include no more than four most important results in a brief executive summary, and support your statements with graphs and exhibits in the appendix.
4. Focus on business development trend, as opposed to over emphasis on specific numbers or the details of the model. Keep in mind that DFA is only an estimate of what might happen.
5. Support the DFA analysis with other available information within the company.

Financial Statement Analysis

Financial statement analysis (or financial analysis) is the process of reviewing and analyzing a company's financial statements to make better economic decisions. These statements include the income statement, balance sheet, statement of cash flows, and a statement of retained earnings. Financial statement analysis is a method or process involving specific techniques for evaluating risks, performance, financial health, and future prospects of an organisation.

It is used by a variety of stakeholders, such as credit and equity investors, the government, the public, and decision-makers within the organisation. These stakeholders have different interests and apply a variety of different techniques to meet their needs. For example, equity investors are interested in the long-term earnings power of the organisation and perhaps the sustainability and growth of dividend payments. Creditors want to ensure the interest and principal is paid on the organisations debt securities (e.g., bonds) when due.

Common methods of financial statement analysis include fundamental analysis, DuPont analysis, horizontal and vertical analysis and the use of financial ratios. Historical information combined with a series of assumptions and adjustments to the financial information may be used to project future performance. The Chartered Financial Analyst designation in available for professional financial analysts.

History

Benjamin Graham and David Dodd first published their influential book "Security Analysis" in 1934. A central premise of their book is that the market's pricing mechanism for financial securities such as stocks and bonds is based upon faulty and irrational analytical processes performed by many market participants. This results in the market price of a security only occasionally coinciding with the intrinsic value around which the price tends to fluctuate. Investor Warren Buffett is a well-known supporter of Graham and Dodd's philosophy.

The Graham and Dodd approach is referred to as Fundamental analysis and includes: 1) Economic analysis; 2) Industry analysis; and 3) Company analysis. The latter is the primary realm of financial statement analysis. On the basis of these three analyses the intrinsic value of the security is determined.

Horizontal and Vertical Analysis

Horizontal analysis compares financial information over time, typically from past quarters or years. Horizontal analysis is performed by comparing financial data from a past statement, such as the income statement. When comparing this past information one will want to look for variations such as higher or lower earnings.

Vertical analysis is a proportional analysis of financial statements. Each line item listed in the financial statement is listed as the percentage of another line item. For example, on an income statement each line item will be listed as a percentage of gross sales. This technique is also referred to as normalization or common-sizing.

Financial Ratio Analysis

Financial ratios are very powerful tools to perform some quick analysis of financial statements. There are four main categories of ratios: liquidity ratios, profitability ratios, activity ratios and leverage ratios. These are typically analyzed over time and across competitors in an industry.

- *Liquidity ratios* are used to determine how quickly a company can turn its assets into cash if it experiences financial difficulties or bankruptcy. It essentially is a measure of a company's ability to remain in business. A few common liquidity ratios are the current ratio and the liquidity index. The current ratio is current assets/current liabilities and measures how much liquidity is available to pay for liabilities. The liquidity index shows how quickly a company can turn assets into cash and is calculated by: (Trade receivables x Days to liquidate) + (Inventory x Days to liquidate)/Trade Receivables + Inventory.

- *Profitability ratios* are ratios that demonstrate how profitable a company is. A few popular profitability ratios are the breakeven point and gross profit ratio. The breakeven point calculates how much cash a company must generate to break even with their start up costs. The gross profit ratio is equal to (revenue - the cost of goods sold)/revenue. This ratio shows a quick snapshot of expected revenue.
- *Activity ratios* are meant to show how well management is managing the company's resources. Two common activity ratios are accounts payable turnover and accounts receivable turnover. These ratios demonstrate how long it takes for a company to pay off its accounts payable and how long it takes for a company to receive payments, respectively.
- *Leverage ratios* depict how much a company relies upon its debt to fund operations. A very common leverage ratio used for financial statement analysis is the debt-to-equity ratio. This ratio shows the extent to which management is willing to use debt in order to fund operations. This ratio is calculated as: (Long-term debt + Short-term debt + Leases)/ Equity.

DuPont analysis uses several financial ratios that multiplied together equal return on equity, a measure of how much income the firm earns divided by the amount of funds invested (equity).

A Dividend discount model (DDM) may also be used to value a company's stock price based on the theory that its stock is worth the sum of all of its future dividend payments, discounted back to their present value. In other words, it is used to value stocks based on the net present value of the future dividends.

Financial statement analyses are typically performed in spreadsheet software and summarized in a variety of formats.

Recasting Financial Statements

Investors typically are attempting to understand how much cash the company will generate in the future and its rate of profit growth, relative to the amount of capital deployed. Analysts may modify ("recast") the financial statements by adjusting the underlying assumptions to aid in this computation. For example, operating leases (treated like a rental transaction) may be recast as capital leases (indicating ownership), adding assets and liabilities to the balance sheet. This affects the financial statement ratios.

Recasting financial statements requires a solid understanding of accounting theory. Once the cash flow in future years is projected, a discount rate or interest rate will be applied to measure the value of the company and its stock or debt.

Certifications

Financial analysts typically have finance and accounting education at the undergraduate or graduate level. Persons may earn the Chartered Financial Analyst (CFA) designation through a series of challenging examinations.

Portfolio Optimization

Portfolio optimization is the process of choosing the proportions of various assets to be held in a portfolio, in such a way as to the portfolio better than any other according to some criterion. The criterion will combine, directly or indirectly, considerations of the expected value of the portfolio's rate of return as well as of the return's dispersion and possibly other measures of financial risk.

Efficient Portfolios

Modern portfolio theory, fathered by Harry Markowitz in the 1950s, assumes that an investor wants to maximize a portfolio's expected return contingent on any given amount of risk, with risk measured by the standard deviation of the portfolio's rate of return. For portfolios that meet this criterion, known as efficient portfolios, achieving a higher expected return requires taking on more risk, so investors are faced with a trade-off between risk and expected return. This risk-expected return relationship of efficient portfolios is graphically represented by a curve known as the efficient frontier. All efficient portfolios, each represented by a point on the efficient frontier, are well-diversified.

Methods of Portfolio Optimization

Different approaches to portfolio optimization measure risk differently. In addition to the traditional measure, standard deviation, or its square (variance), which are not robust risk measures, other measures include the Sortino ratio and the CVaR (Conditional Value at Risk).

Often, portfolio optimization takes place in two stages: optimizing weights of asset classes to hold, and optimizing weights of assets within the same asset class. An example of the former would be choosing the proportions placed in equities versus bonds, while an example of the latter would be choosing the proportions of the stock sub-portfolio placed in stocks X, Y, and Z. Equities and bonds have fundamentally different financial characteristics and have different systematic risk and hence can be viewed as separate asset classes; holding some of the portfolio in each class provides some diversification, and holding various specific assets within each class affords further diversification. By using such a two-step procedure one eliminates non-systematic risks both on the individual asset and the asset class level.

One approach to portfolio optimization is to specify a von Neumann-Morgenstern utility function defined over final portfolio wealth; the expected value of utility is to be maximized. To reflect a preference for higher rather than lower returns, this objective function is increasing in wealth, and to reflect risk aversion it is concave. For realistic utility functions in the presence of many assets that can be held, this approach, while theoretically the most defencible, can be computationally intensive.

Optimization Constraints

Often portfolio optimization is done subject to constraints, which may be regulatory constraints, the lack of a liquid market, or any of many others.

Regulation and Taxes

Investors may be forbidden by law to hold some assets. In some cases, unconstrained portfolio optimization would lead to short-selling of some assets. However short-selling can be forbidden. Sometimes it is impractical to hold an asset because the associated tax cost is too high. In such cases appropriate constraints must be imposed on the optimization process.

Transaction Costs

Transaction costs are the costs of trading in order to change the portfolio weights. Since the optimal portfolio changes with time, there is an incentive to re-optimize frequently. However, too frequent trading would incur too-frequent transactions costs; so the optimal strategy is to find the frequency of re-optimization and trading that appropriately trades off the avoidance of transaction costs with the avoidance of sticking with an out-of-date set of portfolio proportions. This is related to the topic of tracking error, by which stock proportions deviate over time from some benchmark in the absence of re-balancing.

Mathematical Tools Used in Portfolio Optimization

The complexity and scale of optimizing all but the simplest portfolio requires that the work be done by computer. Central to this optimization is the construction of the covariance matrix for the rates of return on the assets in the portfolio.

Techniques include:

- Quadratic programming
- Nonlinear programming
- Mixed integer programming
- Meta-Heuristic Methods

Issues with Portfolio Optimization

Investment is a forward looking activity, and thus the covariances of returns and risk levels must be forecast rather than observed. Portfolio optimization assumes the investor may have some risk aversion and the stock prices may exhibit significant differences between their historical or forecast values and what is experienced.

In particular, financial crises are characterized by a significant increase in correlation of stock price movements which may seriously degrade the benefits of diversification.

Financial Models with Long-Tailed Distributions and Volatility Clustering

Financial models with long-tailed distributions and volatility clustering have been introduced to overcome problems with the realism of classical financial models. These classical models of financial time series typically assume homoskedasticity and normality cannot explain stylized phenomena such as skewness, heavy tails, and volatility clustering of the empirical asset returns in finance. In 1963, Benoit Mandelbrot first used the stable (or α-stable) distribution to model the empirical distributions which have the skewness and heavy-tail property. α Since -stable distributions have infinite α-th moments for all $p > \alpha$, the tempered stable processes have been proposed for overcoming this limitation of the stable distribution.

On the other hand, GARCH models have been developed to explain the volatility clustering. In the GARCH model, the innovation (or residual) distributions are assumed to be a standard normal distribution, despite the fact that this assumption is often rejected empirically. For this reason, GARCH models with non-normal innovation distribution have been developed.

Many financial models with stable and tempered stable distributions together with volatility clustering have been developed and applied to risk management, option pricing, and portfolio selection.

Infinitely Divisible Distributions

A random variable Y is called *infinitely divisible* if, for each $n = 1, 2, \ldots$, there are independent and identically-distributed random variables

$$Y_{n,1}, Y_{n,2}, \ldots, Y_{n,n}$$

such that

$$Y \stackrel{d}{=} \sum_{k=1}^{n} Y_{n,k},$$

where $\stackrel{d}{=}$ denotes equality in distribution.

A Borel measure ν on $\mathbb{R}$ is called a *Lévy measure* if $\nu(0) = 0$ and

$$\int_{\mathbb{R}} (1 \wedge |x^2|)\nu(dx) < \infty.$$

If Y is infinitely divisible, then the characteristic function $\phi_Y(u) = E[e^{iuY}]$ is given by

$$\phi_Y(u) = \exp\left(i\gamma u - \frac{1}{2}\sigma^2 u^2 + \int_{-\infty}^{\infty} (e^{iux} - 1 - iux1_{|x|\le 1})\nu(dx) \right), \sigma \ge 0,\ \gamma \in \mathbb{R}$$

where $\sigma \ge 0$, $\gamma \in \mathbb{R}$ and υ is a Lévy measure. Here the triple (σ^2, ν, γ) is called a *Lévy triplet of* Y. This triplet is unique. Conversely, for any choice (σ^2, ν, γ) satisfying the conditions above, there exists an infinitely divisible random variable Y whose characteristic function is given as .

α-Stable Distributions

An real-valued random variable X is said to have an α *-stable distribution* if for any $n \ge 2$, there are a positive number C_n and a real number D_n such that

$$X_1 + \cdots + X_n \stackrel{d}{=} C_n X + D_n,$$

where $X_1, X_2, \ldots, X_n$ are independent and have the same distribution as that of X. All stable random variables are infinitely divisible. It is known that $C_n = n^{1/\alpha}$ for some $0 < \alpha \le 2$. A stable random variable X with index α is called an α*-stable random variable.*

Let X be an α-stable random variable. Then the characteristic function ϕ_X of X is given by

$$\phi_X(u) = \begin{cases} \exp\left(i\mu u - \sigma^\alpha |u|^\alpha \left(1 - i\beta \operatorname{sgn}(u) \tan\left(\frac{\pi\alpha}{2}\right)\right)\right) & \text{if } \alpha \in (0,1) \cup (1,2) \\ \exp\left(i\mu u - \sigma |u| \left(1 + i\beta \operatorname{sgn}(u) \left(\frac{2}{\pi}\right) \ln(|u|)\right)\right) & \text{if } \alpha = 1 \\ \exp\left(i\mu u - \frac{1}{2}\sigma^2 u^2\right) & \text{if } \alpha = 2 \end{cases}$$

for some $\mu \in \mathbb{R}$, $\sigma > 0$ and $\beta \in [-1,1]$.

Tempered Stable Distributions

An infinitely divisible distribution is called a *classical tempered* stable (CTS) distribution *with parameter* $(C_1, C_2, \lambda_+, \lambda_-, \alpha)$, if its Lévy triplet (σ^2, ν, γ) is given by $\sigma = 0$, $\gamma \in \mathbb{R}$ and

$$\nu(dx) = \left(\frac{C_1 e^{-\lambda_+ x}}{x^{1+\alpha}} 1_{x>0} + \frac{C_2 e^{-\lambda_- |x|}}{|x|^{1+\alpha}} 1_{x<0} \right) dx,$$

where $C_1, C_2, \lambda_+, \lambda_- > 0$ and $\alpha < 2$.

This distribution was first introduced by under the name of *Truncated Lévy Flights* and has been called the *tempered stable* or the *KoBoL* distribution. In particular, if $C_1 = C_2 = C > 0$, then this distribution is called the CGMY distribution which has been used for financial modelling.

The characteristic function ϕ_{CTS} for a tempered stable distribution is given by

$$\phi_{CTS}(u) = \exp\left(iu\mu + C_1\Gamma(-\alpha)((\lambda_+ - iu)^\alpha - \lambda_+^\alpha) + C_2\Gamma(-\alpha)((\lambda_- + iu)^\alpha - \lambda_-^\alpha)\right),$$

for some $\mu \in \mathbb{R}$. Moreover, ϕ_{CTS} can be extended to the region .

$$\{z \in \mathbb{C} : \operatorname{Im}(z) \in (-\lambda_-, \lambda_+)\}$$

Rosiñski generalized the CTS distribution under the name of the *tempered stable distribution.* The KR distribution, which is a subclass of the Rosiñski's generalized tempered stable distributions, is used in finance.

An infinitely divisible distribution is called a *modified tempered stable (MTS) distribution* with parameter $(C,\lambda_+,\lambda_-,\alpha)$, if its Lévy triplet (σ^2,ν,γ) is given by $\sigma=0$, $\gamma\in\mathbb{R}$ and

$$\nu(dx)=C\left(\frac{q_\alpha(\lambda_+|x|)}{x^{\alpha+1}}1_{x>0}+\frac{q_\alpha(\lambda_-|x|)}{|x|^{\alpha+1}}1_{x<0}\right)dx,$$

where $C,\lambda_+,\lambda_->0,\alpha<2$ and

$$q_\alpha(x)=x^{\frac{\alpha+1}{2}}K_{\frac{\alpha+1}{2}}(x).$$

Here $K_p(x)$ is the modified Bessel function of the second kind. The MTS distribution is not included in the class of Rosiñski's generalized tempered stable distributions.

Volatility Clustering with Stable and Tempered Stable Innovation

In order to describe the volatility clustering effect of the return process of an asset, the GARCH model can be used. In the GARCH model, innovation (ϵ_t) is assumed that $\epsilon_t=\sigma_t z_t$, where $z_t\sim iid\,N(0,1)$ and where the series σ_t^2 are modelled by

$$\sigma_t^2=\alpha_0+\alpha_1\epsilon_{t-1}^2+\cdots+\alpha_q\epsilon_{t-q}^2=\alpha_0+\sum_{i=1}^{q}\alpha_i\epsilon_{t-i}^2$$

and where $\alpha_0>0$ and $\alpha_i\geq 0,i>0$.

However, the assumption of $z_t\sim iid\,N(0,1)$ is often rejected empirically. For that reason, new GARCH models with stable or tempered stable distributed innovation have been developed. GARCH models with α-stable innovations have been introduced. Subsequently, GARCH Models with tempered stable innovations have been developed.

Martingale Pricing

Martingale pricing is a pricing approach based on the notions of martingale and risk neutrality. The martingale pricing approach is a cornerstone of modern quantitative finance and can be applied to a variety of derivatives contracts, e.g. options, futures, interest rate derivatives, credit derivatives, etc.

In contrast to the PDE approach to pricing, martingale pricing formulae are in the form of expectations which can be efficiently solved numerically using a Monte Carlo approach. As such, Martingale pricing is preferred when valuing highly dimensional contracts such as a basket of options. On the other hand, valuing American-style contracts is troublesome and requires discretizing the problem (making it like a Bermudan option) and only in 2001 F. A. Longstaff and E. S. Schwartz developed a practical Monte Carlo method for pricing American options.

Measure Theory Representation

Suppose the state of the market can be represented by the filtered probability space, $(\Omega, (\mathcal{F}_t)_{t\in[0,T]}, \widetilde{\mathbb{P}})$. Let $\{S(t)\}_{t\in[0,T]}$ be a stochastic price process on this space. One may price a derivative security, $V(t, S(t))$ under the philosophy of no arbitrage as,

$$D(t)V(t,S(t)) = \widetilde{\mathbb{E}}[D(T)V(T,S(T)) \mid \mathcal{F}_t], \qquad dD(t) = -r(t)D(t)\,dt$$

where $\widetilde{\mathbb{P}}$ is the risk-neutral measure.

$(r(t))_{t\in[0,T]}$ is an $\mathcal{F}_t$-measurable (risk-free, possibly stochastic) interest rate process.

This is accomplished through almost sure replication of the derivative's time T payoff using only underlying securities, and the risk-free money market (MMA). These underlyings have prices that are observable and known. Specifically, one constructs a portfolio process $\{X(t)\}_{t\in[0,T]}$ in continuous time, where he holds $\Delta(t)$ shares of the underlying stock at each time t, and $X(t) - \Delta(t)S(t)$ cash earning the risk-free rate $r(t)$. The portfolio obeys the stochastic differential equation

$$dX(t) = \Delta(t)\,dS(t) + r(t)(X(t) - \Delta(t)S(t))\,dt$$

One will then attempt to apply Girsanov theorem by first computing $\frac{d\widetilde{\mathbb{P}}}{d\mathbb{P}}$; that is, the Radon–Nikodym derivative with respect to the observed market probability distribution. This ensures that the discounted replicating portfolio process is a Martingale under risk neutral conditions.

If such a process $\Delta(t)$ can be well-defined and constructed, then choosing $V(0,S(0)) = X(0)$ will result in $\widetilde{\mathbb{P}}[X(T) = V(T)] = 1$, which immediately implies that this happens $\mathbb{P}$-almost surely as well, since the two measures are equivalent.

Extreme Value Theory

Extreme value theory or extreme value analysis (EVA) is a branch of statistics dealing with the extreme deviations from the median of probability distributions. It seeks to assess, from a given ordered sample of a given random variable, the probability of events that are more extreme than any previously observed. Extreme value analysis is widely used in many disciplines, such as structural engineering, finance, earth sciences, traffic prediction, and geological engineering. For example, EVA might be used in the field of hydrology to estimate the probability of an unusually large flooding event, such as the 100-year flood. Similarly, for the design of a breakwater, a coastal engineer would seek to estimate the 50-year wave and design the structure accordingly.

Data Analysis

Two approaches exist for practical extreme value analysis. The first method relies on deriving block maxima (minima) series as a preliminary step. In many situations it is customary and convenient to extract the annual maxima (minima), generating an "Annual Maxima Series" (AMS). The second method relies on extracting, from a continuous record, the peak values reached for any period during which values exceed a certain threshold (falls below a certain threshold). This method is generally referred to as the "Peak Over Threshold" method (POT) and can lead to several or no values being extracted in any given year.

For AMS data, the analysis may partly rely on the results of the Fisher–Tippett–Gnedenko theorem, leading to the generalized extreme value distribution being selected for fitting. However, in practice, various procedures are applied to select between a wider range of distributions. The theorem here relates to the limiting distributions for the minimum or the maximum of a very large collection of independent random variables from the same arbitrary distribution. Given that the number of relevant random events within a year may be rather limited, it is unsurprising that analyses of observed AMS data often lead to distributions other than the generalized extreme value distribution being selected.

For POT data, the analysis involves fitting two distributions: one for the number of events in a basic time period and a second for the size of the exceedances. A common assumption for the first is the Poisson distribution, with the generalized Pareto distribution being used for the exceedances. Some further theory needs to be applied in order to derive the distribution of the most extreme value that may be observed in a given period, which may be a target of the analysis. An alternative target may be to estimate the expected costs associated with events occurring in a given period.

An alternative approach is the tail-fitting approach based on the Pickands–Balkema–de Haan theorem. This concentrates on the distribution of the size of an event, given that one has occurred.

Applications

Applications of extreme value theory include predicting the probability distribution of:

- Extreme floods
- The amounts of large insurance losses
- Equity risks
- Day to day market risk
- The size of freak waves
- Mutational events during evolution
- Large wildfires
- It can be applied to some characterization of the distribution of the maxima of incomes, like in some surveys done in virtually all the National Offices of Statistics
- Estimate fastest time humans are capable of running the 100 metres sprint.
- Pipeline failures due to pitting corrosion.

History

The field of extreme value theory was pioneered by Leonard Tippett (1902–1985). Tippett was employed by the British Cotton Industry Research Association, where he worked to make cotton thread stronger. In his studies, he realised that the strength of a thread was controlled by the strength of its weakest fibres. With the help of R. A. Fisher, Tippet obtained three asymptotic limits describing the distributions of extremes. Emil Julius Gumbel codified this theory in his 1958 book *Statistics of Extremes*, including the Gumbel distributions that bear his name.

A summary of historically important publications relating to extreme values theory can be found on the article List of publications in statistics.

Univariate Theory

Let $X_1,\ldots,X_n$ be a sequence of independent and identically distributed variables with distribution function F and let $M_n = \max(X_1,\ldots,X_n)$ denote the maximum.

In theory, the exact distribution of the maximum can be derived:

$$\begin{aligned}\Pr(M_n \le z) &= \Pr(X_1 \le z,\ldots,X_n \le z) \\ &= \Pr(X_1 \le z)\cdots\Pr(X_n \le z) = (F(z))^n.\end{aligned}$$

The associated indicator function $I_n = I(X_n > z)$ is a Bernoulli process with a success probability $p(z) = (1-(F(z))^n)$ that depends on the magnitude *z* of the extreme event. The number of extreme events within *n* trials thus follows a binomial distribution and the number of trials until an event occurs follows a geometric distribution with expected value and standard deviation of the same order $O(1/p(z))$.

In practice, we might not have the distribution function *F* but the Fisher–Tippett–Gnedenko theorem provides an asymptotic result. If there exist sequences of constants $a_n > 0$ and $b_n \in \mathbb{R}$ such that

$$\Pr\{(M_n - b_n)/a_n \le z\} \to G(z)$$

as $n \to \infty$ then

$$G(z) \propto \exp\left[-(1+\zeta z)^{-1/\zeta}\right]$$

where ζ depends on the tail shape of the distribution. When normalized, *G* belongs to one of the following non-degenerate distribution families:

Weibull law: $G(z) = \begin{cases} \exp\left\{-\left(-\left(\frac{z-b}{a}\right)\right)^{\alpha}\right\} & z < b \\ 1 & z \ge b \end{cases}$ when the distribution of M_n has a light tail with finite upper bound. Also known as Type 3.

Gumbel law: $G(z) = \exp\left\{-\exp\left(-\left(\frac{z-b}{a}\right)\right)\right\}$ for $z \in \mathbb{R}$. when the distribution of M_n has an exponential tail. Also known as Type 1

Fréchet Law: $G(z) = \begin{cases} 0 & z \le b \\ \exp\left\{-\left(\frac{z-b}{a}\right)^{-\alpha}\right\} & z > b. \end{cases}$ when the distribution of M_n has a heavy tail (including polynomial decay). Also known as Type 2.

In all cases, $\alpha > 0$.

Historical Simulation (Finance)

Historical simulation in finance's value at risk (VaR) analysis is a procedure for predicting the value at risk by 'simulating' or constructing the cumulative distribution function (CDF) of assets returns over time. Unlike parametric VaR models, historical simulation does not assume a particular distribution of the asset returns. Also, it is relatively easy to implement. However, there are a couple of shortcomings of historical simulation. First of all, it imposes a restriction on the estimation assuming that asset returns are independent and identically-distributed random variables, which is not the case: from empirical evidence, it is known that asset returns are clearly not independent, as they exhibit certain patterns such as volatility clustering. The second restriction relates to time: historical simulation applies equal weight to all returns of the whole period; this is inconsistent with the diminishing predictability of data that are further away from the present. These two shortcomings lead economists and financial experts to further develop other non-parametric, semi-parametric and parametric models.

Weighted Historical Simulation

Weighted historical simulation applies decreasing weights to returns that are further away from the present, which overcomes the inconsistency of historical simulation with diminishing predictability of data that are further away from the present. However, weighted historical simulation still assumes independent and identically-distributed (iid) asset returns.

Filtered Historical Simulation

Filtered historical simulation is a semi-parametric technique in forecasting VaR. Here the returns are no longer assumed iid, rather there is an additional innovation term v is now assumed to be iid instead. This allows the means and variances to be 'filtered away', coupled with an empirically estimated CDF, it becomes a more realistic model in predicting VaR.

Monte Carlo Methods in Finance

Monte Carlo methods are used in finance and mathematical finance to value and analyze (complex) instruments, portfolios and investments by simulating the various sources of uncertainty affecting their value, and then determining their average value over the range of resultant outcomes. This is usually done by help of stochastic asset models. The advantage of Monte Carlo methods over other techniques increases as the dimensions (sources of uncertainty) of the problem increase.

Monte Carlo methods were first introduced to finance in 1964 by David B. Hertz through his *Harvard Business Review* article, discussing their application in Corporate Finance. In 1977, Phelim Boyle pioneered the use of simulation in derivative valuation in his seminal *Journal of Financial Economics* paper.

This article discusses typical financial problems in which Monte Carlo methods are used. It also touches on the use of so-called "quasi-random" methods such as the use of Sobol sequences.

Overview

The Monte Carlo Method encompasses any technique of statistical sampling employed to approximate solutions to quantitative problems. Essentially, the Monte Carlo method solves a problem by directly simulating the underlying (physical) process and then calculating the (average) result of the process. This very general approach is valid in areas such as physics, chemistry, computer science etc.

In finance, the Monte Carlo method is used to simulate the various sources of uncertainty that affect the value of the instrument, portfolio or investment in question, and to then calculate a representative value given these possible values of the underlying inputs. ("Covering all conceivable real world contingencies in proportion to their likelihood.") In terms of financial theory, this, essentially, is an application of risk neutral valuation.

Some Examples:

- In Corporate Finance, project finance and real options analysis, Monte Carlo Methods are used by financial analysts who wish to construct "stochastic" or probabilistic financial models as opposed to the traditional static and deterministic models. Here, in order to analyze the characteristics of a project's net present value (NPV), the cash flow components that are (heavily) impacted by uncertainty are modelled, incorporating any correlation between these, mathematically reflecting their "random characteristics". Then, these results are combined in a histogram of NPV (i.e. the project's probability distribution), and the average NPV of the potential investment - as well as its volatility and other sensitivities - is observed. This distribution allows, for example, for an estimate of the probability that the project has a net present value greater than zero (or any other value).
- In valuing an option on equity, the simulation generates several thousand possible (but random) price paths for the underlying share, with the associated exercise value (i.e. "payoff") of the option for each path. These payoffs are then averaged and

discounted to today, and this result is the value of the option today.

- To value fixed income instruments and interest rate derivatives the underlying source of uncertainty which is simulated is the short rate - the annualized interest rate at which an entity can borrow money for a given period of time. For example for bonds, and bond options, under each possible evolution of interest rates we observe a different yield curve and a different resultant bond price. To determine the bond value, these bond prices are then averaged; to value the bond option, as for equity options, the corresponding exercise values are averaged and present valued. A similar approach is used in valuing swaps and swaptions. (Note that whereas these options are more commonly valued using lattice based models, for path dependent interest rate derivatives - such as CMOs - simulation is the *primary* technique employed.; note also that "to create realistic interest rate simulations" Multi-factor short-rate models are sometimes employed.)
- Monte Carlo Methods are used for portfolio evaluation. Here, for each sample, the correlated behaviour of the factors impacting the component instruments is simulated over time, the resultant value of each instrument is calculated, and the portfolio value is then observed. As for corporate finance, above, the various portfolio values are then combined in a histogram, and the statistical characteristics of the portfolio are observed, and the portfolio assessed as required. A similar approach is used in calculating value at risk.
- Monte Carlo Methods are used for personal financial planning. For instance, by simulating the overall market, the chances of a 401(k) allowing for retirement on a target income can be calculated. As appropriate, the worker in question can then take greater risks with the retirement portfolio or start saving more money.
- Discrete event simulation can be used in evaluating a proposed capital investment's impact on existing operations. Here, a "current state" model is constructed. Once operating correctly, having been tested and validated against historical data, the simulation is altered to reflect the proposed capital investment. This "future state" model is then used to assess the investment, by evaluating the improvement in performance (i.e. return) relative to the cost (via histogram as above); it may also be used in stress testing the design.

Although Monte Carlo methods provide flexibility, and can handle multiple sources of uncertainty, the use of these techniques is nevertheless not always appropriate. In general, simulation methods are preferred to other valuation techniques only when there are several state variables (i.e. several sources of uncertainty). These techniques are also of limited use in valuing American style derivatives.

Applicability

Level of Complexity: Many problems in mathematical finance entail the computation of a particular integral (for instance the problem of finding the arbitrage-free value of a particular derivative). In many cases these integrals can be valued analytically, and in still more cases they can be valued using numerical integration, or computed using a partial differential equation (PDE). However when the number of dimensions (or degrees of freedom) in the problem is large, PDEs and numerical integrals become intractable, and in these cases Monte Carlo methods often give better results.

For more than three or four state variables, formulae such as Black Scholes (i.e. analytic solutions) do not exist, while other numerical methods such as the Binomial options pricing model and finite difference methods face several difficulties and are not practical. In these cases, Monte Carlo methods converge to the solution more quickly than numerical methods, require less memory and are easier to program. For simpler situations, however, simulation is not the better solution because it is very time-consuming and computationally intensive.

Monte Carlo methods can deal with derivatives which have path dependent payoffs in a fairly straight forward manner. On the other hand Finite Difference (PDE) solvers struggle with path dependence.

American Options

Monte-Carlo methods are harder to use with American options. This is because, in contrast to a partial differential equation, the Monte Carlo method really only estimates the option value assuming a given starting point and time.

However, for early exercise, we would also need to know the option value at the intermediate times between the simulation start time and the option expiry time. In the Black–Scholes PDE approach these prices are easily obtained, because the simulation runs backwards from the expiry date. In Monte-Carlo this information is harder to obtain, but it can be done for example using the least squares algorithm of Carriere which was made popular a few years later by Longstaff and Schwartz.

Monte Carlo Methods

Mathematically: The fundamental theorem of arbitrage-free pricing states that the value of a derivative is equal to the discounted expected value of the derivative payoff where the expectation is taken under the risk-neutral measure . An expectation is, in the language of pure mathematics, simply an integral with respect to the measure. Monte Carlo methods are ideally suited to evaluating difficult integrals.

Thus if we suppose that our risk-neutral probability space is P and that we have a derivative H that depends on a set of underlying instruments $S_1,...,S_n$. Then given a sample ω from the probability space the value of the derivative is $H(S_1(\omega),S_2(\omega),\ldots,S_n(\omega)) =: H(\omega)$. Today's value of the derivative is found by taking the expectation over all possible samples and discounting at the risk-free rate. I.e. the derivative has value:

$$H_0 = DF_T \int_\omega H(\omega) d\mathbb{P}(\omega)$$

where DF_T is the discount factor corresponding to the risk-free rate to the final maturity date T years into the future.

Now suppose the integral is hard to compute. We can approximate the integral by generating sample paths and then taking an average. Suppose we generate N samples then

$$H_0 \approx DF_T \frac{1}{N} \sum_{\omega \in \text{sample set}} H(\omega)$$

which is much easier to compute.

Sample Paths for Standard Models

In finance, underlying random variables (such as an underlying stock price) are usually assumed to follow a path that is a function of a Brownian motion . For example in the standard Black–Scholes model, the stock price evolves as

$$dS = \mu S\, dt + \sigma S\, dW_t.$$

To sample a path following this distribution from time 0 to T, we chop the time interval into M units of length δt, and approximate the Brownian motion over the interval dt by a single normal variable of mean 0 and variance . This leads to a sample path of

$$S(k\delta t) = S(0)\exp\left(\sum_{i=1}^{k}\left[\left(\mu - \frac{\sigma^2}{2}\right)\delta t + \sigma\varepsilon_i\sqrt{\delta t}\right]\right)$$

for each k between 1 and M. Here each ε_i is a draw from a standard normal distribution.

Let us suppose that a derivative H pays the average value of S between 0 and T then a sample path ω corresponds to a set $\{\varepsilon_1,\ldots,\varepsilon_M\}$ and

$$H(\omega) = \frac{1}{M}\sum_{k=1}^{M} S(k\delta t).$$

We obtain the Monte-Carlo value of this derivative by generating N lots of M normal variables, creating N sample paths and so N values of H, and then taking the average. Commonly the derivative will depend on two or more (possibly correlated) underlyings. The method here can be extended to generate sample paths of several variables, where the normal variables building up the sample paths are appropriately correlated. It follows from the central limit theorem that quadrupling the number of sample paths approximately halves the error in the simulated price (i.e. the error has order $\epsilon = \mathcal{O}\left(N^{-1/2}\right)$ convergence in the sense of standard deviation of the solution).

In practice Monte Carlo methods are used for European-style derivatives involving at least three variables (more direct methods involving numerical integration can usually be used for those problems with only one or two underlyings.

Greeks

Estimates for the "Greeks" of an option i.e. the (mathematical) derivatives of option value with respect to input parameters, can be obtained by numerical differentiation. This can be a time-consuming process (an entire Monte Carlo run must be performed for each "bump" or small change in input parameters). Further, taking numerical derivatives tends to emphasize the error (or noise) in the Monte Carlo value - making it necessary to simulate with a large number of sample paths. Practitioners regard these points as a key problem with using Monte Carlo methods.

Variance Reduction

Square root convergence is slow, and so using the naive approach described above requires using a very large number of sample paths (1 million, say, for a typical problem) in order to obtain an accurate result. Remember that an estimator for the price of a derivative is a random variable, and in the framework of a risk-management activity, uncertainty on the price of a portfolio of derivatives and/or on its risks can lead to suboptimal risk-management decisions.

This state of affairs can be mitigated by variance reduction techniques.

Antithetic Paths

A simple technique is, for every sample path obtained, to take its antithetic path — that is given a path $\{\varepsilon_1,\ldots,\varepsilon_M\}$ to also take $\{-\varepsilon_1,\ldots,-\varepsilon_M\}$. Not only does this reduce the number of normal samples to be taken to generate N paths, but also, under same conditions, reduces the variance of the sample paths, improving the accuracy.

Control Variate Method

It is also natural to use a control variate. Let us suppose that we wish to obtain the Monte Carlo value of a derivative *H*, but know the value analytically of a similar derivative I. Then *H** = (Value of *H* according to Monte Carlo) + B*[(Value of *I* analytically) – (Value of *I* according to same Monte Carlo paths)] is a better estimate, where B is covar(H,I)/var(H).

The intuition behind that technique, when applied to derivatives, is the following: note that the source of the variance of a derivative will be directly dependent on the risks (e.g. delta, vega) of this derivative. This is because any error on, say, the estimator for the forward value of an underlier, will generate a corresponding error depending on the delta of the derivative with respect to this forward value. The simplest example to demonstrate this consists in comparing the error when pricing an at-the-money call and an at-the-money straddle (i.e. call+put), which has a much lower delta.

Therefore, a standard way of choosing the derivative *I* consists in choosing a replicating portfolios of options for *H*. In practice, one will price *H* without variance reduction, calculate deltas and vegas, and then use a combination of calls and puts that have the same deltas and vegas as control variate.

Importance Sampling

Importance sampling consists of simulating the Monte Carlo paths using a different probability distribution (also known as a change of measure) that will give more likelihood for the simulated underlier to be located in the area where the derivative's payoff has the most convexity (for example, close to the strike in the case of a simple option). The simulated payoffs are then not simply averaged as in the case of a simple Monte Carlo, but are first multiplied by the likelihood ratio between the modified probability distribution and the original one (which is obtained by analytical formulas specific for the probability distribution). This will ensure that paths whose probability have been arbitrarily enhanced by the change of probability distribution are weighted with a low weight (this is how the variance gets reduced).

This technique can be particularly useful when calculating risks on a derivative. When calculating the delta using a Monte Carlo method, the most straightforward way is the *black-box* technique consisting in doing a Monte Carlo on the original market data and another one on the changed market data, and calculate the risk by doing the difference. Instead, the importance sampling method consists in doing a Monte Carlo in an arbitrary reference market data (ideally one in which the variance is as low as possible), and calculate the prices using the weight-changing technique described above. This results in a risk that will be much more stable than the one obtained through the *black-box* approach.

Quasi-Random (Low-Discrepancy) Methods

Instead of generating sample paths randomly, it is possible to systematically (and in fact completely deterministically, despite the "quasi-random" in the name) select points in a probability spaces so as to optimally "fill up" the space. The selection of points is a low-discrepancy sequence such as a Sobol sequence. Taking averages of derivative payoffs at points in a low-discrepancy sequence is often more efficient than taking averages of payoffs at random points.

Notes

1. Frequently it is more practical to take expectations under different measures, however these are still fundamentally integrals, and so the same approach can be applied.
2. More general processes, such as Lévy processes, are also sometimes used. These may also be simulated.

Quasi-Monte Carlo Methods in Finance

High-dimensional integrals in hundreds or thousands of variables occur commonly in finance. These integrals have to be computed numerically to within a threshold ϵ. If the integral is of dimension d then in the worst case, where one has a guarantee of error at most ϵ, the computational complexity is typically of order ϵ^{-d}. That is, the problem suffers the curse of dimensionality. In 1977 P. Boyle, University of Waterloo, proposed using Monte Carlo (MC) to evaluate options. Starting in early 1992, J. F. Traub, Columbia University, and a graduate student at the time, S. Paskov, used quasi-Monte Carlo (QMC) to price a Collateralized mortgage obligation with parameters specified by

Goldman Sachs. Even though it was believed by the world's leading experts that QMC should not be used for high-dimensional integration, Paskov and Traub found that QMC beat MC by one to three orders of magnitude and also enjoyed other desirable attributes. Their results were first published in 1995. Today QMC is widely used in the financial sector to value financial derivatives.

QMC is not a panacea for all high-dimensional integrals. A number of explanations have been proposed for why QMC is so good for financial derivatives. This continues to be a very fruitful research area.

Monte Carlo and Quasi-Monte Carlo Methods

Integrals in hundreds or thousands of variables are common in computational finance. These have to be approximated numerically to within an error threshold ϵ. It is well known that if a worst case guarantee of error at most ϵ is required then the computational complexity of integration may be exponential in *d*, the dimension of the integrand. To break this curse of dimensionality one can use the Monte Carlo (MC) method defined by

$$\varphi^{\mathrm{MC}}(f) = \frac{1}{n}\sum_{i=1}^{n} f(x_i),$$

where the evaluation points x_i are randomly chosen. It is well known that the expected error of Monte Carlo is of order $n^{-1/2}$. Thus the cost of the algorithm that has error ϵ is of order ϵ^{-2} breaking the curse of dimensionality. Of course in computational practice pseudo-random points are used. Figure depicted earlier, shows the distribution of 500 pseudo-random points on the unit square.

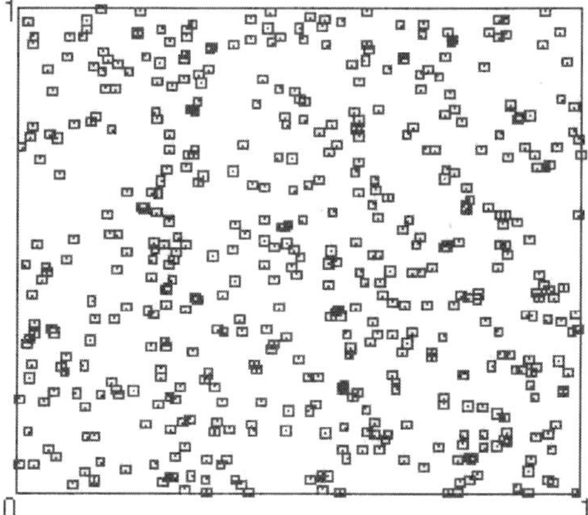

Figure: *500 pseudo-random points*

Note there are regions where there are no points and other regions where there are clusters of points. It would be desirable to sample the integrand at uniformly distributed points. A rectangular grid would be uniform but even if there were only 2 grid points in each Cartesian direction there would be 2^d points. So the desideratum should be as few points as possible chosen as uniform as possible.

It turns out there is a well-developed part of number theory which deals exactly with this desideratum. Discrepancy is a measure of deviation from uniformity so what one wants are low discrepancy sequences (LDS). Numerous LDS have been created named after their inventors, e.g.

- Halton
- Hammersley
- Sobol
- Faure
- Niederreiter

Figure gives the distribution of 500 LDS points.

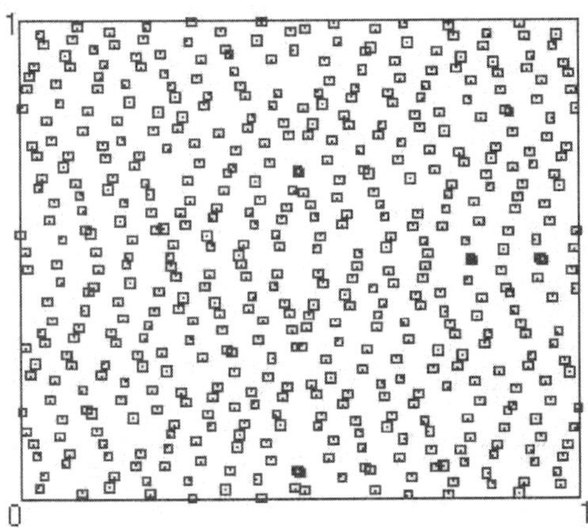

Figure: *500 low discrepancy points*

The quasi-Monte Carlo (QMC) method is defined by

$$\varphi^{\mathrm{QMC}}(f) = \frac{1}{n}\sum_{i=1}^{n} f(x_i),$$

where the x_i belong to an LDS. The standard terminology quasi-Monte Carlo is somewhat unfortunate since MC is a randomized method whereas QMC is purely deterministic.

The uniform distribution of LDS is desirable. But the worst case error of QMC is of order

$$\frac{(\log n)^d}{n},$$

where n is the number of sample points. The rate of convergence of LDS may be contrasted with the expected rate of convergence of MC which is $n^{-1/2}$. For d small the rate of convergence of QMC is faster than MC but for d large the factor $(\log n)^d$ is devastating. For example, if $d = 360$, then even with $\log n = 2$ the QMC error is proportional to 2^{360}. Thus it was widely believed by the world's leading experts that QMC should not be used for high-dimensional integration. For example, in 1992 Bratley, Fox and Niederreiter performed extensive testing on certain mathematical problems. They conclude "in high-dimensional problems (say $d > 12$), QMC seems to offer no practical advantage over MC". In 1993, Rensburg and Torrie compared QMC with MC for the numerical estimation of high-dimensional integrals which occur in computing virial coefficients for the hard-sphere fluid. They conclude QMC is more effective than MC only if $d < 10$. As we shall see, tests on 360-dimensional integrals arising from a collateralized mortgage obligation (CMO) lead to very different conclusions.

WoŸniakowski's 1991 paper showing the connection between average case complexity of integration and QMC led to new interest in QMC. WoŸniakowski's result received considerable coverage in the scientific press . In early 1992, I. T. Vanderhoof, New York University, became aware of WoŸniakowski's result and gave WoŸniakowski's colleague J. F. Traub, Columbia University, a CMO with parameters set by Goldman Sachs. This CMO had 10 tranches each requiring the computation of a 360 dimensional integral. Traub asked a Ph.D. student, Spassimir Paskov, to compare QMC with MC for the CMO. In 1992 Paskov built a software system called FinDer and ran extensive tests. To the Columbia's research group's surprise and initial disbelief Paskov reported that QMC was always superior to MC in a number of ways. Details are given below. Preliminary results were presented by Paskov and Traub to a number of Wall Street firms in Fall 1993 and Spring 1994. The firms were initially skeptical of the claim that QMC was superior to MC for pricing financial derivatives. A January 1994 article in Scientific American by Traub and WoŸniakowski discussed the theoretical issues and reported that "Preliminary results obtained by testing certain finance problems suggests the superiority of the deterministic methods in practice". In Fall 1994 Paskov wrote a

Columbia University Computer Science Report which appeared in slightly modified form in 1997.

In Fall 1995 Paskov and Traub published a paper in the "Journal of Portfolio Management". They compared MC and two QMC methods. The two deterministic methods used Sobol and Halton points. Since better LDS were created later, no comparison will be made between Sobol and Halton sequences. The experiments drew the following conclusions regarding the performance of MC and QMC on the 10 tranche CMO:

- QMC methods converge significantly faster than MC
- MC is sensitive to the initial seed
- The convergence of QMC is smoother than the convergence of MC. This makes automatic termination easier for QMC.

To summarize, QMC beats MC for the CMO on accuracy, confidence level, and speed.

This paper was followed by reports on tests by a number of researchers which also led to the conclusion the QMC is superior to MC for a variety of high-dimensional finance problems. This includes papers by Caflisch and Morokoff (1996), Joy, Boyle, Tan (1996), Ninomiya and Tezuka (1996), Papageorgiou and Traub (1996), Ackworth, Broadie and Glasserman (1997).

Further testing of the CMO was carried out by Anargyros Papageorgiou, who developed an improved version of the FinDer software system. The new results include the following:

- Small number of sample points: For the hardest CMO tranche QMC using the generalized Faure LDS due to S. Tezuka achieves accuracy 10^{-2} with just 170 points. MC requires 2700 points for the same accuracy. The significance of this is that due to future interest rates and prepayment rates being unknown, financial firms are content with accuracy of .
- Large number of sample points: The advantage of QMC over MC is further amplified as the sample size and accuracy demands grow. In particular, QMC is 20 to 50 times faster than MC with moderate sample sizes, and can be up to 1000 times faster than MC when high accuracy is desired QMC.

Theoretical Explanations

The results reported so far in this article are empirical. A number of possible theoretical explanations have been advanced. This has been a very research rich area leading to powerful new concepts but a definite answer has not been obtained. A possible explanation of why QMC is good for finance is the following. Consider a tranche of the CMO mentioned earlier. The integral gives expected future cash flows from a basket of 30 year mortgages at 360 monthly intervals. Because of the discounted value of money variables representing future times are increasingly less important. In a seminal paper I. Sloan and H. WoŸniakowski introduced the idea of weighted spaces. In these spaces the dependence on the successive variables can be moderated by weights. If the weights decrease sufficiently rapidly the curse of dimensionality is broken even with a worst case guarantee. This paper led to a great amount of work on the tractability of integration and other problems. A problem is tractable when its complexity is of order ϵ^{-p} and p is independent of the dimension.

On the other hand, *effective dimension* was proposed by Caflisch, Morokoff and Owen as an indicator of the difficulty of high-dimensional integration. The purpose was to explain the remarkable success of quasi-Monte Carlo (QMC) in approximating the very-high-dimensional integrals in finance. They argued that the integrands are of low effective dimension and that is why QMC is much faster than Monte Carlo (MC). The impact of the arguments of Caflisch et al. was great. A number of papers deal with the relationship between the error of QMC and the effective dimension.

It is known that QMC fails for certain functions that have high effective dimension. However, low effective dimension is not a necessary condition for QMC to beat MC and for high-dimensional integration to be tractable. In 2005, Tezuka exhibited a class of functions of d variables, all with maximum effective dimension equal to d. For these functions QMC is very fast since its convergence rate is of order n^{-1}, where n is the number of function evaluations.

Isotropic Integrals

QMC can also be superior to MC and to other methods for isotropic problems, that is, problems where all variables are equally important. For example, Papageorgiou and Traub reported test results on the model integration problems suggested by the physicist B. D. Keister

$$\left(\frac{1}{2\pi}\right)^{d/2} \int_{\mathbb{R}^d} \cos(\| x \|) e^{-\|x\|^2} \, dx,$$

where $\|\cdot\|$ denotes the Euclidean norm and $d = 25$. Keister reports that using a standard numerical method some 220,000 points were needed to obtain a relative error on the order of 10^{-2}. A QMC calculation using the generalized Faure low discrepancy sequence (QMC-GF) used only 500 points to obtain the same relative error. The same integral was tested for a range of values of d up to $d = 100$. Its error was

$$c \cdot n^{-1},$$

$c < 110$, where n is the number of evaluations of f. This may be compared with the MC method whose error was proportional to $n^{-1/2}$.

These are empirical results. In a theoretical investigation Papageorgiou proved that the convergence rate of QMC for a class of d-dimensional isotropic integrals which includes the integral defined above is of the order

$$\sqrt{\log n} / n.$$

This is with a worst case guarantee compared to the expected convergence rate of $n^{-1/2}$ of Monte Carlo and shows the superiority of QMC for this type of integral.

In another theoretical investigation Papageorgiou presented sufficient conditions for fast QMC convergence. The conditions apply to isotropic and non-isotropic problems and, in particular, to a number of problems in computational finance. He presented classes of functions where even in the worst case the convergence rate of QMC is of order

$$n^{-1+p(\log n)^{-1/2}},$$

where $p \geq 0$ is a constant that depends on the class of functions.

Chapter 6

Cash Forecast

What is a Cash Budget

A cash budget is an accounting device that is used to effectively monitor and manage the immediate cash flow of a home or business budget. Many people choose to employ a cash approach as a quick and easy way to monitor the financial condition of the household or a small business on a daily, weekly, or monthly basis. Generally, cash budgets are used to manage short-term cash flow by creating an organised means of keeping up with cash receipts and balancing them against cash disbursements during the accounting period.

Part of the genius of a cash budget is the simplicity of the approach. Often, it is possible to employ this principle by using a basic spreadsheet. Creating columns that make it possible to record basic information, it is possible to tell at a glance how much money came in for the period, and how much went out. This is accomplished by recording each cash receipt and cash disbursement on the spreadsheet. Often, the date, amount, and a brief description of the transaction is all that is necessary.

The cash budget is such a simplistic tool that even people who feel they lack any real accounting acumen can employ this approach. Because it is possible to track the cash in and cash out in the same format that is used for a standard check register, most people will find that the process takes very little time. A simply designed budget will provide a helpful look at how well the entity is doing in staying within the approved expenses for the period.

It is possible to keep a cash budget in a simple accounting ledger, or design one using spreadsheet software. Most accounting software programs are also equipped with a simple budgeting feature that will gather data from within the database and provide a quick snapshot of the period under consideration. For persons who do not need a professional level accounting database but do not feel competent to design a cash budget template using a spreadsheet, there are several free downloadable budgeting programs available.

What are the Advantages of a Cash Budget?

The cash budget is a tool companies can use to track all the movements of cash within their firms. Both inflows and outflows are written down in the budget; this information will usually come from the company's normal business operations. Advantages of the cash budget include discovering the amount of expected cash received from customers, calculating the amount of credit the company can extend to clients, estimating expenses, and providing focus for management. This budget can also help companies reduce expenditures and begin to control costs.

High sales revenue does not always equal high cash flows; this increases the importance of the cash budget. Companies can often take their amount of sales each month and calculate the amount of cash they expect to receive. This process is especially important for companies that allow customers to purchase items on credit. Each company will often have a historical percentage that indicates how much cash it can expect to collect from sales. The remaining amount may be uncollectable, indicating the company will lose this amount of money.

Through the calculation of received cash from sales, companies can determine how much credit to extend to customers. For example, if a company has $100,000 US Dollars (USD) in sales and expects to collect $95,000 USD, the company cannot extend credit above $95,000 USD without experiencing cash flow problems. If the normal time to collect receivables is 30 days, the company must plan to have enough cash to last this amount of time without having to borrow money.

Estimating expenses is another advantage of the cash budget. Companies can write the amount of normal expenditures they experience each month to produce revenue. Then all ancillary cash outflows need recording in the budget. This allows the company to determine how much it spends on activities that do not add value to the firm. A reduction in expenditures or decreasing cash budget cap limits can help the company increase its gross profit.

Not all managers care cash-savvy in a business. In fact, very few managers may have a good understanding of accounting processes. Creating a cash budget allows owners and executive managers to involve all individuals within the firm and help them understand the importance of the cash budget.

Involving all managers in the budget process can help give each one a sense of purpose. Managers can then help the company reduce expenditures and refine the company's operations. This will help ensure the company does not become cash poor during its operational lifetime.

What is a Cash Flow Plan?

A cash flow plan is a specific outline of the expected inflows or outflows in future time periods. Both individuals and companies will use these plans, albeit somewhat differently in form and function. While a personal cash flow plan often focuses on creating a personal budget based on wages and household expenditures, a business cash plan can include a budget, capital structure plan for debt and equity financing, net present value calculations for new business opportunities, and other detailed forecasts or formulas.

Individuals will typically start a cash flow plan by listing their total monthly income they receive from jobs, interest received on investments, and other sources of cash. The plan will also include a budget, which represents a detailed list of all expenditures during a certain time period. Expenses include rent or mortgage payments, car loan payments, food, clothing, insurance, utilities, childcare or school payments, and miscellaneous items. Individuals can create an expected budget or one based on historical information. Either way, individuals will have a clear picture of the cash flow related to their lifestyle.

Most businesses use a cash management function as part of their cash flow plan. A cash management function can be the designated duty of a specific employee, or it may be a set of additional tasks attached to an employee's responsibilities. While companies will also use budgets as part of their plans, they are often quite extensive. Companies typically create budgets based on departmental expenditures. Therefore, the sales, accounting, production, information technology and marketing department will all have a specific budget. Each of these individual budgets will then roll into one large master budget, which will outline all the future expenditures for the upcoming year.

Another aspect of a company's cash flow plan is their capital structure. Most companies will use a mix of debt and equity financing to pay for large-scale business purchases. External financing allows a company to retain the cash from its standard operations for regular expenditures. Each portion of the capital structure will affect a company's cash flow differently. For example, a traditional bank loan often requires companies to follow a strict repayment schedule, which includes making payments on the loan's principle and interest in fixed intervals. Equity financing is usually more flexible. Companies can use an investment contract with venture capitalists to secure specific terms for the investment. This allows the company to avoid immediate cash outflows through monthly repayments. Most often, companies will repay investments at a designated point in the future.

What is a Cash Flow Budget?

A cash flow budget shows how much money a business expects to make and spend over the course of a year. The cash flow budget calculates actual cash purchases or payments made or received. A business uses cash flow to estimate how much it will make after the cost of expenses and to see when it will need to borrow money. It can also use a cash flow budget to estimate when it can repay loans.

Each year a business should try cash flow budgeting to estimate its expected cash inflow and cash outflow for the year. Cash inflow is all the money a business will make that year and cash outflow is all the money it will spend. A business that expects to spend more than it makes has a problem and needs to find a more efficient way to budget.

After each month and year is over, it's important to look at cash flow. Unlike the cash flow budget, cash flow shows the actual amount of money in and out of the business; the cash flow budget is usually an estimate. Cash flow shows the change in cash from start to finish of a year or month. For example, if a business started the month with $20,000 US Dollars (USD) and ended with $30,000 USD, its cash flow is a positive $10,000 USD.

Cash flow is calculated by subtracting the amount of cash outflow from the amount of cash inflow. For the above example, the business made $10,000 USD, so the amount is positive. If the business had spent more than it made or had in savings, then the amount would be negative.

Once a business has tracked its cash inflow and outflow for a year, it can use a cash flow budget to estimate what its cash flow will look like for the upcoming year. Net cash flow is a term used to describe the ratio of cash earned and spent over a period of time. Knowing how much a business can expect to make helps it make important decisions, such as whether or not to invest in new technology.

Individuals may use a cash flow budget in a home business. When starting a small business, the owner needs to know how much she's spent and how much she's made. This information helps her better prepare for the coming year. She can decide if her prices are high enough and whether or not she can afford to buy new materials that would make production faster.

Cash Flow Forecasting

Cash flow forecasting or cash flow management is a key aspect of financial management of a business, planning its future cash requirements to avoid a crisis of liquidity.

Cash flow forecasting is important because if a business runs out of cash and is not able to obtain new finance, it will become insolvent. Cash flow is the life-blood of all businesses—particularly start-ups and small enterprises. As a result, it is essential that management forecast (predict) what is going to happen to cash flow to make sure the business has enough to survive. How often management should forecast cash flow is dependent on the financial security of the business. If the business is struggling, or is keeping a watchful eye on its finances, the business owner should be forecasting and revising his or her cash flow on a daily basis. However, if the finances of the business are more stable and 'safe', then forecasting and revising cash flow weekly or monthly is enough. Here are the key reasons why a cash flow forecast is so important:

- Identify potential shortfalls in cash balances in advance—think of the cash flow forecast as an "early warning system". This is, by far, the most important reason for a cash flow forecast.
- Make sure that the business can afford to pay suppliers and employees. Suppliers who don't get paid will soon stop supplying the business; it is even worse if employees are not paid on time.
- Spot problems with customer payments—preparing the forecast encourages the business to look at how quickly customers are paying their debts. Note—this is not really a problem for businesses (like retailers) that take most of their sales in cash/credit cards at the point of sale.
- As an important discipline of financial planning—the cash flow forecast is an important management process, similar to preparing business budgets.
- External stakeholders such as banks may require a regular forecast. Certainly, if the business has a bank loan, the bank will want to look at the cash flow forecast at regular intervals.

Corporate Finance

In the context of corporate finance, cash flow forecasting is the modelling of a company or entity's future financial liquidity over a specific timeframe. *Cash* usually refers to the company's total bank balances, but often what is forecast is treasury position which is cash plus short-term investments minus short-term debt. Cash flow is the change in cash or treasury position from one period to the next period.

Methods

The direct method of cash flow forecasting schedules the company's cash receipts and disbursements (R&D). Receipts are primarily the collection of accounts receivable from recent sales, but also include sales of other assets, proceeds of financing, etc. Disbursements include payroll, payment of accounts payable from recent purchases, dividends and interest on debt. This direct R&D method is best suited to the short-term forecasting horizon of 30 days or so because this is the period for which actual, as opposed to projected, data is available.

The three indirect methods are based on the company's projected income statements and balance sheets.

- The adjusted net income (ANI) method starts with operating income (EBIT or EBITDA) and adds or subtracts changes in balance sheet accounts such as receivables, payables and inventories to project cash flow.
- The pro-forma balance sheet (PBS) method looks straight at the projected book cash account; if all the other balance sheet accounts have been correctly forecast, cash will be correct, too.

Both the ANI and PBS methods are best suited to the medium-term (up to one year) and long-term (multiple years) forecasting horizons. Both are limited to the monthly or quarterly intervals of the financial plan, and need to be adjusted for the difference between accrual-accounting book cash and the often-significantly-different bank balances.

- The third indirect approach is the accrual reversal method (ARM), which is similar to the ANI method. But instead of using projected balance sheet accounts, large accruals are reversed and cash effects are calculated based upon statistical distributions and algorithms. This allows the forecasting period to be weekly or even daily. It also eliminates the cumulative errors inherent in the direct, R&D method when it is extended beyond the short-term horizon. But because the ARM allocates both accrual reversals and cash effects to weeks or days, it is more complicated than the ANI or PBS indirect methods. The ARM is best suited to the medium-term forecasting horizon.

Uses

A cash flow projection is an important input into valuation of assets, budgeting and determining appropriate capital structures in LBOs and leveraged recapitalizations. [3]

Entrepreneurial

Definition

In the context of entrepreneurs or managers of small and medium enterprises, cash flow forecasting may be somewhat simpler, planning what cash will come into the business or business unit in order to ensure that outgoing can be managed so as to avoid them exceeding cashflow coming in. Entrepreneurs need to learn fast that "Cash is king" and, therefore, they must become good at cashflow forecasting.

Methods

The simplest method is to have a spreadsheet that shows cash coming in from all sources out to at least 90 days, and all cash going out for the same period. This requires that the quantity and timings of receipts of cash from sales are reasonably accurate, which in turn requires judgement honed by experience of the industry concerned, because it is rare for cash receipts to match sales forecasts exactly, and it is also rare for customers all to pay on time. These principles remain constant whether the cash flow forecasting is done on a spreadsheet or on paper or on some other IT system.

A danger of using too much corporate finance theoretical methods in cash flow forecasting for managing a business is that there can be non cash items in the cashflow as reported under financial accounting standards. This goes to the heart of the difference between financial accounting and management accounting.

Uses

The point of making the forecast of incoming cash is to manage the outflow of cash so that the business remains solvent. The section of the spreadsheet that shows cash out is thus the basis for what-if modelling, for instance, "what if we pay our suppliers 30 days later?"

Financial Investment

Financial Investment - Meaning, its Need and Different Types of Investments

It is human nature to plan for rainy days. An individual must plan and keep aside some amount of money for any unavoidable circumstance which might arise in days to come. Future is uncertain and one must invest wisely to avoid financial crisis in any point of time.

Let Us First Understand What is Investment ?

Investment is nothing but goods or commodities purchased today to be used in future or at the times of crisis. An individual must plan his future well to ensure happiness for himself as well as his immediate family members. Consuming everything today and saving nothing for the future is foolish. Not everyday is a bed of roses, you never know what your future has in store for you.

What is Financial Investment ?

Financial investment refers to putting aside a fixed amount of money and expecting some kind of gain out of it within a stipulated time frame.

What is Important in Financial Investment ?

Planning plays a pivotal role in Financial Investment. Don't just invest just for the sake of investing. Understand why you really need to invest money? Investing just because your friend has said you to do so is foolish. Careful analysis and focused approach are mandatory before investing. Explore all the investment plans available in the market. Go through the pros and cons of each plan in detail. Analyze the risk factors carefully before finalizing the plan. Invest in something which will give you the maximum return. Appoint a good financial planning manager who takes care of all your investment needs. He must understand your requirement, family income, stability etc to decide the best plan for you.

One needs to be a little careful and sensible while investing. An individual must read the documents carefully before investing.

Types of Financial Investment

An individual can invest in any of the following:

- Mutual Funds
- Fixed Deposits
- Bonds
- Stock
- Equities
- Real Estate (Residential/Commercial Property)
- Gold /Silver
- Precious stones

Need for Financial Investment

Financial Investment ensures all your dreams turn real and you enjoy life to the fullest without actually worrying about the future. Financial investment ensures you save for rainy days. Careful investment makes your future secure. Financial investment controls an individual's spending pattern. It decides how and what amount one should spend so that he has sufficient money for future.

Tips for Financial investment

Don't just blindly trust your financial advisor. Read the terms and conditions and go through all the related documents carefully before signing. Check out risk factors, tenure, clauses etc before selecting the plan. Avoid cash transactions. It is always advisable to issue an account payee cheque in favour of the company rather than giving cash to your advisor. You never know when he disappears with all your hard earned money. Carefully staple all the related documents and put it in a folder. Keep it at a proper and safe place. Loosing even a single paper might land you in trouble later on.

Make sure your investment plan is the best in the market and guarantees sufficient return in future. If you plan to invest in property, ensure it is at a prime location and would have takers in the near future. Investing in non approved properties is worthless.

What is a Financial Market ?

A market is a place where two parties are involved in transaction of goods and services in exchange of money. The two parties involved are:

- Buyer
- Seller

In a market the buyer and seller comes on a common platform, where buyer purchases goods and services from the seller in exchange of money.

What is a Financial Market ?

A place where individuals are involved in any kind of financial transaction refers to financial market. Financial market is a platform where buyers and sellers are involved in sale and purchase of financial products like shares, mutual funds, bonds and so on.

Let Us Go through the Various Types of Financial Market

Capital Market: A market where individuals invest for a longer duration i.e. more than a year is called as capital market. In a capital market various financial institutions raise money from individuals and invest it for a longer period.

Capital Market is Further Divided into

i. Primary Market: Primary Market is a form of capital market where various companies issue new stock, shares and bonds to investors in the form of IPO's (Initial Public Offering). Primary Market is a form of market where stocks and securities are issued for the first time by organisations.

ii. Secondary Market: Secondary market is a form of capital market where stocks and securities which have been previously issued are bought and sold.

Types of Capital Market

1. Stock Markets: Stock Market is a type of Capital market which deals with the issuance and trading of shares and stocks at a certain price.
2. Bond Markets: Bond Market is a form of capital market where buyers and sellers are involved in the trading of bonds.
3. Commodity Market: A market which facilitates the sale and purchase of raw goods is called a commodity market.

   Commodity market like any other market includes a buyer and a seller. In such a market buyer purchases raw products like rice, wheat, grain, cattle and so on from the seller at a mutually agreed rate.
4. Money Market: As the name suggests, money market involves individuals who deal with the lending and borrowing of money for a short time frame.
5. Derivatives Market: The market which deals with the trading of contracts which are derived from any other asset is called as derivative market.
6. Future Market: Future market is a type of financial market which deals with the trading of financial instruments at a specific rate where in the delivery takes place in future.
7. Insurance Market: Insurance market deals with the trading of insurance products. Insurance companies pay a certain amount to the immediate family members of owner of the policy in case of his untimely death.
8. Foreign Exchange Market: Foreign exchange market is a globally operating market dealing in the sale and purchase of foreign currencies.

9. Private Market: Private market is a form of market where transaction of financial products takes place between two parties directly.
10. Mortgage Market: A type of market where various financial organisations are involved in providing loans to individuals on various residential and commercial properties for a specific duration is called a mortgage market. The payment is made to the individual concerned on submitting certain necessary documents and fulfilling certain basic criteria.

Shares and Stock Market - An Overview

An organisation in order to raise money divides its entire capital into small units of equal value. Each unit is called a share.

A share is nothing but an indivisible unit of a company's capital to be sold among individuals to increase profit of the organisation.

Shareholder

An individual owning one or more than one share of an organisation is called a shareholder. In simpler words, an individual purchasing one or more than one share from any private or public organisation is called a shareholder.

- A shareholder can sell his shares anytime depending on the current value of the share.
- He/she can purchase any new share issued by any other or same organisation.
- A shareholder has the right to declared dividend.

Dividend

Why Do People Invest in Shares?: An organisation pays the shareholders for investing in their company's shares. The income earned by an individual by investing in an organisation's share (private or public) is called as dividend.

What is Retained Earnings?: The profit earned by an organisation is put into use in the following two ways:

- It is paid to the shareholders as dividend.
- The profit earned by the organisation is not distributed amongst the shareholders but is retained and reinvested in the organisation. This portion of the income is called retained earnings.

What is a Share Certificate ?

When an individual purchases shares from any organisation, he/she is issued a certificate as a proof of his investment. Such a certificate issued by an organisation to the shareholders is called a share certificate.

Types of Shares

1. Equity Shares: Equity shares also called as ordinary shares are the shares where the payment of dividend is directly proportional to the profits earned by the organisation. Higher the profits earned, higher the dividend, lower the profits, and lower the dividend. In an equity share, dividends are paid at a fluctuating/floating rate.
2. Preference Shares: Shares which enjoy preference over payment of dividends are called preference shares. Shareholders enjoy fixed rate of dividends in case of preference shares.
3. Founder Shares: Shares held by the management or founders of the organisation are called as founder shares.
4. Bonus Shares: Bonus shares are often issued to the shareholders when the organisation earns surplus profits. The company officials may decide to pay the extra profits to the shareholders either as cash (dividend) or issue a bonus share to them.

Bonus shares are often issued by organisations to the shareholders free of charge as a gift in proportion to their existing shares with the organisation.

How to Buy Shares ?

- Find a good broker for yourself. Make sure he has good knowledge about the share market and can guide you properly.
- To invest in shares one needs to open a DEMAT Account for online trading. A DEMAT Account is mandatory for sale and purchase of shares anytime and anywhere.
- An individual needs to have his PAN Card, a bank account, other necessary Identity proofs, address proofs and so on.

What is a Stock Market ?

A stock market is a platform for trading of company's shares at an agreed rate.

The Promise and Perils of High Frequency Trading or HFT

What is HFT or High Frequency Trading ?

HFT or High Frequency Trading is a process where trading in equities, bonds, derivatives, and just about all financial instruments is done through computers driven by algorithms that determine the trading patterns rather than humans trading on the basis of information. In other words, HFT means that trading in financial instruments is done through computers talking to each other that are powered by complex algorithms that map how trading has to be done. HFT is a recent phenomenon that arose from the need to make sense of the increasingly complex nature of financial markets.

HFT resembles the 21st century trading paradigm where information is obtained real time and those market participants who can use the information instantaneously benefit more than those who are late to the react to the developments. Since computers driven by Artificial Intelligence or AI have the ability to react in real time to changing market trends, HFT has revolutionized the way in which financial markets operate in the West and especially on Wall Street. As we shall discuss subsequently, there are advantages and disadvantages of HFT.

The Promise of HFT

The promise of HFT lies in the fact that humans cannot make sense of the rapidly changing market trends and the accelerating changes in financial markets in real time. On the other hand, computers powered by AI have the ability to respond in real time to the changes and the flows of information. Since asymmetries of information are the real reason why financial markets are imperfect, it is believed that HFT would do away with this anomaly or shortcoming and lead to markets that are more efficient. Further, it is believed that handling the ever increasingly complexity and the explosion in the volumes of financial products that are traded can only be managed through computers that pack in a lot of punch with their computing power. Indeed, this is the best argument and the justification that is made for the use of HFT as it has the power to revolutionize the way in which financial markets operate. Indeed, in the west and on Wall Street, HFT has engineered a revolution in the way Wall Street brokers' trade with each other and financial firms operate. The use of HFT is being adopted worldwide following the success of its venture in the West.

The Perils of HFT

However, there are many perils of using HFT as well. For starters, chances of the computer programs going haywire and large-scale swings in the markets is one big danger that HFT poses. As can be seen from the various flash crashes where the DOW and the NASDAQ crashed abysmally within a few minutes on several occasions within the last couple of years, the potential for dangerous situations to manifest themselves is very high. Further, as computers make the decisions on trading rather than humans and the AI can sometimes encounter a situation where human intervention is needed, HFT cannot be the solution all the time. The preferred method would be for a system where the actual human traders have the overall decision-making power rather than the computers alone wherein any potential for the software going haywire is immediately rectified through prompt human intervention. The other danger that HFT poses is that it elbows out the individual investor and the jobbers or the small traders and bestows all the benefits on large financial firms. Considering the fact that financial markets are supposed to work for the benefit of everybody, HFT moves away from democratization of the market.

Concluding Remarks

Finally, when one considers the promise and the perils of HFT, it is clear that the balance is even and hence, one has to watch how the future of trading in financial markets evolves to a situation that is more in tune with market participants and their desires.

Chapter 7

Building Blocks of Finance

Mutual Fund

A mutual fund is a type of professionally managed collective investment scheme that pools money from many investors to purchase securities. While there is no legal definition of the term *mutual fund*, it is most commonly applied only to those collective investment vehicles that are regulated and sold to the general public. They are sometimes referred to as "investment companies" or "registered investment companies". Most mutual funds are *open-ended*, meaning stockholders can buy or sell shares of the fund at any time by redeeming them from the fund itself, rather than on an exchange. Hedge funds are not considered a type of mutual fund, primarily because they are not sold publicly.

In the United States, mutual funds must be registered the Securities and Exchange Commission, overseen by a board of directors (or board of trustees if organised as a trust rather than a corporation or partnership) and managed by a registered investment adviser. Mutual funds, like other registered investment companies, are also subject to an extensive and detailed regulatory regime set forth in the Investment Company Act of 1940. Mutual funds are not taxed on their income and profits if they comply with certain requirements under the U.S. Internal Revenue Code.

Mutual funds have both advantages and disadvantages compared to direct investing in individual securities. They have a long history in the United States. Today they play an important role in household finances, most notably in retirement planning.

There are 3 types of U.S. mutual funds: open-end, unit investment trust, and closed-end. The most common type, the open-end fund, must be willing to buy back shares from investors every business day. Exchange-traded funds (ETFs) are open-end funds or unit investment trusts that trade on an exchange. Open-end funds are most common, but exchange-traded funds have been gaining in popularity.

Mutual funds are generally classified by their principal investments. The four main categories of funds are money market funds, bond or fixed income funds, stock or equity funds and hybrid funds. Funds may also be categorized as index or actively managed.

Investors in a mutual fund pay the fund's expenses, which reduce the fund's returns and performance. There is controversy about the level of these expenses. A single mutual fund may give investors a choice of different combinations of expenses (which may include sales commissions or loads) by offering several different types of share classes.

Structure

In the US, a mutual fund is registered with the Securities and Exchange Commission (SEC) and is overseen by a board of directors (if organised as a corporation) or board of trustees (if organised as a trust). The board is charged with ensuring that the fund is managed in the best interests of the fund's investors and with hiring the fund manager and other service providers to the fund.

The fund manager, also known as the fund sponsor or fund management company, trades (buys and sells) the fund's investments in accordance with the fund's investment objective. A fund manager must be a registered investment advisor. Funds that are managed by the same fund manager and that have the same brand name are known as a *fund family* or *fund complex.*

Mutual funds are not taxed on their income and profits as long as they comply with requirements established in the U.S. Internal Revenue Code. Specifically, they must diversify their investments, limit ownership of voting securities, distribute a high percentage of their income and capital gains (net of capital losses) to their investors annually, and earn most of the income by investing in securities and currencies.

Mutual funds pass taxable income on to their investors by paying out dividends and capital gains at least annually. The characterization of that income is unchanged as it passes through to the shareholders. For example, mutual fund distributions of dividend income are reported as dividend income by the investor. There is an exception: net losses incurred by a mutual fund are not distributed or passed through to fund investors but are retained by the fund to be able to offset future gains.

Mutual funds may invest in many kinds of securities. The types of securities that a particular fund may invest in are set forth in the fund's prospectus, which describes the fund's investment objective, investment approach and permitted investments. The investment objective describes the type of income that the fund seeks. For example, a *capital appreciation* fund generally looks to earn most of its returns from increases in the prices of the securities it holds, rather than from dividend or interest income. The investment approach describes the criteria that the fund manager uses to select investments for the fund.

A mutual fund's investment portfolio is continually monitored by the fund's portfolio manager or managers.

Hedge funds are not considered a type of (unregistered) mutual fund. While they are another type of collective investment vehicle, they are not governed by the Investment Company Act of 1940 and are not required to register with the Securities and Exchange Commission (though many hedge fund managers must register as investment advisers).

Advantages and Disadvantages

Mutual funds have advantages compared to direct investing in individual securities. These include:

- Increased diversification: A fund must hold many securities. Diversifying reduces risks compared to holding a single stock, bond, other available instruments.
- Daily liquidity: This concept applies only to open-end funds. Shareholders may trade their holdings with the fund manager at the close of a trading day based on the closing net asset value of the fund's holdings. However, there may be fees and restrictions as stated in the fund prospectus. For holders of individual stocks, bonds, closed-end funds, ETFs, and other available instruments, there may not be a buyer/seller for that instrument every day, making such investments less liquid.
- Professional investment management: A highly variable aspect of a fund discussed in the prospectus. Actively managed funds may have large staffs of analysts who actively trade the fund holdings. Management of an index fund may just passively re-balance holdings to match a market index like the Standard and Poors 500 Index.

- Ability to participate in investments that may be available only to larger investors: Foreign markets, in particular, are rarely open and affordable for individual investors. Moreover, the research required to make sensible foreign investments may require knowledge of another language and the rules of regulations of other markets.
- Service and convenience: This is not a feature of a mutual fund, but rather a feature of the fund management company. Increasingly in recent years, there are funds, notably Exchange Traded Funds (ETFs) that are purely investment instruments without any additional services from the fund management company.
- Government oversight: Largely, the US government's role with mutual funds is to require the publication of a prospectus describing the fund. No such document is required for stock, bonds, currencies, and other investment instruments. There is no governmental oversight of a fund's investment success/failure.
- Ease of comparison: Since mutual funds are available from many providers, it is generally easy to find similar funds and compare features such as expenses.

Mutual funds have disadvantages as well, which include:

- Fees
- Less control over timing of recognition of gains
- Less predictable income
- No opportunity to customize

History

The first mutual funds were established in Europe. One researcher credits a Dutch merchant with creating the first mutual fund in 1774. The first mutual fund outside the Netherlands was the Foreign & Colonial Government Trust, which was established in London in 1868. It is now the Foreign & Colonial Investment Trust and trades on the London stock exchange.

Mutual funds were introduced into the United States in the 1890s. They became popular during the 1920s. These early funds were generally of the closed-end type with a fixed number of shares which often traded at prices above the value of the portfolio.

The first open-end mutual fund with redeemable shares was established on March 21, 1924. This fund, the Massachusetts Investors

Trust, is now part of the MFS family of funds. However, closed-end funds remained more popular than open-end funds throughout the 1920s. By 1929, open-end funds accounted for only 5% of the industry's $27 billion in total assets.

After the stock market crash of 1929, Congress passed a series of acts regulating the securities markets in general and mutual funds in particular. The Securities Act of 1933 requires that all investments sold to the public, including mutual funds, be registered with the Securities and Exchange Commission and that they provide prospective investors with a prospectus that discloses essential facts about the investment. The Securities and Exchange Act of 1934 requires that issuers of securities, including mutual funds, report regularly to their investors; this act also created the Securities and Exchange Commission, which is the principal regulator of mutual funds. The Revenue Act of 1936 established guidelines for the taxation of mutual funds, while the Investment Company Act of 1940 governs their structure.

When confidence in the stock market returned in the 1950s, the mutual fund industry began to grow again. By 1970, there were approximately 360 funds with $48 billion in assets. The introduction of money market funds in the high interest rate environment of the late 1970s boosted industry growth dramatically. The first retail index fund, First Index Investment Trust, was formed in 1976 by The Vanguard Group, headed by John Bogle; it is now called the Vanguard 500 Index Fund and is one of the world's largest mutual funds, with more than $100 billion in assets as of January 31, 2011.

Fund industry growth continued into the 1980s and 1990s, as a result of three factors: a bull market for both stocks and bonds, new product introductions (including tax-exempt bond, sector, international and target date funds) and wider distribution of fund shares. Among the new distribution channels were retirement plans. Mutual funds are now the preferred investment option in certain types of fast-growing retirement plans, specifically in 401(k) and other defined contribution plans and in individual retirement accounts (IRAs), all of which surged in popularity in the 1980s. Total mutual fund assets fell in 2008 as a result of the credit crisis of 2008.

In 2003, the mutual fund industry was involved in a scandal involving unequal treatment of fund shareholders. Some fund management companies allowed favoured investors to engage in late trading, which is illegal, or market timing, which is a practice prohibited by fund policy. The scandal was initially discovered by then-New York

State Attorney General Eliot Spitzer and resulted in significantly increased regulation of the industry.

At the end of 2011, there were over 14,000 mutual funds in the United States with combined assets of $13 trillion, according to the Investment Company Institute (ICI), a trade association of investment companies in the United States. The ICI reports that worldwide mutual fund assets were $23.8 trillion on the same date.

Mutual funds play an important role in U.S. household finances and retirement planning. At the end of 2011, funds accounted for 23% of household financial assets. Their role in retirement planning is particularly significant. Roughly half of assets in 401(k) plans and individual retirement accounts were invested in mutual funds.

Types

There are 3 principal types of mutual funds in the United States: open-end funds, unit investment trusts (UITs); and closed-end funds.

Exchange-traded funds (ETFs) are open-end funds or unit investment trusts that trade on an exchange; they have gained in popularity recently. While the term "mutual fund" may refer to all three types of registered investment companies, it is more commonly used to refer exclusively to the open-end type.

Open-End Funds

Open-end mutual funds must be willing to buy back their shares from their investors at the end of every business day at the net asset value computed that day. Most open-end funds also sell shares to the public every business day; these shares are also priced at net asset value. A professional investment manager oversees the portfolio, buying and selling securities as appropriate. The total investment in the fund will vary based on share purchases, share redemptions and fluctuation in market valuation. There is no legal limit on the number of shares that can be issued.

Open-end funds are the most common type of mutual fund. At the end of 2011, there were 7,581 open-end mutual funds in the United States with combined assets of $11.6 trillion.

Closed-End Funds

Closed-end funds generally issue shares to the public only once, when they are created through an initial public offering. Their shares are then listed for trading on a stock exchange. Investors who no longer wish to invest in the fund cannot sell their shares back to the fund (as they can with an open-end fund). Instead, they must sell their shares to another investor in the market; the price they receive may be significantly different from net asset value. It may be at a "premium" to net asset value (meaning that it is higher than net asset value) or, more commonly, at a "discount" to net asset value (meaning that it is lower than net asset value). A professional investment manager oversees the portfolio, buying and selling securities as appropriate.

At the end of 2011, there were 634 closed-end funds in the United States with combined assets of $239 billion.

Unit Investment Trusts

Unit investment trusts or UITs issue shares to the public only once, when they are created. UITs generally have a limited life span, established at creation. Investors can redeem shares directly with the fund at any time (as with an open-end fund) or wait to redeem upon termination of the trust. Less commonly, they can sell their shares in the open market.

Unit investment trusts do not have a professional investment manager. Their portfolio of securities is established at the creation of the UIT and does not change.

At the end of 2011, there were 6,022 UITs in the United States with combined assets of $60 billion.

Exchange-Traded Funds

A relatively recent innovation, the exchange-traded fund or ETF is often structured as an open-end investment company, though ETFs may also be structured as unit investment trusts, partnerships, investments trust, grantor trusts or bonds (as an exchange-traded note). Most ETFs are index funds that combine characteristics of both closed-end funds and open-end funds. Ideally, ETFs are traded throughout the day on a stock exchange at a price that is close to net asset value of the ETF holdings. ETF shares may be created or liquidated during the trading day by the fund manager working with specialist and institutions that profit from arbitrage trading the slight differences between the ETF trading price and the price of the ETF holdings. This arbitrage is supposed to keep the ETF market price close to net asset value of its holdings, but there is no guarantee especially with thinly traded ETFs. As of March 2014, more than half of ETFs have less than $100 million in assets, and about 20% have assets less than $10 million.).

ETFs have been gaining in popularity. As of March 2014, there were over 1,500 ETFs in the United States with combined assets of in excess of $2.7 trillion.

Investments and Classification

Mutual funds are normally classified by their principal investments, as described in the prospectus and investment objective. The four main categories of funds are money market funds, bond or fixed income funds, stock or equity funds and hybrid funds. Within these categories, funds may be subclassified by investment objective, investment approach or specific focus. The SEC requires that mutual fund names not be inconsistent with a fund's investments. For example, the "ABC New Jersey Tax-Exempt Bond Fund" would generally have to invest, under normal circumstances, at least 80% of its assets in bonds that are exempt from federal income tax, from the alternative minimum tax and from taxes in the state of New Jersey.

Bond, stock and hybrid funds may be classified as either index (passively managed) funds or actively managed funds.

Money Market Funds

Money market funds invest in money market instruments, which are fixed income securities with a very short time to maturity and high credit quality. Investors often use money market funds as a substitute for bank savings accounts, though money market funds are not government insured, unlike bank savings accounts.

Money market funds strive to maintain a $1.00 per share net asset value, meaning that investors earn interest income from the fund but do not experience capital gains or losses. If a fund fails to maintain that $1.00 per share because its securities have declined in value, it is said to "break the buck". Only two money market funds have ever broken the buck: Community Banker's U.S. Government Money Market Fund in 1994 and the Reserve Primary Fund in 2008.

At the end of 2011, money market funds accounted for 23% of open-end fund assets.

Bond Funds

Bond funds invest in fixed income or debt securities. Bond funds can be subclassified according to the specific types of bonds owned (such as high-yield or junk bonds, investment-grade corporate bonds, government bonds or municipal bonds) or by the maturity of the bonds held (short-, intermediate- or long-term). Bond funds may invest in primarily U.S. securities (domestic or U.S. funds), in both U.S. and foreign securities (global or world funds), or primarily foreign securities (international funds).

At the end of 2011, bond funds accounted for 25% of open-end fund assets.

Stock or Equity Funds

Stock or equity funds invest in common stocks which represent an ownership share (or equity) in corporations. Stock funds may invest in primarily U.S. securities (domestic or U.S. funds), in both U.S. and foreign securities (global or world funds), or primarily foreign securities (international funds). They may focus on a specific industry or sector.

A stock fund may be subclassified along two dimensions: (1) market capitalization and (2) investment style (i.e., growth vs. blend/core vs. value). The two dimensions are often displayed in a grid known as a "style box".

Market capitalization ("cap") indicates the size of the companies in which a fund invests, based on the value of the company's stock. Each company's market capitalization equals the number of shares outstanding times the market price of the stock. Market capitalizations are typically divided into the following categories:

- Micro cap
- Small cap
- Mid cap
- Large cap

While the specific definitions of each category vary with market conditions, large cap stocks generally have market capitalizations of at least $10 billion, small cap stocks have market capitalizations below $2 billion, and micro cap stocks have market capitalizations below $300 million. Funds are also classified in these categories based on the market caps of the stocks that it holds.

Stock funds are also subclassified according to their investment style: growth, value or blend (or core). Growth funds seek to invest in stocks of fast-growing companies. Value funds seek to invest in stocks that appear cheaply priced. Blend funds are not biased toward either growth or value.

At the end of 2011, stock funds accounted for 46% of the assets in all U.S. mutual funds.

Hybrid Funds

Hybrid funds invest in both bonds and stocks or in convertible securities. Balanced funds, asset allocation funds, target date or target risk funds and lifecycle or lifestyle funds are all types of hybrid funds.

Hybrid funds may be structured as funds of funds, meaning that they invest by buying shares in other mutual funds that invest in securities. Most fund of funds invest in affiliated funds (meaning mutual funds managed by the same fund sponsor), although some invest in unaffiliated funds (meaning those managed by other fund sponsors) or in a combination of the two. At the end of 2011, hybrid funds accounted for 7% of the assets in all U.S. mutual funds.

Index (Passively Managed) versus Actively Managed

An index fund or passively managed fund seeks to match the performance of a market index, such as the S&P 500 index, while an actively managed fund seeks to outperform a relevant index through superior security selection.

Expenses

Investors in a mutual fund pay the fund's expenses. These expenses fall into five categories: distribution charges (sales loads and 12b-1 fees), the management fee, other fund expenses, shareholder transaction fees and securities transaction fees. Some of these expenses reduce the value of an investor's account; others are paid by the fund and reduce net asset value.

Recurring fees and expenses—specifically the 12b-1 fee, the management fee and other fund expenses—are included in a fund's total expense ratio, or simply the "expense ratio". Because all funds must compute an expense ratio using the same method, it allows investors to compare costs across funds.

Distribution Charges

Distribution charges pay for marketing, distribution of the fund's shares as well as services to investors.

Front-End Load or Sales Charge

A front-end load or sales charge is a commission paid to a broker by a mutual fund when shares are purchased. It is expressed as a percentage of the total amount invested or the "public offering price", which equals the net asset value plus the front-end load per share. The front-end load often declines as the amount invested increases, through breakpoints. The front-end load is paid by the shareholder; it is deducted from the amount invested.

Back-End Load

Some funds have a back-end load, which is paid by the investor when shares are redeemed. If the back-end load declines the longer the investor holds shares, it is called a contingent deferred sales charges (or CDSC). Like the front-end load, the back-end load is paid by the shareholder; it is deducted from the redemption proceeds.

12b-1 Fees

Some funds charge an annual fee to compensate the distributor of fund shares for providing ongoing services to fund shareholders. This fee is called a 12b-1 fee, after the SEC rule authorizing it. The 12b-1 fee is paid by the fund and reduces net asset value.

No-Load Funds

A no-load fund does not charge a front-end load under any circumstances, does not charge a back-end load under any circumstances and does not charge a 12b-1 fee greater than 0.25% of fund assets. An example of this type of fund is a Real estate fund.

Management Fee

The management fee is paid to the fund manager or sponsor who organises the fund, provides the portfolio management or investment advisory services and normally lends its brand name to the fund. The fund manager may also provide other administrative services. The management fee often has breakpoints, which means that it declines as assets (in either the specific fund or in the fund family as a whole) increase. The management fee is paid by the fund and is included in the expense ratio.

The fund's board of directors reviews the management fee annually. Fund shareholders must vote on any proposed increase in the management. However, the fund manager or sponsor may agree to waive all or a portion of the management fee in order to lower the fund's expense ratio.

Other Fund Expenses

A mutual fund may pay for other services including:

- Board of directors or trustees fees and expenses
- Custody fee: paid to a custodian bank for holding the fund's portfolio in safekeeping and collecting income owed on the securities
- Fund administration fee: for overseeing all administrative affairs of the fund such as preparing financial statements and shareholder reports, preparing and filing myriad SEC filings required of registered investment companies, monitoring compliance with investment restrictions, computing total returns and other fund performance information, preparing/ filing tax returns and all expenses of maintaining compliance with state "blue sky" laws

- Fund accounting fee: for performing investment or securities accounting services and computing the net asset value (usually each day the New York Stock Exchange is open)
- Professional services fees: legal and auditing fees
- Registration fees: for 24F-2 fees owed to the SEC for net sales of registered fund shares and state blue sky fees owed for selling shares to residents of states in the US and jurisdictions such as Puerto Rico and Guam
- Shareholder communications expenses: printing and mailing required documents to shareholders such as shareholder reports and prospectuses
- Transfer agent service fees and expenses: for keeping shareholder records, providing statements and tax forms to investors and providing telephone, internet and or other investor support and servicing
- Other/miscellaneous fees

The fund manager or sponsor may agree to subsidize some of these other expenses in order to lower the fund's expense ratio.

Shareholder Transaction Fees

Shareholders may be required to pay fees for certain transactions. For example, a fund may charge a flat fee for maintaining an individual retirement account for an investor. Some funds charge redemption fees when an investor sells fund shares shortly after buying them (usually defined as within 30, 60 or 90 days of purchase); redemption fees are computed as a percentage of the sale amount. Shareholder transaction fees are not part of the expense ratio.

Securities Transaction Fees

A mutual fund pays expenses related to buying or selling the securities in its portfolio. These expenses may include brokerage commissions. Securities transaction fees increase the cost basis of investments purchased and reduce the proceeds from their sale. They do not flow through a fund's income statement and are not included in its expense ratio. The amount of securities transaction fees paid by a fund is normally positively correlated with its trading volume or "turnover".

Controversy

Critics of the fund industry argue that fund expenses are too high. They believe that the market for mutual funds is not competitive and that there are many hidden fees, so that it is difficult for investors to reduce the fees that they pay. They argue that the most effective way for investors to raise the returns they earn from mutual funds is to invest in funds with low expense ratios.

Fund managers counter that fees are determined by a highly competitive market and, therefore, reflect the value that investors attribute to the service provided. In addition, they note that fees are clearly disclosed.

Share Classes

A single mutual fund may give investors a choice of different combinations of front-end loads, back-end loads and 12b-1 fees, by offering several different types of shares, known as *share classes*. All of the shares classes invest in the same portfolio of securities, but each has different expenses and, therefore, a different net asset value and different performance results. Some of these share classes may be available only to certain types of investors.

Funds offering multiple classes often identify them with letters, though they may also use names such as "Investor Class", "Service Class", "Institutional Class", etc., to identify the type of investor for which the class is intended. The SEC does not regulate the names of share classes, so that specifics of a share class with the same name may vary from fund family to fund family.

Typical share classes for funds sold through brokers or other intermediaries are as follows.:

- Class A shares usually charge a front-end sales load together with a small 12b-1 fee.
- Class B shares usually don't have a front-end sales load. Instead they, have a high contingent deferred sales charge, or CDSC that declines gradually over several years, combined with a high 12b-1 fee. Class B shares usually convert automatically to Class A shares after they have been held for a certain period.
- Class C shares usually have a high 12b-1 fee and a modest contingent deferred sales charge that is discontinued after one or two years. Class C shares usually do not convert to another class. They are often called "level load" shares.
- Class I are usually subject to very high minimum investment requirements and are, therefore, known as "institutional" shares. They are no-load shares.
- Class R are usually for use in retirement plans such as 401(k) plans. They typically do not charge loads, but do charge a small 12b-1 fee.

No-load funds often have two classes of shares:

- Class I shares do not charge a 12b-1 fee.
- Class N shares charge a 12b-1 fee of no more than 0.25% of fund assets.

Neither class of shares typically charges a front-end or back-end load.

Definitions: Definitions of key terms.

Net Asset Value or NAV

A fund's net asset value or NAV equals the current market value of a fund's holdings minus the fund's liabilities (sometimes referred to as "net assets"). It is usually expressed as a per-share amount, computed by dividing net assets by the number of fund shares outstanding. Funds must compute their net asset value according to the rules set forth in their prospectuses. Funds compute their NAV at the end of each day that the New York Stock Exchange is open, though some funds compute their NAV more than once daily.

Valuing the securities held in a fund's portfolio is often the most difficult part of calculating net asset value. The fund's board typically oversees security valuation.

Expense Ratio

The expense ratio allows investors to compare expenses across funds. The expense ratio equals the 12b-1 fee plus the management fee plus the other fund expenses divided by average daily net assets. The expense ratio is sometimes referred to as the "total expense ratio" or TER.

Average Annual Total Return

The SEC requires that mutual funds report the average annual compounded rates of return for 1-year, 5-year and 10-year periods using the following formula:

$$P(1+T)^n = ERV$$

Where:

P = a hypothetical initial payment of $1,000.

T = average annual total return.

n = number of years.

ERV = ending redeemable value of a hypothetical $1,000 payment made at the beginning of the 1-, 5-, or 10-year periods at the end of the 1-, 5-, or 10-year periods (or fractional portion).

Turnover

Turnover is a measure of the volume of a fund's securities trading. It is expressed as a percentage of average market value of the portfolio's long-term securities. Turnover is the lesser of a fund's purchases or sales during a given year divided by average long-term securities market value for the same period. If the period is less than a year, turnover is generally annualized.

Exchange-Traded Fund

An exchange-traded fund (ETF) is an investment fund traded on stock exchanges, much like stocks. An ETF holds assets such as stocks, commodities, or bonds, and trades close to its net asset value over the course of the trading day. Most ETFs track an index, such as a stock index or bond index. ETFs may be attractive as investments because of their low costs, tax efficiency, and stock-like features. ETFs are the most popular type of exchange-traded product.

Only *authorized participants*, which are large broker-dealers that have entered into agreements with the ETF's distributor, actually buy or sell shares of an ETF directly from or to the ETF, and then only in *creation units*, which are large blocks of tens of thousands of ETF shares, usually exchanged in-kind with *baskets* of the underlying securities. Authorized participants may wish to invest in the ETF shares for the long-term, but they usually act as market makers on the open market, using their ability to exchange creation units with their underlying securities to provide liquidity of the ETF shares and help ensure that their intraday market price approximates the net asset value of the underlying assets. Other investors, such as individuals using a retail broker, trade ETF shares on this secondary market.

An ETF combines the valuation feature of a mutual fund or unit investment trust, which can be bought or sold at the end of each trading day for its net asset value, with the tradability feature of a closed-end fund, which trades throughout the trading day at prices that may be more or less than its net asset value. Closed-end funds are not considered to be ETFs, even though they are funds and are traded on an exchange. ETFs have been available in the US since 1993 and in Europe since 1999. ETFs traditionally have been index funds, but in 2008 the U.S. Securities and Exchange Commission began to authorize the creation of actively managed ETFs.

Structure

An ETF is a type of *fund*, some entity such as a corporation or trust that owns assets (bonds, stocks, gold bars, etc.) and divides ownership of itself into shares that are held by shareholders. The details of the structure can vary by country, or even by state in the United States. The shareholders indirectly own the assets of the fund, and they will typically get an annual report. Shareholders are entitled to a share of the profits, such as interest or dividends, and they may get a residual value in case the fund is liquidated. Their ownership of the fund can easily be bought and sold.

ETFs are similar in many ways to traditional mutual funds, except that shares in an ETF can be bought and sold throughout the day like stocks on a stock exchange through a broker-dealer. Unlike traditional mutual funds, ETFs do not sell or redeem their individual shares at net asset value (NAV). Instead, financial institutions purchase and redeem ETF shares directly from the ETF, but only in large blocks varying in size from 25,000 to 200,000 shares, called *creation units*. Purchases and redemptions of the creation units generally are in kind, with the institutional investor contributing or receiving a basket of securities of the same type and proportion held by the ETF, although some ETFs may require or permit a purchasing or redeeming shareholder to substitute cash for some or all of the securities in the basket of assets.

The ability to purchase and redeem creation units gives ETFs an arbitrage mechanism intended to minimize the potential deviation between the market price and the net asset value of ETF shares. Existing ETFs have transparent portfolios, so institutional investors will know exactly what portfolio assets they must assemble if they wish to purchase a creation unit, and the exchange disseminates the updated net asset value of the shares throughout the trading day, typically at 15-second intervals.

If there is strong investor demand for an ETF, its share price will temporarily rise above its net asset value per share, giving arbitrageurs an incentive to purchase additional creation units from the ETF and sell the component ETF shares in the open market. The additional supply of ETF shares reduces the market price per share, generally eliminating the premium over net asset value. A similar process applies when there is weak demand for an ETF: its shares trade at a discount from net asset value.

In the United States, most ETFs are structured as open-end management investment companies (the same structure used by mutual funds and money market funds), although a few ETFs, including some of the largest ones, are structured as unit investment trusts. ETFs structured as open-end funds have greater flexibility in constructing a portfolio and are not prohibited from participating in securities lending programs or from using futures and options in achieving their investment objectives.

Under existing regulations, a new ETF must receive an order from the Securities and Exchange Commission (SEC), giving it relief from provisions of the Investment Company Act of 1940 that would not otherwise allow the ETF structure. In 2008, the SEC proposed rules that would allow the creation of ETFs without the need for exemptive orders. Under the SEC proposal, an ETF would be defined as a registered open-end management investment company that:

- issues (or redeems) creation units in exchange for the deposit (or delivery) of basket assets the current value of which is disseminated per share by a national securities exchange at regular intervals during the trading day
- identifies itself as an ETF in any sales literature
- issues shares that are approved for listing and trading on a securities exchange
- discloses each business day on its publicly available web site the prior business day's net asset value and closing market price of the fund's shares, and the premium or discount of the closing market price against the net asset value of the fund's shares as a percentage of net asset value
- either is an index fund, or discloses each business day on its publicly available web site the identities and weighting of the component securities and other assets held by the fund.

The SEC rule proposal would allow ETFs either to be index funds or to be fully transparent actively managed funds. Historically, all ETFs in the United States have been index funds. In 2008, however, the SEC began issuing exemptive orders to fully transparent actively managed ETFs. The first such order was to PowerShares Actively Managed Exchange-Traded Fund Trust, and the first actively managed ETF in the United States was the Bear Stearns Current Yield Fund, a short-term income fund that began trading on the American Stock Exchange under the symbol YYY on March 25, 2008. The SEC rule proposal indicates that the SEC may still consider future applications for exemptive orders for actively managed ETFs that do not satisfy the proposed rule's transparency requirements.

Some ETFs invest primarily in commodities or commodity-based instruments, such as crude oil and precious metals. Although these commodity ETFs are similar in practice to ETFs that invest in securities, they are not investment companies under the Investment Company Act of 1940.

Publicly traded grantor trusts, such as Merrill Lynch's HOLDRs securities, are sometimes considered to be ETFs, although they lack many of the characteristics of other ETFs. Investors in a grantor trust have a direct interest in the underlying basket of securities, which does not change except to reflect corporate actions such as stock splits and mergers. Funds of this type are not investment companies under the Investment Company Act of 1940.

As of 2009, there were approximately 1,500 exchange-traded funds traded on US exchanges. This count uses the wider definition of ETF, including HOLDRs and closed-end funds.

History

ETFs had their genesis in 1989 with Index Participation Shares, an S&P 500 proxy that traded on the American Stock Exchange and the Philadelphia Stock Exchange. This product, however, was short-lived after a lawsuit by the Chicago Mercantile Exchange was successful in stopping sales in the United States.

A similar product, Toronto Index Participation Shares, started trading on the Toronto Stock Exchange (TSE) in 1990. The shares, which tracked the TSE 35 and later the TSE 100 indices, proved to be popular. The popularity of these products led the American Stock Exchange to try to develop something that would satisfy SEC regulation in the United States.

Nathan Most and Steven Bloom, under the direction of Ivers Riley, designed and developed Standard & Poor's Depositary Receipts (NYSE Arca: SPY), which were introduced in January 1993. Known as SPDRs or "Spiders", the fund became the largest ETF in the world. In May 1995 they introduced the MidCap SPDRs (NYSE Arca: MDY).

Barclays Global Investors, a subsidiary of Barclays PLC, entered the fray in 1996 with World Equity Benchmark Shares (WEBS) subsequently renamed iShares MSCI Index Fund Shares. WEBS tracked MSCI country indices, originally 17, of the funds' index provider, Morgan Stanley. WEBS were particularly innovative because they gave casual investors easy access to foreign markets. While SPDRs were organised as unit investment trusts, WEBS were set up as a mutual fund, the first of their kind.

In 1998, State Street Global Advisors introduced "Sector Spiders", which follow nine sectors of the S&P 500. Also in 1998, the "Dow Diamonds" (NYSE Arca: DIA) were introduced, tracking the famous

Dow Jones Industrial Average. In 1999, the influential "cubes" (NASDAQ: QQQ), were launched attempting to replicate the movement of the NASDAQ-100.

In 2000, Barclays Global Investors put a significant effort behind the ETF marketplace, with a strong emphasis on education and distribution to reach long-term investors. The iShares line was launched in early 2000. Within five years iShares had surpassed the assets of any other ETF competitor in the U.S. and Europe. Barclays Global Investors was sold to BlackRock in 2009.

The Vanguard Group entered the market in 2001. The first fund was Vanguard Total Stock Market ETF (NYSE Arca: VTI), which has become quite popular, and they made the Vanguard Extended Market Index ETF (VXF).

iShares made the first bond funds in July 2002, based on US Treasury bonds and corporate bonds, such as iShares iBoxx $ Invst Grade Crp Bond (LQD). They also created a TIPS fund. In 2007, they introduced funds based on junk and muni bonds; about the same time SPDR and Vanguard got in gear and created several of their bond funds.

Since then ETFs have proliferated, tailored to an increasingly specific array of regions, sectors, commodities, bonds, futures, and other asset classes. As of January 2014, there were over 1,500 ETFs traded in the U.S., with over $1.7 trillion in assets.

Investment Uses

ETFs generally provide the easy diversification, low expense ratios, and tax efficiency of index funds, while still maintaining all the features of ordinary stock, such as limit orders, short selling, and options. Because ETFs can be economically acquired, held, and disposed of, some investors invest in ETF shares as a long-term investment for asset allocation purposes, while other investors trade ETF shares frequently to implement market timing investment strategies. Among the advantages of ETFs are the following:

- Lower costs – ETFs generally have lower costs than other investment products because most ETFs are not actively managed and because ETFs are insulated from the costs of having to buy and sell securities to accommodate shareholder purchases and redemptions. ETFs typically have lower marketing, distribution and accounting expenses, and most ETFs do not have 12b-1 fees.
- Buying and selling flexibility – ETFs can be bought and sold at current market prices at any time during the trading day, unlike

mutual funds and unit investment trusts, which can only be traded at the end of the trading day. As publicly traded securities, their shares can be purchased on margin and sold short, enabling the use of hedging strategies, and traded using stop orders and limit orders, which allow investors to specify the price points at which they are willing to trade.

- Tax efficiency – ETFs generally generate relatively low capital gains, because they typically have low turnover of their portfolio securities. While this is an advantage they share with other index funds, their tax efficiency is further enhanced because they do not have to sell securities to meet investor redemptions.
- Market exposure and diversification – ETFs provide an economical way to rebalance portfolio allocations and to "equitize" cash by investing it quickly. An index ETF inherently provides diversification across an entire index. ETFs offer exposure to a diverse variety of markets, including broad-based indices, broad-based international and country-specific indices, industry sector-specific indices, bond indices, and commodities.
- Transparency – ETFs, whether index funds or actively managed, have transparent portfolios and are priced at frequent intervals throughout the trading day.

Some of these advantages derive from the status of most ETFs as index funds.

Types

Index ETFs: Most ETFs are index funds that attempt to replicate the performance of a specific index. Indexes may be based on stocks, bonds, commodities, or currencies. An index fund seeks to track the performance of an index by holding in its portfolio either the contents of the index or a representative sample of the securities in the index. As of June 2012, in the United States, about 1200 index ETFs exist, with about 50 actively managed ETFs. Index ETF assets are about $1.2 trillion, compared with about $7 billion for actively managed ETFs. Some index ETFs, known as leveraged ETFs or inverse ETFs, use investments in derivatives to seek a return that corresponds to a multiple of, or the inverse (opposite) of, the daily performance of the index.

Some index ETFs invest 100% of their assets proportionately in the securities underlying an index, a manner of investing called *replication*. Other index ETFs use *representative sampling*, investing 80% to 95% of their assets in the securities of an underlying index and investing the remaining 5% to 20% of their assets in other holdings, such as futures, option and swap contracts, and securities not in the underlying index, that the fund's adviser believes will help the ETF to achieve its investment objective. There are various ways the ETF can be weighted, such as equal weighting or revenue weighting. For index ETFs that invest in indices with thousands of underlying securities, some index ETFs employ "aggressive sampling" and invest in only a tiny percentage of the underlying securities.

Stock ETFs

The first and most popular ETFs track stocks. Many funds track national indexes; for example, Vanguard Total Stock Market ETF NYSE Arca: VTI tracks the MSCI US Broad Market Index, and several funds track the S&P 500, both indexes for US stocks. Other funds own stocks from many countries; for example, Vanguard Total International Stock Index NYSE Arca: VXUS tracks the MSCI All Country World ex USA Investable Market Index, while the iShares MSCI EAFE Index NYSE Arca: EFA tracks the MSCI EAFE Index, both "world ex-US" indexes.

ETFs can also be sector funds. These can be broad sectors, like finance and technology, or specific niche areas, like green power. They can also be for one country or global. Critics have said that no one *needs* a sector fund. This point is not really specific to ETFs; the issues are the same as with mutual funds. The funds are popular since people can put their money into the latest fashionable trend, rather than investing in boring areas with no "cachet".

Bond ETFs

Exchange-traded funds that invest in bonds are known as bond ETFs. They thrive during economic recessions because investors pull their money out of the stock market and into bonds (for example, government treasury bonds or those issued by companies regarded as financially stable). Because of this cause and effect relationship, the performance of bond ETFs may be indicative of broader economic conditions. There are several advantages to bond ETFs such as the reasonable trading commissions, but this benefit can be negatively offset by fees if bought and sold through a third party.

Commodity ETFs or ETCs

Commodity ETFs (ETCs or CETFs) invest in commodities, such as precious metals, agricultural products, or hydrocarbons. Among the first commodity ETFs were gold exchange-traded funds, which have been offered in a number of countries. The idea of a Gold ETF was first officially conceptualised by Benchmark Asset Management Company

Private Ltd in India when they filed a proposal with the SEBI in May 2002. The first gold exchange-traded fund was Gold Bullion Securities launched on the ASX in 2003, and the first silver exchange-traded fund was iShares Silver Trust launched on the NYSE in 2006. As of November 2010 a commodity ETF, namely SPDR Gold Shares, was the second-largest ETF by market capitalization.

However, generally commodity ETFs are index funds tracking non-security indices. Because they do not invest in securities, commodity ETFs are not regulated as investment companies under the Investment Company Act of 1940 in the United States, although their public offering is subject to SEC review and they need an SEC no-action letter under the Securities Exchange Act of 1934. They may, however, be subject to regulation by the Commodity Futures Trading Commission.

The earliest commodity ETFs, such as SPDR Gold Shares NYSE Arca: GLD and iShares Silver Trust NYSE Arca: SLV, actually owned the physical commodity (e.g., gold and silver bars). Similar to these are NYSE Arca: PALL (palladium) and NYSE Arca: PPLT (platinum). However, most ETCs implement a futures trading strategy, which may produce quite different results from owning the commodity.

Commodity ETFs trade just like shares, are simple and efficient and provide exposure to an ever-increasing range of commodities and commodity indices, including energy, metals, softs and agriculture. However, it is important for an investor to realise that there are often other factors that affect the price of a commodity ETF that might not be immediately apparent. For example, buyers of an oil ETF such as USO might think that as long as oil goes up, they will profit roughly linearly. What isn't clear to the novice investor is the method by which these funds gain exposure to their underlying commodities. In the case of many commodity funds, they simply roll so-called front-month futures contracts from month to month. This does give exposure to the commodity, but subjects the investor to risks involved in different prices along the *term structure*, such as a high cost to roll.

ETC can also refer to exchange-traded *notes*, which are not exchange-traded funds.

Currency ETFs or ETCs

In 2005, Rydex Investments launched the first ever currency ETF called the Euro Currency Trust (NYSE Arca: FXE) in New York. Since then Rydex has launched a series of funds tracking all major currencies under their brand CurrencyShares. In 2007 Deutsche Bank's db x-trackers launched EONIA Total Return Index ETF in Frankfurt tracking the euro, and later in 2008 the Sterling Money Market ETF

(LSE: XGBP) and US Dollar Money Market ETF (LSE: XUSD) in London. In 2009, ETF Securities launched the world's largest FX platform tracking the MSFX℠ Index covering 18 long or short USD ETC vs. single G10 currencies. The funds are total return products where the investor gets access to the FX spot change, local institutional interest rates and a collateral yield.

Actively Managed ETFs

Most ETFs are index funds, but some ETFs do have active management. Actively managed ETFs have been offered in the United States only since 2008. The first active ETF was Bear Stearns Current Yield ETF (Ticker: YYY). Currently, actively managed ETFs are fully transparent, publishing their current securities portfolios on their web sites daily. However, the SEC indicated that it was willing to consider allowing actively managed ETFs that are not fully transparent in the future, and later actively managed ETFs have sought alternatives to full transparency.

The fully transparent nature of existing ETFs means that an actively managed ETF is at risk from arbitrage activities by market participants who might choose to front run its trades as daily reports of the ETF's holdings reveals its manager's trading strategy. The initial actively managed equity ETFs addressed this problem by trading only weekly or monthly. Actively managed debt ETFs, which are less susceptible to front-running, trade their holdings more frequently.

The actively managed ETF market has largely been seen as more favourable to bond funds, because concerns about disclosing bond holdings are less pronounced, there are fewer product choices, and there is increased appetite for bond products. Pimco's Enhanced Short Duration ETF NYSE: MINT is the largest actively managed ETF, with approximately $3.93 billion in assets as of May 16, 2014.

Actively managed ETFs grew faster in their first three years of existence than index ETFs did in their first three years of existence. As track records develop, many see actively managed ETFs as a significant competitive threat to actively managed mutual funds. However, many academic studies have questioned the value of active management. Jack Bogle of Vanguard Group wrote an article in the *Financial Analysts Journal* where he estimated that higher fees as well as hidden costs (such a more trading fees and lower return from holding cash) reduce returns for investors by around 2.66 percentage points a year "a huge differential considering that long-term real returns from American equities have been 6.45%." Even without considering hidden costs, high fees negatively affect long-term performance. In another *Financial Analysts Journal* article, Nobel laureate, Bill Sharpe "calculated that someone who saved via a low-cost fund would have a standard of living in retirement 20% higher than someone who saved in a high-cost fund"

Exchange-Traded Grantor Trusts

An exchange-traded grantor trust share represents a direct interest in a static basket of stocks selected from a particular industry. Such products have some properties in common with ETFs – low costs, low turnover, and tax efficiency – but are generally regarded as separate from ETFs. The leading example was Holding Company Depositary Receipts, or HOLDRs, a proprietary Merrill Lynch product, but these have now disappeared from the scene.

Inverse ETFs

Leveraged ETFs: Leveraged exchange-traded funds (LETFs), or simply *leveraged ETFs*, are a special type of ETF that attempt to achieve returns that are more sensitive to market movements than non-leveraged ETFs. Leveraged index ETFs are often marketed as bull or bear funds. A leveraged bull ETF fund might for example attempt to achieve daily returns that are *2x* or *3x* more pronounced than the Dow Jones Industrial Average or the S&P 500. A leveraged inverse (bear) ETF fund on the other hand may attempt to achieve returns that are -*2x* or -*3x* the daily index return, meaning that it will gain double or triple the *loss* of the market. Leveraged ETFs require the use of financial engineering techniques, including the use of equity swaps, derivatives and rebalancing, and re-indexing to achieve the desired return. The most common way to construct leveraged ETFs is by trading futures contracts.

The rebalancing and re-indexing of leveraged ETFs may have considerable costs when markets are volatile. The rebalancing problem is that the fund manager incurs trading losses because he needs to buy when the index goes up and sell when the index goes down in order to maintain a fixed leverage ratio. A 2.5% daily change in the index will for example reduce value of a -2x bear fund by about 0.18% per day, which means that about a third of the fund may be wasted in trading losses within a year (1-(1-0.18%)=36.5%). Investors may however circumvent this problem by buying or writing futures directly, accepting a varying leverage ratio. A more reasonable estimate of daily market changes is 0.5%, which leads to a 2.6% yearly loss of principal in a 3x leveraged fund.

The re-indexing problem of leveraged ETFs stems from the arithmetic effect of volatility of the underlying index. Take, for example, an index that begins at 100 and a 2X fund based on that index that also starts at 100. In a first trading period (for example, a day), the index rises 10% to 110. The 2X fund will then rise 20% to 120. The index then drops back to 100 (a drop of 9.09%), so that it is now even. The drop in the 2X fund will be 18.18% (2*9.09). But 18.18% of 120 is 21.82. This puts the value of the 2X fund at 98.18. Even though the index is unchanged after two trading periods, an investor in the 2X fund would have lost 1.82%. This decline in value can be even greater for inverse funds (leveraged funds with negative multipliers such as -1, -2, or -3). It always occurs when the change in value of the underlying index changes direction. And the decay in value increases with volatility of the underlying index.

The effect of leverage is also reflected in the pricing of options written on leveraged ETFs. In particular, the terminal payoff of a leveraged ETF European/American put or call depends on the realised variance (hence the path) of the underlying index. The impact of leverage ratio can also be observed from the implied volatility surfaces of leveraged ETF options. For instance, the implied volatility curves of inverse leveraged ETFs (with negative multipliers such as -1, -2, or -3) are commonly observed to be increasing in strike, which is characteristically different from the implied volatility smiles or skews seen for index options or non-leveraged ETF options.

ETFs Compared to Mutual Funds

Costs: Because ETFs trade on an exchange, each transaction is generally subject to a brokerage commission. Commissions depend on the brokerage and which plan is chosen by the customer. For example, a typical flat fee schedule from an online brokerage firm in the United States ranges from $10 to $20, but it can be as low as $0 with discount brokers. Due to this commission cost, the amount invested has a great bearing; someone who wishes to invest $100 per month may have a significant percentage of their investment destroyed immediately, while for someone making a $200,000 investment, the commission cost may be negligible. Generally, mutual funds obtained directly from the fund company itself do not charge a brokerage fee. Thus, when low or no-cost transactions are available, ETFs become very competitive.

ETFs have a lower expense ratio than comparable mutual funds. Not only does an ETF have lower shareholder-related expenses, but because it does not have to invest cash contributions or fund cash redemptions, an ETF does not have to maintain a cash reserve for redemptions and saves on brokerage expenses. Mutual funds can charge 1% to 3%, or more; index fund expense ratios are generally lower, while ETFs are almost always in the 0.1% to 1% range. Over the long term, these cost differences can compound into a noticeable difference.

The cost difference is more evident when compared with mutual funds that charge a front-end or back-end load as ETFs do not have loads at all. The redemption fee and short-term trading fees are examples of other fees associated with mutual funds that do not exist with ETFs. Traders should be cautious if they plan to trade inverse and leveraged ETFs for short periods of time. Close attention should be paid to transaction costs and daily performance rates as the potential combined compound loss can sometimes go unrecognised and offset potential gains over a longer period of time.

Taxation

ETFs are structured for tax efficiency and can be more attractive than mutual funds. In the U.S., whenever a mutual fund realises a capital gain that is not balanced by a realised loss, the mutual fund must distribute the capital gains to its shareholders. This can happen whenever the mutual fund sells portfolio securities, whether to reallocate its investments or to fund shareholder redemptions. These gains are taxable to all shareholders, even those who reinvest the gains distributions in more shares of the fund. In contrast, ETFs are not redeemed by holders (instead, holders simply sell their ETF shares on the stock market, as they would a stock, or effect a non-taxable redemption of a creation unit for portfolio securities), so that investors generally only realise capital gains when they sell their own shares or when the ETF trades to reflect changes in the underlying index.

In most cases, ETFs are more tax-efficient than conventional mutual funds in the same asset classes or categories. Because Vanguard's ETFs are a share-class of their mutual funds, they don't get all the tax advantages if there are net redemptions on the mutual fund shares. Although they do not get all the tax advantages, they get an additional advantage from tax loss harvesting any capital losses from net redemptions.

In the U.K., ETFs can be shielded from capital gains tax by placing them in an Individual Savings Account or self-invested personal pension, in the same manner as many other shares. Because UK-resident ETFs would be liable for UK corporation tax on non-UK dividends, most ETFs which hold non-UK companies sold to UK investors are issued in Ireland or Luxembourg.

Trading

An important benefit of an ETF is the stock-like features offered. A mutual fund is bought or sold at the end of a day's trading, whereas ETFs can be traded whenever the market is open. Since ETFs trade on the market, investors can carry out the same types of trades that they can with a stock. For instance, investors can sell short, use a limit order, use a stop-loss order, buy on margin, and invest as much or as little money as they wish (there is no minimum investment requirement). Also, many ETFs have the capability for options (puts and calls) to be written against them. Covered call strategies allow investors and traders to potentially increase their returns on their ETF purchases by collecting premiums (the proceeds of a call sale or write) on calls written against them. Mutual funds do not offer those features.

Risks

Tracking Error: The ETF tracking error is the difference between the returns of the ETF and its reference index or asset. A non-zero tracking error therefore represents a failure to replicate the reference as stated in the ETF prospectus. The tracking error is computed based on the prevailing price of the ETF and its reference. It is different than the premium/discount which is the difference between the ETF's NAV (updated only once a day) and its market price. Tracking errors are more significant when the ETF provider uses strategies other than full replication of the underlying index. Some of the most liquid equity ETFs tend to have better tracking performance because the underlying is also sufficiently liquid, allowing for full replication. In contrast, some ETFs, such as commodities ETFs and their leveraged ETFs, do not necessarily employ full replication because the physical assets cannot be stored easily or used to create a leveraged exposure, or the reference asset or index is illiquid. Futures-based ETFs may also suffer from negative roll yields, as seen in the VIX futures market.

Effects on Stability

ETFs that buy and hold commodities or futures of commodities have become popular. For example, SPDR Gold Shares ETF (GLD) has 41 million ounces in trust. The silver ETF, SLV, is also very large. The commodity ETFs are in effect consumers of their target commodities, thereby affecting the price in a spurious fashion. In the words of the IMF, "Some market participants believe the growing popularity of exchange-traded funds (ETFs) may have contributed to equity price appreciation in some emerging economies, and warn that leverage embedded in ETFs could pose financial stability risks if equity prices were to decline for a protracted period."

Regulatory Risk

Synthetic ETFs are attracting regulatory attention from the FSB, the IMF, and the BIS. Areas of concern include the lack of transparency in products and increasing complexity; conflicts of interest; and lack of regulatory compliance.

Counterparty Risk

A synthetic ETF has counterparty risk, because the counterparty is contractually obligated to match the return on the index. The deal is arranged with collateral posted by the swap counterparty. A potential hazard is that the investment bank offering the ETF might post its own collateral, and that collateral could be of dubious quality. Furthermore, the investment bank could use its own trading desk as counterparty. These types of set-ups are not allowed under the European guidelines, Undertakings for Collective Investment in Transferable Securities (UCITS), so the investor should look for UCITS III-compliant funds.

Liquidity

ETFs have a wide range of liquidity. Some funds are constantly traded, with tens of millions of shares per day changing hands, while others trade only once in a while, even not trading for some days. There are many funds that do not trade very often. This just means that most *trading* is conducted in the most popular funds. The most active funds (such as SPY, IWM, QQQ, et cetera) are *very* liquid, with high volume and tight spreads. In these cases, the investor is almost sure to get a "reasonable" price, even in difficult conditions. With other funds, it is worthwhile to take some care in execution. This does not mean that less popular funds are not a quality investment. This is in contrast with traditional mutual funds, where everyone who trades on the same day gets the same price.

Criticism

John C. Bogle, founder of the Vanguard Group, a leading issuer of index mutual funds (and, since Bogle's retirement, of ETFs), has argued that ETFs represent short-term speculation, that their trading expenses decrease returns to investors, and that most ETFs provide insufficient diversification. He concedes that a broadly diversified ETF that is held over time can be a good investment.

ETFs are dependent on the efficacy of the arbitrage mechanism in order for their share price to track net asset value. While the average deviation between the daily closing price and the daily NAV of ETFs that track domestic indices is generally less than 2%, the deviations may be more significant for ETFs that track certain foreign indices. The *Wall Street Journal* reported in November 2008, during a period of market turbulence, that some lightly traded ETFs frequently had deviations of 5% or more, exceeding 10% in a handful of cases, although even for these niche ETFs, the average deviation was only a little more than 1%. The trades with the greatest deviations tended to be made immediately after the market opened.

According to a study on ETF returns in 2009 by Morgan Stanley, ETFs missed in 2009 their targets by an average of 1.25 percentage points, a gap more than twice as wide as the 0.52-percentage-point average they posted in 2008. Part of this so-called tracking error is attributed to the proliferation of ETFs targeting exotic investments or areas where trading is less frequent, such as emerging-market stocks, future-contracts based commodity indices and junk bonds. The *tax* advantages of ETFs are of no relevance for investors using tax-deferred accounts (or indeed, investors who are tax-exempt in the first place). However, the lower expense ratios are proving difficult for the proponents of traditional mutual funds to overcome.

In a survey of investment professionals, the most frequently cited disadvantage of ETFs was the unknown, untested indices used by many ETFs, followed by the overwhelming number of choices. Some critics claim that ETFs can be, and have been, used to manipulate market prices, including having been used for short selling that has been asserted by some observers (including Jim Cramer of theStreet.com) to have contributed to the market collapse of 2008.

Financial Adviser

A financial adviser (or advisor) is a professional who renders financial services to clients. According to the U.S. Financial Industry Regulatory Authority (FINRA), terms such as *financial adviser* and *financial planner* are general terms or job titles used by investment professionals and do not denote any specific designations. FINRA describes the main groups of investment professionals who may use the term *financial advisor* to be: brokers, investment advisers, accountants, lawyers, insurance agents and financial planners.

Role

Financial advisors typically provide clients/customers with financial products and services, depending on the licenses they hold and the training they have had. For example, an insurance agent may be qualified to sell both life insurance and variable annuities. A broker may also be a financial planner. A financial advisor may create financial plans for clients or sell financial products, or a combination of both.

Compensation

A financial advisor is generally compensated through fees, commissions, or a combination of both. For example, a financial advisor may be compensated in one or more of the following ways:

- An hourly fee for advisory services
- A flat fee, such as $500 per year, for an annual portfolio review or $2,000 for a financial plan
- A commission on the securities bought or sold, such as $12 per trade
- A commission (sometimes called a "load") based on the amount invested in a mutual fund or variable annuity
- A "mark-up": when one buys "house" products (such as bonds that the broker holds in inventory), or a "mark-down" when they are sold
- A fee for assets under management, such as 1% annually of assets managed

Advisor vs. Adviser

Both spellings, *advisor* and *adviser*, are accepted and denote someone who provides advice. According to one textbook, *adviser* and *advisor* are not interchangeable in the financial services industry, since the term *adviser* is generally used "when referring to legislative acts and their requirements and *advisor* when referring to a practitioner. Since [a financial advisor's practice] is never described as an advisery practice, advisor is preferable when not referencing the law." Congress and the Securities Exchange Commission refer to "investment advisers" when discussing regulation of them in the Investment Advisers Act of 1940.

Bibliography

Anson, Mark J.P.: *The Handbook of Alternative Assets*, John Wiley & Sons, NY, 2006.

Bardsley, N., Cubitt: *Assessing Experimental Economics*, Princeton, Princeton University Press, 2009.

Bateson, J.E.G. : *Managing Services Marketing : Text and Readings*, The Dryden Press, USA, 1991.

Broby, D.: *"A Guide to Fund Management"*, Risk Books, UK, 2010.

Burke, Frank M., *Valuation and Valuation Planning for Closely Held Businesses*, Englewood Cliffs, NJ, Prentice Hall, 1981.

Butler, David; Martin Westlake: *British Politics and European Election*. London: Palgrave Macmillan, 2005.

Cooper, R. and R. Slagmulder : *Interorganizational Cost Management*, Productivity Press, 1999.

Cootner, Paul : *The Random Character of Stock Market Prices*, MIT Press, 1964.

Corbett, Richard: *The European Parliament's Role in Closer EU Integration*. LBasingstoke: Macmillan, 1998.

Dimson, Elroy: *Stock Market Anomalies*, Cambridge University Press, 1988.

Goswami, B. : *Parliament and Administration : Parliament's Control Over Budget and Legislation*, Rawat, Delhi, 2002.

Granger, Clive W. J.: *Empirical Modeling in Economics, Specification and Evaluation*, London, Cambridge University Press, 1999.

Hague, D.C. : *Managerial Economics: Analysis for Business Decisions*, Longman, Harlow, 1977.

Hix, Simon; Abdul Noury, Serard Roland: *Democratic Politics in the European Parliament (Themes in European Governance)*. Cambridge: Cambridge University Press, 2007.

Hoskyns, Catherine; Michael Newman: *Democratizing the European Union: Issues for the twenty-first Century (Perspectives on Democratization*. Manchester University Press, 2000.

Jalal Firoj: *Women in Bangladesh Parliament : A Study on Opinions of the Women MPs*, A H Development, Delhi, 2007.

Johari, J C : *Indian Parliament : A Critical Study of Its Evolution, Composition and Working*, Metropolitan Book, Delhi, 2006.

Kasper, Larry J.: *Business Valuations, Advanced Topics*, Westport, CT, Quorum Books, 1997.

Keller, Kevin Lane : *Conceptualizing, Measuring, and Managing Customer-Based Brand Equity*, Journal of Marketing, 1993.

Lodge, Juliet, : *The 2009 Elections to the European Parliament,* Palgrave Macmillan; 2011.

Loomes, G.: *Current Issues in Microeconomics*, New York: St. Martin's Press, 1989.

Madhav Godbole: *India's Parliamentary Democracy On Trial*, Rupa Publications, Delhi, 2011.

Meyer, M. W.: *Theory of Financial Organizational Structure*, Indianapolis, 1977.

Nizam Ahmed: *Limits of Parliamentary Control : Public Spending in Bangladesh*, The University Press Limited, Delhi, 2006.

Peirson, G., Bird, R., Brown, R., & Howard, P.: *Business Finance*, Roseville, 1990

Purohit H.C. : *Rural Marketing : Challenges and Opportunities*, Shree Pub, Delhi, 2006.

Rao T. Srinivasa : *Changing Lifestyle and Consumer Behaviour*, Deep and Deep, Delhi, 2006.

Taylor, F. W.: *The Principles of Business and Finance*, New York, 1917.

Weber, M.: *The Theory of Social and Economic Organizations*, New York, Oxford University Press, 1947.

West, Thomas L.: and Jeffrey D. Jones: *Handbook of Business Valuation*, New York: Wiley, 1992.

Yegge, Wilbur M., *A Basic Guide for Valuing a Company*, New York, Wiley, 1996.

Index

❑❑❑